The Strange Sound of
CTHULHU

Music Inspired By The Writings of H.P. Lovecraft

by Gary Hill

music street journal

THE STRANGE SOUND OF CTHULHU

Music Inspired by the Writings of H.P. Lovecraft

by Gary Hill

Foreword by S.T. Joshi
Proofreading by Henrik Harksen

ISBN: 978-1-84728-776-2
Printed in the U.S.A.

Cover art by Joseph Vargo. Book design by Christine Filipak.
"Necronomicon" ©2005 Joseph Vargo. Used with permission.
www.noxarcana.com www.monolithgraphics.com

For more musical musings, reviews and interviews by Gary Hill, visit
Music Street Journal at: www.musicstreetjournal.com

This book is dedicated to Howard Phillips Lovecraft and all of the writers, film makers, game designers, artists and musicians who have kept his dark vision alive in the years since his passing.

Contents

Foreword by S.T. Joshi

It is a tribute to H.P. Lovecraft's nearly universal appeal that he can elicit praise from both the preeminent exemplars of "high culture" (Jorge Luis Borges, Joyce Carol Oates) and the most popular figures of pop culture (Stephen King, Clive Barker). Lovecraft's works have been published by the prestigious Library of America, but have also served as the inspiration for a popular role-playing game, The Call of Cthulhu. His imaginary volume of occult lore, the *Necronomicon,* has been cited in Umberto Eco's *Foucault's Pendulum* and also on the television show "The Simpsons." Clearly, different readers draw different types of nourishment from Lovecraft, and this diversity appeal augurs well for his survival well into the twenty-first century.

Now, as Gary Hill's fascinating book attests, Lovecraft has served as the inspiration for a succession of rock musicians over the past forty years or more. Lovecraft himself regretfully admitted that he was not a trained musician and could not appreciate the greatest fruits of Western musical culture—the work of Bach, Beethoven, Brahms, and others—but instead found innocent pleasure in the barbershop tunes of his boyhood or in such popular songs as "Rule, Britannia" or "It's a Long Way to Tipperary." And yet, Lovecraft did inspire at least one classical musician: his friend Alfred Galpin, who upon Lovecraft's death wrote the poignant piece for solo piano, "Lament for H.P.L." Galpin, starting out as a student of French literature, later turned to music and became a composer and pianist, living for most of his adult life in Italy. During a 1977 conference on Lovecraft in Trieste, Galpin played his own composition for the assembled audience of Lovecraft scholars and devotees.

I know of no other instances of Lovecraft inspiring a classical composer or musician, but his influence upon the numerous varieties of rock music—from progressive to heavy metal to punk to Goth—has been well chronicled by Gary Hill. Gary has that rarest of skills among music critics: the ability to describe a song, whether vocal or instrumental, in such a way that readers seem to hear it running through their heads. His coverage—from the 1960s group H.P. Lovecraft to Asmodeus X—is exhaustive and comprehensive, and his sensitivity to the Lovecraftian overtones of songs and albums that do not, at first glance, seem obviously inspired by Lovecraft is impressive. Although my own musical training is largely in the realm of classical music, I gained a real sense of the tremendous impact Lovecraft has had on rock music over the past forty years. Gary has also performed a notable task in interviewing many of the musicians whose work he discusses, so that we have first-hand knowledge of how these artists came upon Lovecraft, what they think of his work, and how their own music is meant to be an homage to the lantern-jawed New England writer.

Perhaps we should not wonder that Lovecraft's work has inspired so many rock musicians. In many ways they have understood the core of Lovecraft's bleak, nihilistic message better than many of the writers who purport to be his posthumous disciples. Aware that Lovecraft saw the universe as a place hostile, or at best cruelly indifferent, to the concerns of humanity, bands such as Black Sabbath, Metallica, and Mercyful Fate have translated that chilling worldview into music that is suitably dark and even at times pessimistic and misanthropic. And yet, as shown by Gary's discussion of the H.P. Lovecraft Historical Society and other such groups, there can also be a lot of fun in dealing with Lovecraftian themes and images. Lovecraft himself was well aware that many of his flamboyant and outlandish conceptions could easily lend themselves to self-parody, and many bands have brought out the sly humour latent in the Lovecraft Mythos.

Lovecraft himself, strait-laced Puritan that he was, may not have looked with favour upon many of the bands who have appropriated his words and ideas, but I think he could not help being flattered by his influence upon an artistic medium so far removed from his own. The lonely writer from Providence, Rhode Island, scribbling his cosmic visions with a free-flowing fountain pen, would have been bemused at how he has inspired music for electric guitar, synthesizer, and drums. If nothing else, he would have seen it as a testament to the inexplicable workings of the human mind.

Chapter 1

H.P. LOVECRAFT:
THE MAN AND HIS MUSICAL LEGACY

Those drawn to this book through their interest in the author H.P. Lovecraft will surely need no introduction to him or his work, but for those whose interest in music has brought them here, a brief introduction will be in order. There have been many biographies and critical analyses of his work published, so that will not be the purpose of this segment. One should view this more as an introduction to who the man was, what his overall contribution to literature has been and an overview of some of the music that has been constructed in the image of his creations. If you want to follow up your quest for more information I highly recommend S.T. Joshi's *H.P. Lovecraft: A Life*. I say this based on the quality of the book, and the suggestion is in no way influenced by Joshi's contribution in the form of the foreword to this book. Indeed, his biography is regarded by most as the ultimate work on Lovecraft's life.

Howard Phillips Lovecraft was born on August 20th, 1890 in Providence, Rhode Island. He was raised in an aristocratic family whose failing wealth did not truly fit his upbringing. This would, in fact, become one of the nearly crippling paradoxes of his life. He regarded himself as one of the "elite class," although his monetary situation throughout the majority of his existence certainly did not live up to those standards. This was especially true during his adult life; while growing up he definitely did not want for much. This disparity caused him to miss many opportunities at financial success, and lead to his living a fairly meager existence in his later years.

As a child Lovecraft developed a love of reading early. According to S.T. Joshi in the *H.P. Lovecraft Centennial Guidebook*, "he was reciting poetry at age two, reading at age three, and writing at age six or seven."[1] His first great literary interest came in the form of *The Arabian Nights* at the age of five. Soon he had also discovered *Bulfinch's Age of Fable*. With that book came a quest for Greek mythology and he made his way through children's editions of the *Iliad* and *Odyssey*. Another piece of importance to Lovecraft's formative literary interest was "The Rime of the Ancient Mariner." This pursuit was brought to life through Lovecraft's own creation of literary works on an almost professional level at a very early age. S.T. Joshi's aforementioned biography documents numerous publications that the young writer produced and apparently sold during his childhood. According to Joshi, there were catalogs and price lists of these stories and poems.

Of course, while all of the previously listed literary works influenced Lovecraft, from most people's way of thinking there is one writer whose work held more power with him than any other. That man was Edgar Allen Poe. Of this influence H.P.L. wrote, "Then I struck EDGAR ALLEN POE!! It was my downfall, and at the age of eight I saw blue firmament of Argos and Sicily darkened by the miasmal exhalation of tomb."[2]

Due to health problems Lovecraft missed much school, but his learning was not hampered because of it. In fact, the time at home allowed him much room to do reading on his own, and by the age of eight he had discovered what was to be another life long love, science. A definite example of this love is the fact that the first instance of Lovecraft's published work was not to be in the fiction vein, but instead a letter in the *The Providence Sunday Journal* that focused on astronomy. This letter was published in 1906. That appearance prompted him to begin writing regular columns, first in *The Pawtuxet Valley Gleaner* on the subject. He later continued this occupation in other publications.

Lovecraft never graduated from High School. This was not due to a lack of academic ability, but rather due to suffering a nervous breakdown, which caused him to withdraw from school in 1908. That particular incident was but the latest in a series of similar episodes that befell the young man. This one was to be the beginning of five years of virtual solitude for him. His only occupation at that time was his continued interest in astronomy and in writing poetry. The year 1913 would, however, find the end to his self-imposed exile.

Finding the stories of Fred Jackson in the *Argosy* to be particularly offensive, Lovecraft created a poem lambasting the writer. When it appeared in the magazine it sparked a feud of words between Lovecraft and Jackson's fans. H.P. continued his side of the argument in the form of poetry. As Joshi describes it, Lovecraft's were "almost always in rollicking heroic couplets reminiscent of Dryden and Pope."[2] In a rather unique turn of events, these letters caught the interest of Edward F. Daas. Daas was the President of the United Amateur Press Association. He invited Lovecraft to join the group, which H.P.L. did in 1914.

Lovecraft himself later described this event in the following way. "In 1914, when the kindly hand of amateurdom was first extended to me, I was as close to the state of vegetation as any animal well can be... With the advent of the United I obtained a renewed will to live; a renewed sense of existence as other than a superfluous weight; and found a sphere in which I could feel that my efforts were not wholly futile. For the first time I could imagine that my clumsy gropings after art were a little more than faint cries lost in the unlistening world."[3]

Indeed, it was through his association with this group that he began to publish his own paper and contributed to numerous works of poetry and essays to various journals. He eventually became President of this organization, and later a rival group. It was to be quite a while before he would again write fiction, though. As mentioned earlier he had penned quite a few works in his younger days, and at the insistence of some of his writing colleagues decided to once again try his hand at the form in 1917. That year saw the creation of both "The Tomb" and "Dagon." Although poetry and non-fiction would remain the bulk of his work for several years, those stories began a slow, but steady journey into the world of fictional literature for the writer.

1923 saw the first publication of many Lovecraft stories in the new magazine *Weird Tales* (begun the same year)—aforementioned "Dagon." Stories of the unusual were to be the most successful output of the rest of Lovecraft's career, although he did have a large number of other professional outlets. He found work as both an editor and a ghostwriter. Perhaps his most notable excursion in this vein was his writing for the famous magician Harry Houdini. He also served as a mentor to a wide number of younger writers including August Derleth, Robert Bloch and Fritz Leiber.

By the time of his death (due to cancer) on March 15th, 1937, Lovecraft had amassed a large number of stories in print, but he never lived to see a collection containing only his stories. Neither did he finish the novel that he had considered writing for years. One of his strongest points, though, was a huge network of fellow writers and correspondents throughout the world with whom he had continued friendships until the end. Many of these relationships were conducted at a distance, communication being in the form of letters (Lovecraft often wrote up to 40 pages in one missive) sent by mail.

It was through these friends that Lovecraft had worked to establish something that would in the end contribute to the lasting power of his work. He had contrived to create a mythos of beings shared between the various writers. These authors included such notables as Robert E. Howard, Frank Belknap Long and Clark Ashton Smith. There are quite a few references in Lovecraft's letters that detail this conspiracy of words. In a letter sent to Howard in 1930, Lovecraft says "[Frank Belknap] Long has alluded to the *Necronomicon* in some things of his—in fact, I think it is rather good fun to have this artificial mythology given an air of verisimilitude by wide citation."[4]

More examples of this collusion in his correspondence include the following from a 1934 letter to William Anger:

> For the fun of building up a convincing cycle of synthetic folklore, all of our gang frequently allude to the pet daemons of the others—thus [Clark Ashton] Smith uses my Yog-Sothoth, while I use his Tsathoggua. Also, I sometimes insert a devil or two of my own in the tales I revise or ghost-write for professional clients. Thus our black pantheon acquires an extensive publicity & pseudo-authoritativeness it would not otherwise get. We never, however, try to put it across as an actual hoax; but always carefully explain to enquirers that it is 100% fiction. In order to avoid ambiguity in my references to the *Necronomicon* I have drawn up a brief synopsis of its "history" . . . All this gives it a sort of air of verisimilitude."[5]

That same year he wrote the following to Margaret Sylvester, dated January 13, 1934, he says:

> Regarding the *Necronomicon*—I must confess that this monstrous & abhorred volume is merely a figment of my own imagination! Inventing horrible books is quite a pastime among devotees of the weird, & ..... many of the regular W.T. [*Weird Tales*] contributors have such things to their credit—or discredit. It rather amuses the different writers to use one another's synthetic demons & imaginary books in their stories—that Clark Ashton Smith often speaks of my *Necronomicon* while I refer to his *Book of Eibon* ... & so on. This pooling of resources tends to build up quite a pseudo-convincing background of dark mythology, legendry, & bibliography—though of course none of us has the least wish actually to mislead readers."[6]

This "pooling of resources," as he puts it, certainly was a continuing factor to the longevity of the appeal of Lovecraft's work. Of course, the quality of the story didn't hurt either. Some readers by now are probably wondering, though, "What does this have to do with music?" At first glance, one can certainly say, "not much." In fact, there are few references in the writing of Lovecraft. One of those references is "The Music of Erich Zann." In that tale music is used as a weapon to keep the monsters away.

> I saw Zann start as from the hint of a horrible shock. Unmistakably he was looking at the curtained window and listening shudderingly. Then I half fancied I heard a sound myself; though it was not a horrible sound, but rather an exquisitely low and infinitely distant musical note, suggesting a player in one of the neighboring houses, or in some abode beyond the lofty wall over which I had never been able to look. Upon Zann the effect was terrible, for, dropping his pencil, suddenly he rose, seized his viol, and commenced to rend the night with the wildest playing I had ever heard from his bow save when listening at the barred door.[8]

One other story, "The Quest of Iranon," includes music in its story. The title character describes himself in this way, "I am Iranon, and come from Aira, a far city that I recall only dimly but seek to find again. I am a singer of songs that I learned in the far city, and my calling is to make beauty with the things remembered of childhood. My wealth is in little memories and dreams, and in hopes that I sing in gardens when the moon is tender and the west wind stirs the lotus-buds."[9] It becomes clear by the climax of the story that these songs and the memories that the man has are what allow him to exist in a sort of unnatural youth.

Looking even to his letters, there are few references to music. The following passage is one of those, from a letter he wrote to August Derleth in November of 1930.

> In matters of music, I would exasperate you—since I am absolutely without the first rudiments of taste. It is simply a blind spot with me, and I candidly recognize the fact. My aesthetic emotions seem to be wholly unreachable except through visual channels. Whenever I seem to appreciate a strain of music, it is purely through *association*—never intrinsically. [10]

Later in the same letter he added that, "But at least I do not fall into the Phillistine's usual pitfall of expressing contempt for an art which I cannot understand. I recognize and regret my limitation in enjoyment capacity, and profoundly congratulate those more broadly favoured by nature."[11]

Two notable articles have been written about the connection of Howard Phillips Lovecraft to music during his lifetime. Both appeared together in 4-5 (a double issue) of *The Romantist*. The first was written by August Derleth and entitled "Lovecraft and Music." In this article Derleth put forth the following statement:

> As in other ways, the late great master of the macabre probably belittled his musical inclinations. Manifestly Lovecraft had no musical education—no genuine education, that is, leading up to a development of authentic interpretation; he had nothing but the dull, monotonous routine of "violin lessons," and his analysis of the effect those lessons had on him is very probably correct to the last detail. What he was misled into under-rating, however—as he—as he under-rated often his other abilities and reactions—was his capacity for the enjoyment of music. [12]

Derleth also asserts his opinion that Lovecraft did in many ways enjoy music. He does, however, add this statement:

> It is probably quite true, however, that, because of his antagonism to music

which became indifference to it, and because he accepted the superficial
indifference as evidence of a "blind spot," Lovecraft did not give himself a
chance to learn to appreciate music, and did not at the time avail himself of
opportunities to listen to music. [13]

The other article from that same publication that addresses H.P.L.'s
relationship with music comes from S.T. Joshi. This one bears the title,
"Further Notes on Lovecraft and Music." While I would again recommend
that the entire article be read to fully understand Joshi's arguments, he does a
nice job of summarizing with the final paragraph. According to Joshi (and
the article served well to demonstrate this by an analysis of the way music
was disseminated in H.P.L.'s day) "the times were, however, against the
possibility of Lovecraft's learning to appreciate Baroque music, and even if
he had lived into the 'forties and 'fifties it is unlikely that his musical taste
would have changed."[14] Joshi further uses Lovecraft's own words in a very
effective manner to drive home this point.

> Of course—if everybody were theoretically perfect in mental and emotional
> balance and sensitiveness, we would all be responsive to every form of art just
> as soon as education opened up our channels of perception and recognition. But
> the human race simply isn't built that way. We are for the most part imperfect
> chance products of varied evolutionary conditions, so that any one of us must be
> content with only part of the aesthetic responsiveness which an ideally perfect
> human being would possess. Some, of course, are lucky enough to possess a
> much wider range than others...but nobody is 100% responsive to all the
> aesthetic stimuli which exist.[15]

Why is it then that the writing of this man has inspired such a wealth of sonic
expression? At least one band, known as "The Darkest of the Hillside
Thickets," is devoted nearly exclusively to paying homage to Lovecraft.
Heavy metal, with its attraction to dark, larger than life imagery seems an
obvious musical form to couple with Lovecraft's writings. Indeed, probably
the greatest wealth of Lovecraft influenced material falls into that genre
including at least passing glances from such artists as Gwar, Mercyful Fate,
Metallica and Entombed. Not even such diverse types of music as
progressive rock (including an entire album by the band Halloween), hard
rock (Blue Öyster Cult), Goth (Fields of the Nephilim), ambient/industrial
(Forma Tadre), psychedelia (one of these 1960s groups even called
themselves "H.P. Lovecraft") and punk (Rudimentary Peni) are untouched by
his mythos.

When the question of what Lovecraft's writing has to contribute to music
is posed to several of the musicians that are featured in this book, the answers

cover a spectrum. Byron of Bal-Sagoth explains that:

> Lovecraft's works stimulate that area of the human mind which aspires to ponder concepts so immeasurably vast as to border on the unthinkable. I believe it is this area of the brain in which the spark of art is also born. Therefore, Lovecraft's grand cosmic concepts of black fathomless gulfs, hinted horrors and immemorial fiends can speak directly to that corner of the mind which channels art from a vague and tenebrous concept to a final and palpable creation. As a result, art which has been so infused with Lovecraftian essence from the point of its very generation will inevitably resonate with and exude those themes which are present in Lovecraft's works. Sometimes, this is a process which occurs so subconsciously as to be almost imperceptible even to the artist himself, which makes the final product all the more potent, and invariably disquieting to the unenlightened.

A somewhat different perspective comes from Smith of the band Babyland.

> What makes the works of Lovecraft great to me is a combination of their own artistic merit, their historical context, and the mythology surrounding the man himself. The appeal of H.P.L. to a contemporary underground artist is almost a cliché: Lovecraft is seen as a pillar of uncompromising integrity. Despite the ghost writing gigs and personal problems, there is this romanticized image of the guy lurking on the edges of society, reporting on its hidden weaknesses and his own wild fantasies through a very personal and unique format that completely stands on its own. The idea that his writing is still effective is something that can give a person hope for their own work—even if it's only ever recognized by a small number of people. Please note that in some ways we value his letters to friends almost as much as we do his official efforts: with H.P.L., it was not about the product, it was about the lifestyle. It's the perfect combination of being accepted by the right people for the right reasons, rather than just some accident of marketing or popular culture.
>
> There is also something about the strange nature of H.P.L.'s philosophy that gives his work an added level of urgency. I get this sense that, like many of the characters in his stories, he fantasized that he really was the doomed "rear guard," facing inevitable oblivion at the hands of hideous outsiders. He seems to be posing as this 18th century character stuck in a time and place that simultaneously fascinates him and repels him—and there is no doubt that race is one of his problems. He obviously rejects all notions of divine intentions (the usual basis for racism), and yet seems to be wholly engrossed by the idea that some people really are better than others—especially if they are Anglo-Saxons who speak English very well. We have to wonder; given the deeply entrenched ideas of racial and linguistic superiority that were popular in this country during his lifetime, why he didn't actually fit in quite well. Then again, his feelings about race might be somewhat hollow: expressions of superiority or xenophobia are constantly undercut by the cold realization that compared to the natural (that is: scientific) world, all human endeavors and differences are just dust. What I

see is a tug of war between his weak public personality (the racist New England gentleman who pretends to be older than he is), and his pathetic but dominant inner reality (the rational but starving artist of great perception, limited means, and feeble constitution). I think that his fear of other people was easier to deal with when he could defend his outer shell with racist language, playing the doomed rearguard as best as he could. What was unbearable was his fear of people who reminded him of himself and his own ultimate shortcomings—and that is the second edge of the racist's blade: ideals of superiority seem to create expectations that can never be achieved, and thus ultimately ensure feelings of failure—if not failure itself.

This loops back a bit onto "Arthur Jermyn." In A.J. and numerous other tales he explores the idea of the inherited curse that is just as biological as it is supernatural, and in the end it seems that almost anyone can carry the taint. To imagine that your own fine ancestry is immune to the brutal facts of history is ignorance, and anyone who looks into the box will see pretty much the same thing. In the end, dominant cultures don't get that way by being inherently pleasant or by being chosen by some god—they get that way by killing and robbing other cultures that were weaker than them. We are all beasts, with fangs and tangled fur and blood on our ugly paws.

What else could we possibly be?

A bit less wordy about the situation, but nonetheless insightful, is Hans Platzgumer of H.P. Zinker. He says that Lovecraft's writing brings to music "the vibe, this haunting psychedelia, these mind twisting aesthetics, these lyrical images he conjures up and that can be translated into music." He added that, "the pictures and the moods he creates are great inspiration to me. I love to let myself fall into that once in a while. It also doesn't grow out of date. I sense that he shared the same fascinations as I do."

Yet a different take is offered by Scott Kesler of Kindred Idol. "I used his writing as a lens for the modern world I grew up in. It gave reality a sense of history in the now. A person can find a quiet corner of a small town and find intrigue and desire. For what, well, I don't know, it's just that feeling or yearning for something more."

Brian Voth, who works as a one-man heavy metal band under the name "Fireaxe" says this:

Lovecraft's haunting visions have inspired a great number of artists to write prose, poetry, and music in that tradition. As why it is popular I think that the answer lies in the fact that Lovecraft was able to capture that state of fear that all of us have experienced when our naive vision of the world was shattered by a frightening reality. Now, of course, none of us discovered that an ancient race of horrible creatures once ruled the earth and will do so again, swatting humans like flies in the process, but if you've ever had the experience of being told that your parents are getting a divorce, or finding out that the places and characters in your favorite TV show were just make-believe, or made the dreadful discovery that one day you were going to die and that there was nothing that you could do about it, then you know that awful feeling of dread and doom pretty well. Since many people into metal appreciate nihilistic themes I think that metal and Lovecraft are a natural fit, but new-age style music can be adapted to horror effectively as well, as Famlende Forsøk have shown.

Niko Skorpio of Thergothon chalks up Lovecraft's appeal to musicians as, "The intense atmosphere of course! Not only horror, though, more than that I've always been more into his way of describing the otherworldly and the style of raising tension by revealing the mystery sparingly. And then there's the distant piping of the accursed flutes to recreate in this world, in honour of the Blind Idiot God..."

These are just a few examples of H.P.L.'s influence on the music of today. As this volume continues forward you will find both additional instances and more detailed examinations of those mentioned here. Indeed, it might be safe to say that as rich and populous as Lovecraft's own wealth of writing is, the music inspired by that work is even more varied. It is without question just one demonstration of how Lovecraft's work continues to live on well beyond his own existence.

Chapter 2

PEACE, LOVE, DUNWICH:
H.P.L's INFLUENCE IN PSYCHEDELIC ROCK

One of the first styles in which the writings of H.P. Lovecraft were to show up was psychedelic rock. Coming in the latter half of the 1960s, the style was named for the psychedelic drugs that its sounds were meant to mimic. Characteristics common to much of the genre include East Indian styled musical scales, long instrumental passages, and effects that were designed to simulate the effects of drug use (included echoey, processed or phased vocals, backwards tracked sounds, distorted and otherwise altered elements.) With much of the genre's lyrical content being devoted to topics like protest, drug use and free love, horror stories might seem an unlikely combination. Still, one band in particular even went so far as to take on the name of the author.

While Providence, Rhode Island was the birthplace of the author H.P. Lovecraft, Chicago, Illinois served the same function for the band H.P. Lovecraft. With that moniker chosen for this original era (formed in 1967) psychedelic rock band, one would assume that much of their material would be based on the works of the author. The full story regarding the taking of the name, though, is provided by band member David Miotke (aka Dave Michaels), explaining both how he discovered the writer and what has kept him as a fan.

> Back in 1967 our two managers were familiar with Lovecraft's writings. After rejecting a whole list of possible group names one evening, we took a break and in collective conversation the name H.P. Lovecraft came up. The name itself, so different and containing the word "love" drew us into naming ourselves after the author. One of the managers, Bill Traut, a graduate of the University of Wisconsin, knew the professor/author August Derleth, who was executor of the Lovecraft body of work. Bill contacted professor Derleth and got permission to use the name. Shortly thereafter, I began reading some of Lovecraft's stories. Wow! What a gifted and talented mind to create such "beyond scary" stuff!

Miotke's band mate Ethan Kenning (aka George Edwards), had a slightly different take on the question of how the group chose their name. He said that, "One of our managers had a dog named 'Yuggoth.' I asked him where the name came from and he replied, 'from H.P. Lovecraft.' It was like the sky opened up... after all, this was 1967." That answer also describes

Kenning's introduction to the author. He further explains how the draw that Lovecraft has had on him, "I hadn't read him until late 1966. Once I started, I couldn't stop. His incredible imagery and the mythos upon which many of the stories are based were beyond anything I'd ever read."

While their name came from the author, only two songs from the band's catalog were truly rooted in his work. The first of these tracks came from their 1967 self-titled debut in the form of "The White Ship." The song comes in with a weird ambient tone that calls to mind both some of the descriptions of sonic oddness that Lovecraft himself described and also the psychedelic chemical influence so common to this musical genre. As it moves forward the cut begins to take on a slow moving, ballad like structure. Those who have not heard it might find similar ground in the music of Procol Harum's "A Whiter Shade of Pale" or "Salty Dog." The vocals have a very classic element to them. The cut moves off into weird spacey jamming later that includes sounds that seem to convey an Eastern mystic tone, which would be somewhat in keeping with much of Lovecraft's writing.

This one takes its title from a Lovecraft tale, and the lyrics definitely draw parallels to the source material, while not being a literal take on the story line. In the band's interpretation the following lines represent the basic premise:

> The white ship has sailed and left me here again / Out in the mist, I was so near again / Sailing on the sea of dreams / How far away it seems / Sailing upon the white ship / On through the night here in my darkened room / Sails of white across the misty moon / Floating across the sky / Burning into my eyes / Sailing upon the white ship.[1]

The original story tells the tale of a lighthouse keeper by the name of Basil Elton. He recounts the following:

> Out of the South it was that the White Ship used to come when the moon was full and high in the heavens. Out of the South it would glide very smoothly and silently over the sea. And whether the sea was rough or calm, and whether the wind was friendly or adverse, it would always glide smoothly and silently, its sails distant and its long strange tiers of oars moving rhythmically. One night I espied upon the deck a man, bearded and robed, and he seemed to beckon me to embark for far unknown shores. Many times afterward I saw him under the full moon, and never did he beckon me.[2]

Mr. Elton is taken on a journey to distant unknown lands and sees many wonders on his voyage. Interestingly enough, another of Lovecraft's few references to music appears in this description. "The man who had beckoned now spoke a welcome to me in a soft language I seemed to know well, and the hours were filled with soft songs of the oarsmen as we glided away into a mysterious South, golden with the glow of that full, mellow moon."[3] Here he seems to be using music to convey both a sense of wonderment and of an alien texture.

Lovecraft makes an allusion later in the story to musical endeavors that again seem to hold similar meanings. "Then came we to a pleasant coast gay with blossoms of every hue, where as far inland as we could see basked lovely groves and radiant arbors beneath a meridian sun. From bowers beyond our view came bursts of song and snatches of lyric harmony, interspersed with faint laughter so delicious that I urged the rowers onward in my eagerness to reach the scene."[4]

Eventually they turn towards a place of legend that again uses the mention of music as way of showing the exotic nature. In his description, Elton believes the place to be as follows:

> And the cities of Cathuria are cinctured with golden walls, and their pavements also are of gold. In the gardens of these cities are strange orchids, and perfumed lakes whose beds are of coral and amber. At night the streets and the gardens are lit with gay lanthorns fashioned from the three-colored shell of the tortoise, and here resound the soft notes of the singer and the lutanist.[5]

With such usage of musical references in the story, then, it seems quite appropriate that the band would create a musical interpretation of this story. The lyrics tell of the wonderment of the journey, although they do not relate the sad and rather horrifying way it is finished out. This book will also leave that conclusion to the further explorations of the reader. It is just one more reason why the reader should seek out Lovecraft's work.

Miotke gave some details about how the band made musical creations of Lovecraftian themes in music in general, and specifically in "The White Ship."

> *Everything comes out of the lyrics. For example, "the White Ship has sailed and left me here again...." invites a tonal effect of "dreamlike separation," linking meter, rhythm, tempo, dynamics, melody and harmonies into a "holistic" concept of serving the vocal poetic imagery. Song lyrics are a unique type of poetic statement, usually very concise. We were, I believe, creating an atmosphere for the lyrics. The actual Lovecraft story with all its detail was only a stepping off point for the songs using titles from his works. Of course, the titles themselves contain a power of meaning in their own right.*

On their second album, entitled *H.P. Lovecraft II*, the band included "At the Mountains of Madness." In this song a flurry of hard edged psychedelic rock, leaning towards the noisy gives way to a main song structure that, while still musically flamboyant, has a more straightforward bluesy rock texture. The vocal arrangement here is the true charm of the track, though. With dual vocal lines carrying nearly the entire track in a very 1960s oriented hippie-like fashion. There are elements of keyboards that come across at points in a fashion that calls to mind The Doors just a bit and a couple instrumental excursions later bring more depth to the track. The second of these (and the longer of the two) turns very noisily psychedelic and twisted and eventually ends the track.

Again, the lyrics to this one seem to capture the tone of the story without actually serving to "retell" the tale. "All alone, there is no release / All you own will not buy you peace / You have lost all sense of touch / In the dark without a crutch / You've arrived at the Mountains of Madness."[6]

Here, the lyrics seem to represent a helplessness, and certainly the story reflects that helplessness in many ways. The third verse moves even further into Lovecraftian thematic territory with this line, "change like this, my friend, will make you go insane."[7] There are many instances in H.P.L.'s work where events cause people to lose their sanity.

Generally only the tone in the lyrics is consistent with the source material. At the Mountains of Madness is one of Lovecraft's most epic works both in terms of depth and length. In length it is a novella, and its story focuses on an expedition to Antarctica. There are numerous horrifying discoveries made on this journey, giving a new perspective on the history of the Earth. To delve into much more detail would be a disservice as, again, this tale is far better when read in Lovecraft's own words.

Kenning described the process of creating music that reflects Lovecraftian textures in the following way:

As it turned out, our other manager was a huge Lovecraft fan, and had just about everything he'd ever written. We began reading the stories at about the same time the band was forming. I really loved the work, and began writing lyrics and general chord progressions to try to capture some of the feeling in the books. David then brought his amazing classical training to bear with the harpsichord section on "The White Ship" and many other textures and colors not common in rock music at that time. Tony was also a big influence in creating the Lovecraft sound. His use of feedback and out of the ordinary melodic lines and rhythms really helped define us. I think it's interesting to note that he did all this without the aid of effects devices of any kind. David and my vocal intervals were also a significant factor. At the Mountains of Madness was the first tune written with a Lovecraftian theme. We worked on it in my apartment, and drove the neighbors crazy... if you remember, Tony is playing mostly feedback throughout, and David and I are singing like men possessed.

"The White Ship" came later. I wrote it in the hallway on a rehearsal break. I think it took fifteen or twenty minutes. When the band came back, we started jamming and Michael Tegza (drummer) started playing it as a "Bolero." Then David brought the harpsichord section, and before the night was over, "The White Ship" was born. On the second album, our engineer Chris Huston became a sixth member of the band for all intents an purposes, as his use of backwards tape effects and other very innovative ideas were a huge part of the sound of that record.

Kenning spoke of what he feels H.P.L.'s work has to offer music, "I think his images and willingness to explore some pretty 'outside' ideas is an inspiration to all writers... there's music and poetry in everything." When asked the same question, Miotke said, "dark expressive sides of imaginative sound landscapes. The feedback effects and dissonant reverse tape sounds served to give that 'otherworldly quality' to many of the tracks."

Both men volunteered their favorite Lovecraft stories. Kenning said, "*At the Mountains of Madness* is my favorite. I also like *The Dream-Quest of Unknown Kadath*, *The Case of Charles Dexter Ward*, 'The White Ship,' and many others." Miotke told me that his favorites are "The White Ship," *At the Mountains of Madness* and "Fungi From Yuggoth." He added that, "It's been a long time since I've read him, so maybe it's time for me to visit the local Berkeley Library and take out a volume."

Another note of interest that Miotke offered was the following:

You're probably aware of the reissue of our two albums (*HP Lovecraft* and *HP Lovecraft II*) on one CD. It's out of England and contains 4 bonus tracks and a well done booklet. On the back of the booklet is a photo I took of our drummer, Mike Tegza, in the Old North Church graveyard in Boston, surrounded by a group of local kids. In hindsight, it captures a certain eerie Lovecraft flavor. We were a pretty carefree and happy bunch touring the country and enjoying each other's company, playing our brand of inventive, improvisatory music, and reaching out to the wonderful crowds for whom we were playing. We also occasionally ran into people who didn't think we conformed or looked the way we should, but in that era things were, of course, "pretty crazy." Kind of like today, although we have, thankfully I feel, made great strides since then. It's just that we have so far to go. "Everyone knows how the wind blows the White Ship."

The band H.P. Lovecraft broke up before recording any albums beyond the first two, although a compilation and live album later surfaced. While they morphed into an outfit simply called "Lovecraft" in the 1970s (not to be confused with the Argentinean heavy metal band by the same name), the only tie that the new group had to H.P.L. was the name.

That band was the only of the 1960s era psychedelic bands to turn to Lovecraft as a source of inspiration, but there were two later bands (part of the psychedelic revival that started in the 1980s) that did the same. The first of the later period (or neo-psychedelia as many call them) groups to hit the scene was The Bevis Frond.

In 1984 Nick Saloman began a project he called "The Bevis Frond." The name applied to recordings written, produced and recorded solely by him. He used his neo-psychedelic leanings to create an original blend of sound that both hearkened back to the older style to which he related and to update it for a modern alternative/indie rock audience. Within this context Saloman created two Lovecraftian songs. Obviously related, the tracks were entitled, respectively "The Miskatonic Variations" and "The Miskatonic Variations II." The term "Miskatonic" is one that often shows up in the work of H.P. Lovecraft, and it refers to a fictional river and a University named for that river (again fictional). Both are frequent visitors to Lovecraft's tales.

Saloman admits that he was drawn to the writer H.P. Lovecraft by discovering the original psychedelic era band of the same name. According to him, "I came to Lovecraft's writings at about the age of 15, having bought both albums by the psychedelic band H.P. Lovecraft. The sleeve notes of the first album explain a bit about the author, so I figured that if they liked him enough to name their band after him, I should check him out! I was immediately hooked by his wonderful use of language, and the incredibly strange stories. I got hold of everything he'd written that was available. I still dip in now and again."

He said that in creating the two tracks, "I guess I was trying to get a feel of epic confusion and chaos that Lovecraft conjures up in his more fantastic tales." Saloman describes the two pieces as "long swirling instrumentals."

The first of these, "The Miskatonic Variations" starts off with feedback and then an echoey guitar with both hints of the blues and lots of psychedelic textures serves as the impetus for a wandering sort of spaced out jam. This becomes a very solid rocker that has a definite classic rock texture. This one is quite meaty, and a real scorcher. It feels a lot like early Hawkwind through a good section of the number. Eventually, about four minutes in, this drops back and gives the guitar plenty of room to get in some tasty soloing, still over the same general themes. It wanders off after a while more into the direction of space, but still the guitar work is full of fiery soloing. At around the six and a half minute mark it drops back a bit and the Hawkwind like elements take over. Through a series of changes it moves out into much more of a spacey arrangement. It seems to wander almost aimlessly at times, but still manages to captivate the listener. Saloman moves it out into an expansive hard rocking variant on the themes a bit later. At almost fifteen minutes in length this one isn't something for a quick music break, but it is worth the time invested. Of the two numbers (both instrumental pieces), I like this one the best.

"The MiskatonicVariations II" begins slowly and very gradually with dramatic waves of echoey sound steadily rising to create a palate of sound. This becomes more and more volumous and powerful as it carries forward. It gets rather noisy at points. There are odd non-lyrical vocals that come across from time to time almost like moans. This cut wanders around seemingly aimlessly in a rather prog rock/freeform jazz style for quite some time, then turns very crunchy and rather cacophonous. It moves into near noise territory for a time. Then it shifts into a bluesy sort of hard rocking jam that feels a bit like Jimi Hendrix, but also like Hawkwind in its spacey overtones. The saxophone in particular brings in that last element. The guitar soloing here is quite tasty. A myriad of instruments eventually run across the surface of this one, including a cool violin line in an accompanied solo. This segment of the track has some of the most accessible and entertaining music, but still manages to maintain a solid weirdness factor. A 1960s style keyboard sound eventually takes over from here, at first playing along with this segment, then dominating the piece, but the violin eventually plays along in neo-classical ways. The cut makes its way after a time back to the harder edged Hawkwind like excursion. It finally dissolves back into the chaotic instrumental work that began the cut to crescendo and end the music. Out of the silence a voice rises with Arabian sounding chant/singing and something that sounds like a flute joins it to serve as the true conclusion to the piece.

Of his interest in the author, Saloman says that:

> My favourite stories are in fact the more 'ghost' based tales. I'm not so keen on the fantasy stuff. I've never been a great fan of science fiction or fantasy writing, but I love the traditional ghost story. M.R. James is another favourite writer. My favourite Lovecraft tale is without doubt "Shadow Over Innsmouth." One very boring day at work many years ago, I actually spent the afternoon creating a street plan of Innsmouth from the description in the story.

He added that, "When The Bevis Frond did our first gig in Providence, I spent an afternoon walking around all the streets named in the stories (Benefit Street etc.) and ended up at the cemetery where I visited Lovecraft's grave. I have to say the rest of the band were somewhat non-plussed, but I was knocked out."

Following not far behind The Bevis Frond came another band from the neo-psychedelic style. Formed in 1989 by Austrian Hans Platzgumer (a child prodigy of sorts, releasing several albums by the age of 15), H.P. Zinker created a unique blend of sounds that merged alternative rock with psychedelia, hard rock and even progressive rock. They released one Lovecraft based number in the title track to their *At the Mountains of Madness* album. The lyrics to the track are taken directly from the story of the same name. The music comes in as a bluesy jam that seems to combine elements of Black Sabbath, Led Zeppelin and Cream, but when the lyrics, with their echoey reading of Lovecraft's words enter, the song takes on a slightly spooky and quite psychedelic tone. This piece features some meaty guitar work and an intriguing retro rock sounding arrangement. It eventually moves into a more jam-band oriented segment that carries it on for quite a while and allows the band to move forward through quite a bit of musical territory while still retaining the original musical themes.

Of H.P. Lovecraft, Platzgumer says that "His texts have this eerie sort of disturbing vibe to it and so I often have in my music. I like that mystery and these psychedelic aspects to it. So when I read Lovecraft or especially when I did use these lyrics I let myself really go into that mood. And when you fall into this feeling then suddenly his words and my music make sense together and go well with each other. I do a lot of soundtrack work, and thus I also there see it a bit like scoring."

It is quite appropriate that Platzgumer chose that particular story to create his musical link as it is his favorite Lovecraft tale. He says of the story:

> It brings together everything that I really appreciate about Lovecraft—this elaborate language and this eerie setting. I am a huge sucker for anything that goes with arctic circumstances as well, so this is an ideal source for me. And it was an ideal inspiration for my album *HP Zinker At the Mountains of Madness*, which dealt with all kinds of abnormalities in human perceptions in big cities. So by using this title and quoting some of Lovecraft lyrics I had a chance to throw a line to some much broader realms than the original concept.

One can really hear the love for the author's work in his words as Platzgumer says, "The Mountains of Madness title inspired our designer Stefan Sagmeister for some exceptional CD artwork that eventually got nominated for a Grammy that year. So you see how Lovecraft's inspiration went a long way. And his words and descriptions are so strong, they will last on!"

While the links to music and the author may have begun with psychedelia, they certainly did not end there. The genre may not have seemed an obvious fit with Lovecraftian themes, but all of these acts managed to do an admirable job of uniting these two, seemingly, disparate forms. The ball had begun to roll, though, with the band H.P. Lovecraft, and it seems in retrospect a foregone conclusion that other musical styles would follow in short order.

Chapter 3

MISKATONIC MELLOTRONS
PROGRESSIVE ROCK AND H.P. LOVECRAFT

Another of the first musical styles which flirted with the works of H.P.L. was progressive rock. "Prog" rock, as it is often called, is a musical style that emerged in the late 1960s. It derives its name from the artists' attempts to create a musical style that "progressed" or pushed the envelope of rock music. The style, which gained prominence in the 1970s, but continues to this day, is typified by complex musical arrangements and extended songs. However, those two elements, like everything else in progressive rock, are not always the case. Certainly this is one style of music in which the rules are meant to be broken. Ultimately, it is a high level of musical ability and the desire to create a higher form of music that are the underlying elements of the form. Much progressive rock owes as much in musical form to jazz and classical as it does to the forebear of mainstream rock—blues.

Progressive rockers Caravan made one musical journey into the land of Lovecraft inspired works. This was the track, "C'thlu Thlu." The unusual spelling is only one aspect of the song that doesn't feel especially in the style of Lovecraft. The opening segment with its bluesy jam has a creepy sort of texture roaming over top. This section (that also makes up the verses) feels a bit like a cross between Peter Green's Fleetwood Mac and the bluesier end of Spinal Tap. It is the chorus and bridge that take away from the Lovecraftian feel of the piece. They are fast paced, almost Beatlesish and very light in tone, feeling quite happy, although the lyrics call the listener to "run away."

Misspellings aside, Lovecraft's Cthulhu is certainly something that would make you want to run away. With its most famous appearance coming from H.P.L.'s story "The Call of Cthulhu," According to *The Encyclopedia Cthulhiana*, Cthulhu is "an amorphous Great Old One who most frequently resembles a clawed octopus-headed humanoid with great batlike wings. Cthulhu sleeps in a deathlike trance beneath the Pacific Ocean, but he will one day awaken to rule the world."[1]

Caravan was part of the "Canterbury" movement in progressive rock. The genre is named for the city in England where most of the bands originated. This subset of the progressive rock genre was one of the earliest, and the bands are characterized by both their fascination with complex musical structures and a very "English" sound. Caravan itself is one of the original Canterbury bands, formed in 1968. The track covered here was released on their sixth album, *For Girls Who Grow Plump in the Night*, which was released in 1972. The disc was sort of a reunion album, bringing back some original members and a renewed vitality after tensions within the band had caused splinterings of both personnel and musical form.

Originally going by the name of "Uriel," the four members of the next act, Arzachel, included Dave Stewart (not the Dave Stewart made famous by his work in the Eurythmics) and Steve Hillage. They recorded one album, a self-titled release, but the credits to the record included pseudonyms due to contractual problems. This disc that seemed to sit on the line between psychedelia and progressive rock included the track "Azathoth." The track seems rather fitting to its Lovecraftian roots, feeling like a psychotic, psychedelic funeral dirge throughout much of the piece.

In a rather confusing turn of events, two German bands shared the name Necromonicon. When you add in one Canadian metal band whose name is NecromonicoN, the situation becomes even more perplexing to sort through. Still, the first band to use that moniker was a German progressive rock band that formed in 1971. The group recorded only one true album, and the name is the only real influence Lovecraft had on these rockers.

Progressive rock band Univers Zero was formed in Belgium in 1974. They entered the realm of Lovecraft inspired music in 1981 with the song "La Musique d'Erich Zann" from their 1980 album *Ceux du Dehors*. According to the liner notes, the song is "a collective improvisation inspired by a short story by H.P. Lovecraft."[2] The track (an instrumental) begins with atmospheric tones and violin, appropriately, enters slowly. The mode here is disjointed. For a time only the violin carries the piece becoming more and more powerful as it does. Eventually, though, other instruments join. Finally this becomes a swirling noisy cacophonic movement that rises up and then ends abruptly. A frantic, yet quiet scratching across the string ends the piece.

Band leader and cofounder Daniel Denis says this about the track and its origins:

> The piece entitled "La musique d'Erich Zann" was a rather interesting experiment. We were trying to record a spontaneous and improvised piece, taking advantage of all the musicians being present in the studio while we were staying in Switzerland recording *Ceux du Dehors*. I asked everyone in the band to briefly read the short story and immerse themselves in its atmosphere. The result was a very mysterious piece which I believe Lovecraft would have liked. And even though I haven't read any of his short stories in many years, I believe Cthulhu, Nyarlathotep or Yog-Sothoth are still there in some remote region of my brain, and from time to time they resurface.

Denis says that it was "through Jean-Luc Manderlier, the keyboard player in Arkham, that I first discovered Lovecraft." He continues, "I found his work amazing and I became immersed in this kind of literature for many years, also reading Belgian science-fiction/fantasy writers like Jean Ray, Thomas Owen, and E.A. Poe too of course. I was particularly attracted at the time to literature and other forms of fantasy art like painting and cinema; it was a source of inspiration that suited me fine." He added that the lure of Lovecraft for him (and what has kept him as a fan) was that "there is something magic about his ability to gradually embark you in his world, from which you never return unscathed... For instance, when I was immersed in reading his books, I remember everything that surrounded me suddenly took on another meaning. I was really transported into one of his stories. That's really 'fantasy' in all its splendor!"

According to Denis, the contribution of Lovecraft's work to music is "enormous, because his writings, even though they are very precise in the descriptions and details, still leave a lot to the reader's imagination." Denis says that it is not possible for him to pick a favorite H.P.L. story, though, because, "I think all his short stories are related and they overlap in such a way that they form one enormous puzzle. They are all interesting."

Since Denis made the mention of Arkham, it seems that this would be an appropriate place to bring up that band. Denis was in this band with the aforementioned Manderlier before forming Univers Zero. While the name calls to mind Lovecraft's Mythos, Manderlier said, "the name Arkham was only a way of pointing an interesting place to visit (if one ever could)." He also has some different opinions on the concept of uniting music and Lovecraftian literature than the other musicians mentioned here. He said the following:

> Of course I've read Lovecraft books but I wouldn't say it has some influence on my music; my point of view is that music has specific rules and that composing has mainly to work with facing those rules and trying to trace your own way through them—a mix of abstraction and physical impact altogether. Writing books or novels is another world with its own rules and I don't think both can really meet.

Beginning in 1983, French band Halloween created a dark form of progressive rock. Their first album, 1988's *Part One*, included the song "Outsider." The number starts tentatively with atmospheric textures, and then begins to rise up with a very classical approach. This runs through for the introduction, then the band turn it into a classically-tinged driving progressive rock motif. The vocals on the verse are nearly spoken, but have a bit of bluesy snarl at times. The chorus gains a lot of potency from over layers and a more "sung" vocal line. A very dramatic and majestic (with a hint of mystery) instrumental break ensues later. The cut ends with a short classically dominated instrumental burst after another verse/chorus combo.

The lyrics here are very directly tied to the story "The Outsider." "I've never known where I was born / But the castle seems very old / I must have lived years in this place / But I can't remember well..."[3] Compare that to this passage from the original story, and there's no question of the tie. "I know not where I was born, save that the castle was infinitely old and infinitely horrible, full of dark passages and having high ceilings where the eye could find only cobwebs and shadows."[4] This segment of Lovecraft's work shows another aspect of the origins of the lyrical verse, "I must have lived years in this place, but I cannot measure the time."[5]

A later verse includes these lines, "... I've never heard a voice / And in fact not even mine / Don't even know my face / There's no mirror here..." [6] Compare those words to the following from the original story:

> No teacher urged or guided me, and I do not recall hearing any human voice in all those years—not even my own; for although I had read of speech, I had never thought to try to speak aloud. My aspect was a matter equally unthought of, for there were no mirrors in the castle, and I merely regarded myself by instinct as akin to the youthful figures I saw drawn and painted in the books.[7]

Lovecraft's story continues later with this description:

> But what I observed with chief interest and delight were the open windows - gorgeously ablaze with light and sending forth sound of the gayest revelry. Advancing to one of these I looked in and saw an oddly dressed company indeed; making merry, and speaking brightly to one another. I had never, seemingly, heard human speech before and could guess only vaguely what was said. Some of the faces seemed to hold expressions that brought up incredibly remote recollections, others were utterly alien.
>
> I now stepped through the low window into the brilliantly lighted room, stepping as I did so from my single bright moment of hope to my blackest convulsion of despair and realization. The nightmare was quick to come, for as I entered, there occurred immediately one of the most terrifying demonstrations I had ever conceived. Scarcely had I crossed the sill when there descended upon the whole company a sudden and unheralded fear of hideous intensity, distorting every face and evoking the most horrible screams from nearly every throat. Flight was universal, and in the clamour and panic several fell in a swoon and were dragged away by their madly fleeing companions. Many covered their eyes with their hands, and plunged blindly and awkwardly in their race to escape, overturning furniture and stumbling against the walls before they managed to reach one of the many doors. [8]

That scene is recreated in the song by the following lines: "Looked through window and saw people / But when I stepped into the room / Everybody flew away..." [9]

With the follow-up *Laz* (1980), the band continued creating Lovecraft based music. This time they devote the majority of the album to the author. The disc opens with "The Wood," and the lyrics are taken from the Lovecraft poem of the same name. Musically this one falls somewhat in the neighborhood of both UK and early Genesis. "A drunken minstrel in his careless verse / spoke the vile word that should not see the light / and stirred the shadows of an ancient curse."[10] This mistaken utterance dooms the minstrel's wondrous city.

With "The Waltz," the band creates a song that has a bit of that Genesis flair, but also features a good deal of spooky tones and a spoken word segment that works quite well. The lyrics are a combination of two Lovecraft poems, "Clouds" and "Psychopompos: A Tale in Rhyme."

After a brief instrumental piece, the group return to Lovecraft-based material with "Yule Horror." This one takes its lyrics from "The Festival" by H.P.L. The words speak of a dark celebration of the pagan holiday, "... for these pow'rs are the pow'rs of the dark / from the graves of / the lost druid-folk..." [11] This has one of the darkest textures of the disc, but still manages to pull off definite progressive rock intensity, Genesis like textures and a great jazz oriented musical excursion.

Three tracks, two of them instrumentals, come in before the final, title track. This one features lyrics from Lovecraft's "The Nightmare Lake." In what may be the strongest piece on the disc, the group include a strong progressive rock introduction followed by a moody main song structure. Several instrumental breaks bring in neo-classical elements, and later an almost funky prog interplay serves as the backdrop for a continuation of the poetry recital. After another potent instrumental segment it drops to a haunting violin solo that ends both the composition and the album.

When Djam Karet released the album *Burning* the *Hard City* in 1991, it included the track "At the Mountains of Madness." Chuck Oken, the band's drummer and the member responsible for picking the title to that song says of the song:

> The feel of the entire song was very majestic and twisted especially in its manic breakdown in the end. Many of our songs have nature references "Swimming in the Big Sky," "Alone With the River Man," etc. I often write down phrases and/or titles and later see how they fit with songs. As we were mixing it, the H.P. Lovecraft title came to mind and it was a match for me to the intensity of the story and the song. It fit, I felt the song was one of our best at the time, and so it was named.

Djam Karet is a progressive rock outfit from California that was founded in 1984. Their music is typically a powerful instrumental montage that captures a lot of emotion and interesting textures into their soundscapes. Their music can be entrancing, but also borders at times on cacophony. The blend has made them a favorite of the underground prog rock scene.

Oken related that he was a fan of H.P.L. "in my high school, college, and post college days. As I have a family, work, and play music I find myself unfortunately having less time for pleasure reading these days and have not kept up with many of the literary authors I devoured in my earlier years."

Their song "At the Mountains of Madness" is an instrumental that starts in a bluesy tone. As it carries forward it takes on a nature that many might be familiar with in the works of Frank Zappa with a bit of the sound of King Crimson thrown into the mix. As Oken suggested, much of the piece has a very majestic tone to it, and a lot of character. This is one that also shows a lot of elements of fusion.

There are those who have said that one Marillion song ("Grendel"), which contains the phrase "Lurker on the Threshold," is derived from the works of H.P.L. Fish, who was the lead singer and lyricist for the band in those days, told me that the line was "just a passing phrase in my life." I believe, since the man's lyrics typically include clever double meanings, that the dual interpretation of this comment was intended—essentially a play on words. He also said about the story that it "was the only one I ever read when I was a kid so I don't think I could talk about him as an influence!"

A rather obscure act, Germany's Payne's Gray only existed for a little while in the 1990s. While many may not have heard of them, their one full album, *Kadath Decoded*, is a full-on Lovecraftian treatment. Their music falls pretty securely between progressive metal (see the next chapter for more information on heavy metal and its various incarnations) and progressive rock, but I would probably consider them more the latter than the former—hence their inclusion in this chapter. As one can well guess, this album focuses on H.P.L.'s story *The Dream-Quest of Unknown Kadath*. While not all the tracks are explicitly Lovecraftian, I will nonetheless address them all here; after all, it is a concept album built around this story line. It's also important to note that even the liner booklet (more of a fold out poster) is full of images and pieces of text surrounding the story, making it a "must have" for Lovecraft collectors.

Hagen Schmidt, who was the band's singer, tells the story of the creation of this disc (including the cover) very eloquently:

> About 12 years ago, I was reading *The Dream-Quest of Unknown Kadath*, a book I had already read once before and which had struck me as Lovecraft's

masterpiece, putting in one book all of his facets, moods and, if one wants to see it, wisdom and knowledge on what life is about. My father, who also is a big Lovecraft fan, came up with the idea of putting the story into music and wrote lyrics based on *The Dream-Quest*... What I did then was to read the book again and the fascinating thing that happened was that I could practically hear the music right out of Lovecraft's writing! I bought another 5 copies of the book and gave them to the other band members so they'd read it too—and the same thing happened to them. I guess Lovecraft simply inspires musicians.

To create the Lovecraft type texture, it was clear we had to use as many different musical styles and sounds as Lovecraft used moods and descriptions. Basically, we tried to be Randolph Carter and express musically what he was feeling. The words to the music mostly followed the author's narration while the music we played expressed what was happening in Carter's heart and mind while he was experiencing all sorts of sensations. The only problem we had was to fit the whole thing into less than 70 minutes of music, as that is all a CD could hold in good sound quality and we couldn't afford recording two—it was expensive enough the way we did it...

The packaging of the CD was the other thing we thought to be very important, and there it happened to be that a Payne's Gray fan, an airbrush artist, Michael Bähre, who also is a Lovecraft fan, read about what we were doing in a magazine and decided he was going to be the one to paint the cover for the album. After he described to me how much thought he was putting into the idea, I let him do it, and eventually he came up with a painting which is just as much a rendition of the whole book as the music we created. The painting having so many details, we decided to have it as a poster and I still think that no other cover could have fit our music and Lovecraft's book better.

Schmidt lists his favorite Lovecraft stories as *The Dream-Quest of Unknown Kadath*, "The Cats of Ulthar," "The Festival," "The Music of Erich Zann" and "Ibid." of that last one he says it is "because it is funny and therefore not so typical." If you haven't already seen that article/story, by all means check it out. While, as Schmidt says, it is not typical H.P.L., it is nonetheless brilliant. Schmidt talks of his interest in the author in the following way:

I started reading short stories by Lovecraft at the age of 14, I think my father or my uncle gave me some anthology of horror stories in which there was "Pickman's Model" and "The Rats in the Walls." My favourites at the time were Poe and Byron and other dark or gothic authors, so it was no wonder that Lovecraft hit me like a hammer. Since then I have read just anything I could get by him, and though today I don't read as much as I used to (life seems to take more time to live), I still do read some Lovecraft once in a while and it strikes me just anytime I do. His writing just draws me in and to me it is a complete escape from whatever is happening around me. I'd even say this only happens to me when I read Lovecraft. Only music does the same thing to me: music can suck me in and let me feel unconscious of my surroundings in exactly the same way. I don't know why that is so, but I have seen other people being just drawn in the same way by our musical rendition of *The Dream-Quest...*, even when they hadn't read the book. On the other hand there are people that are entirely insensitive to this phenomenon, so I guess it must be a gift or just simply individual taste.

Leading off the disc is the instrumental track "Dream Sequence." This starts with piano in a pretty, yet dark and somber mode. As the cut carries forward it resembles a classical music piece with symphonic orchestration joining in a gentle yet melancholy melody that, while still managing to grow, is very cohesive. It segues directly into the next number.

That next track is "Sunset City," and it comes in amidst the melody from the last piece. As it moves on, though, acoustic guitar based progressions take over. The lyrics speak of the city that Randolph Carter seeks in the story. They move this through in a ballad-like manner for quite some time, but other elements gradually emerge. Eventually it bursts up into a very powerful more full progressive rock texture, but this is never fully realized. This is another that is both beautiful and sad. It turns later into an instrumental segment that merges progressive rock textures with classical ones, then moves out into a very pleasing (almost flamenco-textured) instrumental excursion. At just about five and a half minutes, it's rather amazing the amount of complexity and changes they infuse into this one. It varies between more sedate and more fully powered sections as it carries forward, and (as on the entire album) the vocal arrangement with two similar voices at times paired at times seeming to dance around each other is especially effective. Once again they pull this directly into the next number.

Comparing the opening paragraph of Lovecraft's tale to the first verse of the song gives a strong vision of how the group are re-telling the story in their own words. Here is the original Lovecraft prose:

Three times Randolph Carter dreamed of the marvelous city, and three times was he snatched away while still he paused on the high terrace above it. All golden and lovely it blazed in the sunset, with walls, temples, colonnades and arched bridges of veined marble, silver-basined fountains of prismatic spray in broad squares and perfumed gardens, and wide streets marching between delicate trees and blossom-laden urns and ivory statues in gleaming rows; while on steep northward slopes climbed tiers of red roofs and old peaked gables harbouring little lanes of grassy cobbles. It was a fever of the gods, a fanfare of supernal trumpets and a clash of immortal cymbals. Mystery hung about it as clouds about a fabulous unvisited mountain; and as Carter stood breathless and expectant on that balustraded parapet there swept up to him the poignancy and suspense of almost-vanished memory, the pain of lost things and the maddening need to place again what once had been an awesome and momentous place.[12]

When reformatted to fit the song it opens up with the following verse: "All the domes, arched gates and flights of stair / Flooded with red beams from sun's sinking chair – / Who is hindering my will / To reach this place—oh, so tranquil?"[13]

Continuing the lyrical theme, "The Caverns of Flame" is next in line. For those familiar with Lovecraft's story the title, and indeed the links in the words of the song should be clear. The reference is drawn from one section of the story that begins in this way, "In light slumber he descended the seventy steps to the cavern of flame and talked of this design to the bearded priests Nasht and Kaman-Thah."[14] Looking now to the lyrics, once again it is easy to see how deftly it has been adapted here. "Down ten times seven in lightest slumber / To where the bearded priests pray / In the shadow of the flame / Where none has seen the light of day." [15]

The song comes in with the most rocking structure displayed thus far, feeling a lot like jazz fusion. The rhythmic structure, and indeed the overall sound, seems just a bit odd. In other words it works well, but feels slightly off from the concepts that one things of as "mainstream music." Instead the focus is on a hard-edged sort of sound. They work through almost two minutes of instrumental music before they drop it to a more metallic texture for the main song structure. Even then, though, the arrangement is full of odd angles that seem fitting with the story line. A nice keyboard solo is thrown in the midst of this, followed by a short guitar showcase. The whole band then launch into a heavy, but powerfully progressive rock oriented journey. It drops to a rather strange segment with just percussion and dueling voices later, then bursts out into another instrumental movement that carries the band through a number of interesting changes. This is a very dynamic and wondrous piece of music. It eventually drops back to an almost classical mellow ballad section that serves as the composition's eventual conclusion.

"Moonlight Waters" is next in sequence and comes straight out of the song that precedes it. The lyrical connection here is a little less direct, but there nonetheless. One has to skip ahead in the story quite a bit to find it, though. The first clue comes in the first two lines of the song, "Through the gates of cataract / Black galleys leap their way."[16] Two more of the elements that seem most relevant in showing what part of the tale is being retold come in the third stanza of the lyrics. It begins with these two lines, "Captive held and offered meal / No human dares to eat."[17] Looking to Lovecraft's words for reference we find these passages in the story that correspond nicely. Keep in mind, though, that the sequence is not the same as in the original text, but rather rearranged to the order of the song. In regard to a description of the place in which these events take place, these are the words the band alludes to:

Past all these gorgeous lands the malodourous ship flew unwholesomely, urged by the abnormal strokes of those unseen rowers below. And before the day was done Carter saw that the steersman could have no other goal than the Basalt Pillars of the West, beyond which simple folk say splendid Cathuria lies, but which wise dreamers well know are the gates of a monstrous cataract wherein the oceans of earth's dreamland drop wholly to abysmal nothingness and shoot through the empty spaces toward other worlds and other stars and the awful voids outside the ordered universe where the daemon sultan Azathoth gnaws hungrily in chaos amid pounding and piping and the hellish dancing of the Other Gods, blind, voiceless, tenebrous, and mindless, with their soul and messenger Nyarlathotep.[18]

The concept of captivity, though, actually comes from within the two paragraphs of the story that precede that passage:

Carter felt that the lore of so far a traveller must not be overlooked. He bade him therefore be his guest in locked chambers above, and drew out the last of the Zoogs' moon-wine to loosen his tongue. The strange merchant drank heavily, but smirked unchanged by the draught. Then he drew forth a curious bottle with wine of his own, and Carter saw that the bottle was a single hollowed ruby, grotesquely carved in patterns too fabulous to be comprehended. He offered his wine to his host, and though Carter took only the least sip, he felt the dizziness of space and the fever of unimagined jungles. All the while the guest had been smiling more and more broadly, and as Carter slipped into blankness the last thing he saw was that dark odious face convulsed with evil laughter and something quite unspeakable where one of the two frontal puffs of that orange turban had become disarranged with the shakings of that epileptic mirth.

Carter next had consciousness amidst horrible odours beneath a tent-like awning on the deck of a ship, with the marvellous coasts of the Southern Sea flying by in unnatural swiftness. He was not chained, but three of the dark sardonic merchants stood grinning nearby, and the sight of those humps in their turbans made him almost as faint as did the stench that filtered up through the sinister hatches.[19]

The final element referred to in the song comes from a later passage in the story, still during Carter's non-voluntary voyage.

At the set of sun the merchants licked their excessively wide lips and glared hungrily and one of them went below and returned from some hidden and offensive cabin with a pot and basket of plates. Then they squatted close together beneath the awning and ate the smoking meat that was passed around. But when they gave Carter a portion, he found something very terrible in the size and shape of it; so that he turned even paler than before and cast that portion into the sea when no eye was on him.[20]

It is important to note at this point that it's quite understandable if those unfamiliar with the story do not understand all of the references, but I have included the text for comparison to the lyrics, not as a "cliff-notes" version of the tale. By all means, read the original. It is actually a fairly complex story and not the easiest thing to do justice to in a short synopsis. That is a disservice to you that I have desire to attempt.

At over nine minutes in length, this is the second longest track on the disc. A pretty acoustic guitar based ballad melody begins this one with a very dramatic and mysterious texture. Vocals are added to supplement this feeling, and later keyboards also bring in more of a sense of wonder. The cut breaks out for a moment into a neo-classical movie soundtrack sort of texture. Then guitar takes it in metallic directions, but even though there is a lot of crunchiness present there are still plenty of progressive rock oriented, more melodic elements in play, too. As they build on this, the whole arrangement takes on a sound that feels like a hard rocking take on movie soundtrack symphonic textures. Then it drops back for an acoustic guitar solo with keyboards and choral like vocals as accompaniment. It drops back to just acoustic guitar and the vocals of the verse enter. They build on this general theme for a time. It eventually powers up into a hard rocking segment as it carries forward. Then they launch into another rock music based symphonically arranged movement. The keys take the lead for a while, weaving waves of dramatic melody. This gets incredibly powerful, and then moves into a slightly dissonant fusion related journey. They work through several new jams with this general motif to carry forward. This one has as many twists and turns as cityscapes in Lovecraft's tales often possess. It drops eventually to a pretty keyboard dominated section to carry on, after which it jumps up to one of the most metallic passages of the whole CD. A crescendo takes the piece to more atmospheric territory that both ends it and transitions directly into the next number.

An instrumental piece, that number is "Procession." It is also incredibly weird. At just over two minutes it is the shortest piece on the album as well. This composition is composed of strange sound effects, keyboards and other elements woven together into a mélange that is slightly pretty, but extremely unsettling. It ends with noisy wailing of cats. That conclusion is quite appropriate considering the next number is entitled "A Hymn to the Cats." It is even more appropriate given this later section of the story:

> Then through that star-specked darkness there did come a normal sound. It rolled from the higher hills, and from all the jagged peaks around it was caught up and echoed in a swelling pandaemoniac chorus. It was the midnight yell of the cat, and Carter knew at last that the old village folk were right when they

made low guesses about the cryptical realms which are known only to cats, and to which the elders among cats repair by stealth nocturnally, springing from high housetops.[21]

In fact, there is an even more telling paragraph from within Lovecraft's text to tie both the instrumental piece and the cats in to the tale.

Now much of the speech of cats was known to Randolph Carter, and in this far terrible place he uttered the cry that was suitable. But that he need not have done, for even as his lips opened he heard the chorus wax and draw nearer, and saw swift shadows against the stars as small graceful shapes leaped from hill to hill in gathering legions. The call of the clan had been given, and before the foul procession had time even to be frightened a cloud of smothering fur and a phalanx of murderous claws were tidally and tempestuously upon it. The flutes stopped, and there were shrieks in the night. Dying almost-humans screamed, and cats spit and yowled and roared, but the toad-things made never a sound as their stinking green ichor oozed fatally upon that porous earth with the obscene fungi.[22]

As "A Hymn to the Cats" opens, a pretty acoustic guitar based melody begins it in a peaceful ballad format. Tying into the chapter referenced directly above, flute comes in over the top of the arrangement, until then just guitar and keyboards. This builds upward in very pleasing patterns becoming both foreign in texture and extremely powerful. The vocals come in with a pattern that feels a bit like the more classical oriented of 1960s' folk music. These sounds don't stay long, though because as the intensity of the piece grows the singing takes on more standard rock textures. In the next instrumental segment acoustic guitar gets an impressive solo. This piece is another that has a lot of intriguing things going on within it. The variations on this one are more subtle, though moving within over-layers and growing textures and counter-melodies. They move languidly through changes taking them between the more powered sounds and those leaning more heavily into the sedate. They crescendo then atmospheric sounds are left in the midst. A dramatic, movie theme like movement takes it gradually building and segueing it into the next track. It is a track whose title, "The Way to Ngranek," refers to the story directly. The following paragraph shows from whence the name originates.

Then Carter did a wicked thing, offering his guileless host so many draughts of the moon-wine which the Zoogs had given him that the old man became irresponsibly talkative. Robbed of his reserve, poor Atal babbled freely of forbidden things; telling of a great image reported by travellers as carved on the solid rock of the mountain Ngranek, on the isle of Oriab in the Southern Sea, and hinting that it may be a likeness which Earth's gods once wrought of their own features in the days when they danced by moonlight on that mountain. And he hiccoughed likewise that the features of that image are very strange, so that one might easily recognize them, and that they are sure signs of the authentic race of the gods.

Now the use of all this in finding the gods became at once apparent to Carter. It is known that in disguise the younger among the Great Ones often espouse the daughters of men, so that around the borders of the cold waste wherein stands Kadath the peasants must all bear their blood. This being so, the way to find that waste must be to see the stone face on Ngranek and mark the features; then, having noted them with care, to search for such features among living men. Where they are plainest and thickest, there must the gods dwell nearest; and whatever stony waste lies back of the villages in that place must be that wherein stands Kadath. [23]

There is much in that segment which is referenced fairly directly in the lyrics—as these excerpts will show. "Want to find the destination ultimate? / Thou must climb the crags of Ngranek / Whereas hidden through the idols jealous haste..."[24] "This carved count'nance is to point, here / Where God's and mortals race may mingle / Live at places which are near the unknown KADATH." [25]

The music on this track comes in resembling some sort of tribal old world music with distinct Middle Eastern feel. The group build the structure of the song on this basis with layers upon layers of sound creating a wall of sonic textures. This one is an exotic musical tapestry. It doesn't wander far, instead seeming content simply to create this other world out of the sonic elements of the piece. A crescendo of sorts eventually turns to an outro that is composed mostly of atmospheric keyboards that connect it to the next track, another instrumental.

"Within the Vault" is that cut, and it comes in as a noisy (not to be confused with metallic) bit of chaotic music that seems barely under control. The track moves through a number of varying segments and eventually drops back to just piano to carry it on. Then the group move this out into another piece of almost overly busy jamming. This one definitely isn't for everyone, but if you give it the chance it can grab you. It is definitely the least accessible piece of music on the album. Still there are some quite powerful sections and the display of talent on this one is impressive. It's just not extremely cohesive and at times rather abrasive. The truth is, though, since the section of the story which the title seems to point towards is especially harrowing, it is an appropriate tone. There is, though, a sense of relief when it ends and the next piece takes over.

Keyboard tones, somewhat pretty, yet still unsettling, start this one, one of the longest on the CD. "Reaching Kadath" is the title for this number. While those disquietening, yet at the same time pretty sounds carry it for a time, eventually the band shift this out into a rather expansive and somewhat hard edged jam that is very dramatic. This has a neo-classical texture merged with heavy metal like sounds. This is also one of the most dynamic songs on the album, moving through varying melodies for a time, then shifting gears completely. It alternates between metallic passages, those that are more jazz oriented and mellower pretty ballad-like segments. Still, there is a cohesiveness to the number, never feeling like a number of different songs simply strung together.

"Nyarlathotep's Reception" is next in line. It starts with classical instrumentation in a processional type movement. It grows ever so slowly. Next it shifts to a progressive rock type of slow moving jam that has elements of the sounds of spaghetti western theme music. It moves around a bit taking on rather fusion-like elements and the keys find the chance to solo. Eventually this crescendoes out to a false ending. Then a dramatic, dark ballad-like section enters and begins slowly growing. A distorted, evil sounding spoken vocal comes over before the group launch into a killer hard rocking prog jam that is very dynamic and extremely dense with layers of percussion, instrumentation and vocals. It drops back down later, just a bit, and then bursts quickly back up into a metallic crunchy sort of progression. This one leans towards the heavier elements, but features enough prog textures to keep it from being considered heavy metal. The group resolve this out then turn it back into the segment that came before. Eventually, though, this gives way to a very tasty and melodic movement that carries the cut forward. Lots of soloing is worked into this format. Weird spoken vocals come in later to carry it onward. This is definitely one of the odder cuts on show here. It is also one of the most dynamic and has some of the disc's most frightening moments. At almost nine and a half minutes, it's the longest one on show too. The lyrics to this one tie in fairly directly to the story, and also points to later parts of it. For those who haven't read it, I'd rather not spoil any surprise. So, I'll just say that they even include a verse taken directly out of H.P.L.'s text.

An odd rhythmic, melodic pattern starts off the next track, "Riding the Shantak," but they quickly move this out into a dramatic progressive rock jam that has a lot of fusion elements. This instrumental number takes its name from a type of bird mentioned in the story. This one is another dynamic and quite powerful piece of music.

They close out the album with "Finale: Sunset City Part 2." Another instrumental, this one starts off with very sedate elements and gradually grows those into a powerful, yet quick classically oriented progressive rock jam. A false ending eventually gives way to a period of silence followed by a flourish of sound that ends the journey.

While I'm not going to pass judgment on the bulk of the output of this artist, Septimania has one Lovecraftian track and I would put that piece into the territory of progressive rock. The song, "Cthulhu Rising" is part of a three pronged suite entitled "Visitors 1, Universe 0." It was released on the 2001 album *Welcome to Septimania*. The piece is roughly nine minutes in length and is a bombastic and dynamic number that seems to combine elements of King Crimson, Frank Zappa and Birdsongs of the Mesozoic into a mélange that is quite entertaining, if a bit weird. This one features several varying segments and some odd vocals that are just barely audible (but not really enunciated/produced high enough to comprehend) and some rather awesome instrumental work. This number is both strange and tasty.

Septimania is a creation of a gent named Jonathan Thomas who writes and performs much of the music. He also happens to reside in Providence, Rhode Island. When asked about his favorite Lovecraft stories, Thomas said, "I'd rather not play favorites. Different stories have different strengths. Depending on whatever spirit or circumstances move me, I've reread (or re-reread) some, and hope to reread them all sooner or later." When asked about how he worked to create a Lovecraftian texture to his music, Thomas was more willing to illuminate:

> Within a science-fantasy suite titled "Visitors 1, Universe 0," "Cthulhu Rising" is a multilobed structure clocking in at 8:47. In keeping with the Old One in question, the overall texture is dissonant, amorphous, and chaotic. The nightmarish consistency is portioned in terms of several repeating keyboard phrases. The first connotes a sinister descent, in good Gothic tradition, whether of Francis Wayland Thurston in his doomed researches or any of his hapless fellow characters. In the second phrase, something oozes and shambles, with bass and drums adding a sense of lumbering mass. Another brief, more precipitous descent approximates that of Cthulhu or R'lyeh beneath the Pacific. The final relentless phrase implies cultish resurgence, with vocals in particular conveying the spread of insanity until "the stars are right" again.
>
> The keyboard phrases were written beforehand, and recorded with Providence band V.Majestic (arguably the best band in Providence, ever) in their rehearsal space. V.Majestic collectively improvised their parts (in what amounted to "spontaneous composition"), and the resultant eight-track tapes were collated, edited, and processed by Frank Difficult and J. Thomas. The V.Majestic lineup on "Cthulhu Rising" is Robert Jazz, guitar; Stu Powers, drums and vocal; Gerry Heroux, trumpet and vocal; Vinyl von Ricci, bass; and Frank Difficult, Kurzweil K2000 (and nothing says "cosmic dread" like the sound of mellotron). The rest of "Visitors 1, Universe 0" was in collaboration with Steven Ventura (electronics and manipulations).

When the question of what Lovecraft's work has to offer to music in general, Thomas said this:

> If nothing else, basing lyrics on Lovecraft helps avoid a lot of boy-girl rubbish, insofar as H.P.L. had no patience for hack romance. Musically, H.P.L.'s work has been used to inspire a much wider range of atmospheres than seems to be acknowledged: the aura of horror and menace in Univers Zéro's "La Musique d'Erich Zann," but also the pulp-fiction levity of Caravan's "C'thlu" [sic], and the melancholy of the band HP Lovecraft's "The White Ship" or (psychedelicized) sense of wonder in its "At the Mountains of Madness." Four decades along, I imagine a lot of potential remains to be tapped. Maybe a crew like Art Zoyd could work up *The Case of Charles Dexter Ward* as an opera.

Of his introduction to Lovecraft and the lasting draw of his work, Thomas said:

> At age 12, in 1967, I bought a Lancer paperback called *The Colour Out of Space and Others*, with a flaming skull on the cover. Setting horror in familiar landscapes (I might qualify as "ethnic Swamp Yankee") made an impression on me, which was heightened on moving to Providence during college and thereafter (in particular by *The Case of Charles Dexter Ward*), and when writing my own horror stories. Over time, I've come to appreciate more and more about H.P.L.'s wealth of personality. This is from "Miscellaneous Impressions of H.P.L." by Marian F. Barner: "It was his custom to read aloud the plays of Shakespeare with his [aunt Annie Gamwell]. The more cruel the part, the better he liked it, and would shout it out to be heard by the neighbors. I have heard neighbors tell me of his 'quarrels,' but I know that it was only Shakespeare being read." What a card!

John Petrucci is probably best known as the guitarist in the neo-progressive rock band Dream Theater, but his credits also include work with G3 (with Joe Satriani and Steve Vai), Liquid Tension Experiment and others. He makes his way into the Lovecraft vein with the song, "Necromonicon." This instrumental, written for the Sega Saturn game of the same name really only shares a title with Lovecraft's works, though. Petrucci revealed that he has not read any of Lovecraft's work and simply wrote the music for the game. It is a very dynamic piece that features both Eastern tones and mysterious sounds at times. It also manages to get quite powerful and magical. It is overall a frantic hard-edged progressive rock excursion. Its title is of course related to the book that is said to contain all sort of horrifying mysteries and which is a key element of the Lovecraftian mythos.

While there have definitely been plenty of progressive rock ties to H.P. Lovecraft, it is truly the heavy metal genre that embraces it more than any other. There is one other group, Nox Arcana, that fits loosely into prog rock still to be addressed, but they will be covered in a separate chapter later. The next analysis will be focused on heavy metal.

Chapter 4

THE CRUNCH MEETS CTHULHU:
HEAVY METAL AND LOVECRAFT—PART ONE

As previously mentioned, the form of music that has most widely utilized Lovecraftian elements is without question heavy metal. In fact, there are so many instances of H.P.L. inspired music in this genre that while other genres only have one chapter devoted to them, there is no way to really look at this form in that short a space. Heavy metal is an aggressive form of rock music normally played with distorted guitars. The sound first emerged in the late 1960s and grew throughout the 1970s before peaking in the '80s. While that period was its apex, heavy metal is still alive and well. The genre has perhaps spawned the largest number of sub-styles (at least easily definable sub-styles) of any form. In this section whenever a new style is mentioned there will be an attempt made to explain to the uninitiated what the term mentioned means.

As with any musical style, there are arguments as to what album or band constituted the origin of heavy metal. However, in many minds (including the author of this book) the first example of the genre was Black Sabbath and their self-titled debut. It is therefore fitting considering the impact Lovecraft has had on the genre that that album featured Sabbath's one link to his work.

With their first album, Black Sabbath established both their sound and a small following that was to grow over the years. Formed in the late 1960s that first self-titled disc contained the track "Behind the Wall of Sleep." Although this is not a direct quote from the title of the Lovecraft story, bassist Geezer Butler was certainly responsible for bringing his literary influences into the fold and paying tribute to Lovecraft on the number. Those words do not explicitly point to the story, either, but rather seem to be more of a mood setting nature. "Feel your spirit rise with the breeze / Feel your body falling to its knees / Sleeping wall of remorse / Turns your body to a corpse..."[1] Musically, the track is firmly rooted in the dark and bluesy sound that Sabbath made a mainstay of their trademark, but it includes a triumphant metal section that also would be destined to show up frequently in their music. This is proto Sabbath at its best.

Some have said that the lyrics to the band's song "Planet Caravan" are also inspired by H.P.L. I see even less of a connection to the works of the author on this one than the previous cut. The number comes from the follow up album, *Paranoid*, but really I just don't buy the Lovecraft connection on that one at all. It so happens that after the present book had pretty much been wrapped up, I got a response from Geezer Butler on the issue. Out of respect to both Mr. Butler and the truth I make a point of working his reply into the book, to make the situation absolutely clear. Here is what he said:

> I think I may have borrowed the title "Behind the Wall of Sleep" from "Beyond the Wall of Sleep" (of which I have a first edition), but it's so long ago, I can't really remember. The lyrics came from a dream I had, hence the title. Most of my inspiration in those days came from books by Dennis Wheatley, rather than Lovecraft or Poe. "Planet Caravan" had nothing whatsoever to do with Lovecraft.

Perhaps one of the most amazing things about the metal connection is the gap that follows. While the album that probably started the genre features a Lovecraft inspired track, it was to be quite some time until another group would follow the lead. In fact, while that self-titled Black Sabbath album was released in the last year of the 1960s, no other metal band would wander into Lovecraft territory until the 1980s. Once his work was embraced, though, it was done like most things in heavy metal—with a vengeance. While Sabbath was without question the most influential band of their era of metal, the next Lovecraftian connection in metal would come from arguably the most influential band of the 1980s metal sound.

A behemoth of the heavy metal scene, Metallica is probably best known to the general public as the artist responsible for suing Napster. That analysis certainly does not give credit to the legacy of the band, though. The group, practicing a high speed, precision based form of heavy metal known as "thrash" came into existence in 1981. Although they did not invent thrash, they were definitely the band who brought it into the limelight. As the group's popularity soared, they eventually moved away from that style, but not before popularizing it and bringing a wide range of musical prodigies into their shadow.

Metallica has been responsible for two Lovecraft related songs. The first came from their first major label release *Ride the Lightning*. It was a song entitled "The Call of K'Tulu." The instrumental begins with a mysterious acoustic guitar melody. That is moved through various melodic changes for a while before the harder edged sounds take over, bringing up both the intensity and pace of the piece. At nearly nine minutes in length it is meaty, if a bit repetitive. It really feels little like the type of music that Cthulhu might inspire.

With their next excursion into the territory of Lovecraft, though, the band seem to have truly gotten it right. "The Thing That Should Not Be" comes from their next album *Master of Puppets*. While the title is not so obvious a nod to Lovecraft, the song is far more relevant. Feeling dark and mysterious, acoustic tones start this one. As the thrash guitar enters, it carries the melody that was begun in the introduction. This also includes an appropriately psychotic sounding guitar solo. The lyrics are quite a well-written homage to the Cthulhu legends. "Hybrid children watch the sea / Pray for Father, roaming free."[2] Later we get to hear the lines, "He watches / Lurking beneath the sea / Great Old One / Forbidden site / He searches / Hunter of the Shadows is rising / Immortal."[3] Later lyrics include, "Crawling Chaos, underground / Cult has summoned, twisted sound."[4] The song even includes a direct quote from Lovecraft in the form of what is probably the author's most famous couplet, "Not dead which eternal lie / Stranger aeons Death may die."[5] Although this quotation is slightly altered, (Lovecraft's version from the story "The Nameless City" reads "That is not dead which can eternal lie, And with strange aeons even death may die."[6]) fans of H.P.L. can certainly enjoy this homage.

Formed in the early 1980s, German band Rage was originally called "Avenger" and released two discs under that name. Since there was also a British outfit using that moniker they opted for a name change. The group have released several tracks that fit into H.P. Lovecraft inspired territory. Their album *Trapped!* was the first to feature one such cut. That was the song "Beyond the Wall of Sleep." Looking to the lyrics of this track it is obvious that the song is inspired by the story of the same name. "... In a mysterious landscape / Far beyond my belief / In a shape that I can't face / I have found the real me / I have the one desire, / it sets my soul afire / There's something waiting in the deep / Beyond the wall of sleep..."[7]

The Lovecraft story which shares a title with this song is an interesting tale that fits into what many call Lovecraft's "Dream Cycle." All of these works, this one included, revolve around the concept of an alternate form of reality which can be accessed through dreams. In this particular story a curious investigator finds an entity whose true life is within this existence, but also touches upon our world.

Rage's disc *Black in Mind* included not just one track which touches on Lovecraftian territory, but three. The first is "The Crawling Chaos." While the lyrics have distinctly Lovecraftian tones, they do not have a lot to do with the story from which the term originates. "... A giant maelstrom, absorbing what we'd left back, / the deserts of cadaverous, mortal loam / and jungles of decay and decadence, where once had been the homelands of my people, / temples of my ancestors, / they were gone, dead and gone..."[8]

In H.P.L.'s written world, The Crawling Chaos is another name for an entity known as "Nyarlathotep." According to *The Encyclopedia Cthulhiana* this being is "the soul and messenger of the Outer Gods."[9] It also says that "The Crawling Chaos acts as an intermediary between The Great Old Ones and their worshippers, as well as taking messages between the Great Old Ones themselves."[10]

Musically this one pounds in quite heavy with a 1980s metal approach. The verse is rather stripped down in texture, but still quite chunky. This one has a little bit of a raw edge, but the chorus is very anthemic. There is an exceptionally tasty lead guitar solo on this one and the band soars in a jam out of that for a short time. Then a movement with an almost prog metal, neo-classical texture takes it from there. The closing section, with its combination of epic sounding vocals and meaty guitar soloing all over is very effective.

"Shadow Out of Time" is somewhat of an epic piece coming in at over ten minutes in length. It starts with the sounds of wind that carry the track forward for a while. Then an acoustic based, dramatic, ballad type style begins to slowly rise from there. After a time, a driving metal crunch takes over from there, working through a few minor variations. With a staccato sort of approach, this segment serves as a sparse backdrop for the first vocals. The verses run in this manner, while the first chorus is in a somewhat more filled out approach to the same basic musical concept. As it moves into the second chorus, the ante is raised by turbo-charging the arrangement, making this the most effective segment of the track thus far. It moves back to the mode that preceded it for the next verse, then charges out in a Metallica-like progression that gives way to a more epic metal texture from there. They carry it forward in a melodic, but still quite heavy romp after this, and then move into an instrumental segment with both some challenging changes and tasty guitar work. This gives way to a crescendo, then a creepy sort of acoustic guitar based mode moves this onward. The texture here is both pretty and twisted. This interlude runs through for a time until hints of more crunchy metal begin to appear. Then the band launch back out into one of the thrashy segments with a noisy guitar soloing over the top for a short time. This is one of the most aggressive sections of the track. This motif holds the track for quite some time until it drops back to a stripped down percussion and vocals mode for a brief period. Then it fires right back up to where it was before. Another segment of meaty soloing takes it over the top of this later, at points accompanying the vocals. A crescendo gives way to a reprise of the acoustically driven intro segment, then wind sounds come in to end the cut as they began it.

The lyrics to "Shadow Out of Time" also fall well into Lovecraft territory, and come closer to the story whose name it bears.

> "Like a shadow out of time it's injected in my mind, / like a shadow out of time. / Like a vision in disguise it took hold of all my ways, / like a shadow out of time. / They have told me I've reacted like I was not from this earth. / I guess this something inside me was not. / When I've got these visions that I look down at myself I get scared. / This is not my body, but it's ... what ?" [11]

In the Lovecraft tale, much as in these lyrics, a man is convinced that his mind is being transposed with another entity. At times it happens in dream and at others during periods of amnesia. In the following excerpt he relates the concept in a way that shows parallels to Rage's take on it:

> Had I, in full, hideous fact, been drawn back to a pre-human world of a hundred and fifty million years ago in those dark, baffling days of the amnesia? Had my present body been the vehicle of a frightful alien consciousness from palaeogean gulfs of time?
>
> Had I, as the captive mind of those shambling horrors, indeed known that accursed city of stone in its primordial heyday, and wriggled down those familiar corridors in the loathsome shape of my captor? Were those tormenting dreams of more than twenty years the offspring of stark, monstrous memories? [12]

Rounding out the Lovecraft content of the *Black In Mind* disc was the cut "In A Nameless Time." The lyrics to this one are more intricate and extensive than the other two Rage attempts at Lovecraft territory. Like the one before, it turns towards H.P.L.'s "The Shadow Out of Time" for inspiration. It begins by putting the listener deep into the story. "Awakening this curse was the least of all my fears. / If I could turn back time to free me from this crime. / It started back in time when something stole my mind / and led me through aeons to place and time unknown..." [13] At first the narrator says, "Take me back home from these cryptic walls. / I wait for a sign from my own reality, I wait here / in a nameless time..." [14] Later, though, his wishes change, "Take me away to these cryptic walls. / I wait for a sign from this old reality, / it calls me from a nameless time. / Take me back to these cryptic walls, / to this desert place and this strange reality, / it calls me from a nameless time..." [15] The next section of the song is entitled, "The Expedition," and that is precisely what the lyrics tell about. "... I broke up to find this place, find those from the elder race. / In this unknown desert land I was digging in the sand. / Found these ruins, blocks of stone, older than the Egypt ones..." [16] As the narrator continues his search he finds, "these enchanted books, pages that I've known too well..." [17] The "Finding Out" section details just that, the narrator's dark realizations. "... Although the most I knew I needed a final proof / if I'd been one of them. And then these pages came / My written words! So I'd been here in one of them..."[18] This is a very direct interpretation of Lovecraft's story. While I won't give you the texts that show this, as it would ruin any first surprise of the tale for you, rest assured that this is quite an accurate retelling.

2003's *Soundchaser* was a concept album and the whole story involved a modernized tale that was based on ideas from H.P.L. According to the liner notes, the theme of the album is based around the creatures on the cover, which the band has dubbed "Soundchasers." To quote that source, "these biomechanoids were created by an alien intelligence, as described by the American author H.P. Lovecraft."[19] This is certainly a special adaptation of Lovecraft's ideas and has as much in common with Lovecraft's original tales as the film "From Beyond" has with that story. For those not familiar with that film or the original story only the first five or so minutes of the movie came, albeit modified, from the original text, the rest being an all new creation based on some of the concepts hinted at in the tale. Still, the story they create from these beginnings is intriguing and the album is entertaining. Again from the liner notes, "the origins of life lead back to the Great Old Ones, an unknown species from out of space."[20] So begins the Soundchaser story.

The disc opens with "Orgy of Destruction (Intro)." Sounds of thunder begin this, then a heavy, mystical sounding pounding metal texture takes it. Spoken distorted words come overtop. Neo classically tinged progressions take over from there.

"War of Worlds" is next, and a hard-edged jam makes up the elements of this track. It is a strong metal rocker with an anthemic chorus. It has a very tasty, albeit '80s metal styled, instrumental segment.

With a title like "Great Old Ones," the Lovecraft connection on the next piece is obvious. This one stomps in and again has a metal technique that is rooted in the 1980s. It is rather catchy and has a sing along type nature. It also includes a meaty main riff. It drops later to a rather creepy sounding sparse arrangement, then jumps up to more anthemic territory.

The next number is "Defenders of the Ancient Life." This cut is a somewhat generic older styled metal number. It is fast and potent, but just a bit too much like the other material on the album to maintain its own identity.

A change of pace comes with "Secrets in a Weird World," the next track on the CD. This, although heavy and definitely metallic, is very dramatic and features an almost progressive rock arrangement. It has much more in common with neo-prog bands like Dream Theater than with the '80s metal that much of the album resembles. This has an epic and mysterious texture and features an ever-changing song structure. Piano is all over this, but it also finds plenty of room to stomp in sheer metal fury. It ends with a brief piano solo.

"Flesh and Blood" is up next. It comes in balladic and dramatic. It quickly ramps up, but still maintains an air of mystery. It drops to just guitar and vocals for the verse back to ballad territory. It jumps up to a meaty progression for the building of the next segment of the tune. This is one that doesn't stay in one place long, wandering through varying musical themes and styles. It features one of the strongest vocal performances of the disc.

With "Human Metal" the band drop the momentum they had going on the last couple. While it's not a bad song, it is much in the same vein as the bulk of the album. This one is pretty much pure 1980s styled metal.

With a very meaty riff and a cool guitar solo, one would think that "See You In Heaven or Hell" would be a step back up. While those two elements do add to the piece, the track is still too generic to really stand out.

"Falling From Grace—Wake the Nightmares (Pt. 1)" comes next. This starts with a pretty and intricate acoustic guitar solo. The opening vocals are laid over top of this. As it builds, it's in a pretty and powerful ballad style. It then shifts gear to a pounding metal progression that blazes forth fast and heavy. This portion is just an instrumental break, though, the track dropping back down to balladic to carry forward. After the next verse they bump that up, speeding it up and intensifying it, infusing the solid metal elements into this format. Then they move it fairly strictly into a full on heavy metal arrangement. This gets quite heavy and powerful and includes some exceptionally tasty guitar work. Then it moves into more melodic and neo-classical territory as another instrumental break runs through. This then gives way again to the straightforward metal chorus. A quick shift in the progression segues this directly into the final track of the album.

They close out the album with "Death Is On Its Way." Starting with the short metallic instrumental foray that came out of the last number, this quickly drops back to potent balladic textures from the opening vocals. The metallic themes come back after the verse. This song feels very much like a marriage of progressive rock and metal during the next vocal segment. Then a frantic, more purely metallic, instrumental section takes it with a noisy guitar solo wailing over top. It drops to a new riff, at first back in the mix. Then the whole band screams out in this new progression. A newer metal groove takes it later. Then a progressive rock like section ends to an acoustic guitar based section that finally ends it. This also ends Rage's contribution to Lovecraftian music to date.

Witchita, Kansas might not seem the most likely location to give birth to one of the most legendary cult metal bands, but Manilla Road came out of just such a location. The group, formed in 1980, has released quite a number of pieces with fairly direct Lovecraft influences since 1987.

Their first Lovecraftian foray came with the track "Children of the Night" from *Mystification*. The link on this track comes in the following verse: "Forgotten through the years / Born of The Ancient Ones / In The Forest of our fears / Cthulhu still is here..."[21] While the reference is definite, it is also fairly nonspecific as to Lovecraft story, seeming more a general continuation of the Mythos. Musically, this one is fast and furious, feeling at times like early Rush, but with more aggression. There are other points, where the music, but not the vocals, seems to call to mind King Diamond. This closes with a noisy and somewhat chaotic outro.

The title track of the disc is another that has Lovecraft leanings, although a bit more subtly. "Through the winds of time / A poet found the key / To the Elder Rhyme / Some call the song mystic."[22] From a musical point of view, this track starts off in a mellower ballad-like mode. As it jumps up into it is into a more old school heavy metal mode ala Judas Priest. This is a more melodic and catchy song than "Children of the Night."

1988's *Out of* the *Abyss* is rife with Lovecraft links. Even the liner notes speak directly of Lovecraft's pantheon.

> THE MYTHOS: The true gods of Earth existed long before our ancestors crawled mindless upon the shore. Yog-Sothoth, Shub-Niggurath and many more insatiate monsters, whose ultimate throne is chaos. Greatest of all is he called Cthulu. Only in ancient blasphemous manuscripts can that name be found in many forms. This is one of the terrifying tales in the everlasting sago of The Old Ones. [23]

The first number on the disc to show a tie to the author is the title cut. On that song again it is a reference to "Cthulu" that brings in the connection. "... Out of The Hell / Comes Cthulu's rage..."[24] Musically this one comes in frantically fast. It jumps about in an arrangement that feels like a cross between thrash and the music of Primus. It includes a screaming guitar solo.

With "Return of the Old Ones," certainly the title shows a link right at the start, but the lyrics also contain more references. At one point the group sings, "The Old Ones shall return / Cthulu's words still burn / Into the etchings of all time..."[25] Then later the listener hears the following words, "Through death comes life / Blindness to sight, into the light / Here in the darkness / Black dreams of Chaos / I hear Cthulu's call / Forever The Old Ones / Shall be upon us / Until they devour us all."[26] In this song, those are the closing lines. The music to this one starts in a dark ballad style before changing to a heavy stomping metal sound. It drops down to a mellow, almost bluesy segment at points. This feels at times like Dio and at other times like Mercyful Fate. The ballad-based section, sometimes including spoken vocals, comes back in later. The piece includes a smoking guitar solo. This is very dynamic and dramatic. It dissolves to mellow, but dark, atmospheric sounds to carry on. This section eventually ends it.

From the same disc, "Black Cauldron" adds several different Lovecraft references, some a bit less direct than others, to the mix. The song begins with the following lines, "Dark angel of Chaos / Cthulu comes / Bringer of evil..."[27] The next section might be a reference to "Herbert West Reanimator." However, were it not for the other Lovecraft nods on the disc, it would seem more likely that it is simply a coincidental use of language, "... The Black Cauldron / Dead placed in the Cauldron / Re-animate..."[28]

If the references in these quotes are less obvious, the connections in the next segment are unmistakable. "Doorway to Hades / The Old Ones' gate / The Old Ones bring Chaos to earth / Conjuring Yog-Sothoth's birth..."[29] As the track continues the images of the Old Ones and the reanimated dead are united into one theme, as we find that these formerly dead are reviving "... To war for their master / Cthulu's pride..."[30]

In the track "War in Heaven" it seems that there is a battle between Cthulhu's forces and those of Valhalla (home of the Norse Gods). The sole reference to the old one comes in the following portion, "... Here the horde of Chaos passes / Blindly following Cthulu's call..."[31] of the battle we are told, "... The sacred words are spoken / The Seventh Seal is broken / Valhalla's doors are open / The Fires of Mars burn on / All warring gods are destined / To fight until they fall..."[32]

Manilla Road continued showing their love for H.P.L. with 1990's *The Courts of Chaos*. The reference here, though, comes indirectly, through a movie based on the writings. It comes in the form of the song "From Beyond." Looking at the lyrics to this one it is fairly obvious that the Stuart Gordon film, based extremely loosely on the Lovecraft story, is the true inspiration here. "Computations are figured / The tuning forks are set / Turn on the Resonator / Start the experiment / The forks begin vibrating / Dimensional walls gone / The machine is emanating / Resonations from beyond..."[33] This one has a unique texture at first, sort of guitar dominated progressive rock with a funky sort of groove to it. The signing has a touch of a whine to them. The chorus takes on a heavier, more traditional heavy metal approach. This sound is fully realized on the instrumental break, which is a scorcher. As they launch out "from beyond" that segment, the song is fully energized into a metallic stomper with screaming vocals. From this point forward the cut scorches forward as a thrasher. It almost feels like a different band. The lead guitar solo segment that comes out of this is purely awesome with neo-classical tinges, but nothing taking away from the sheer power.

The Lovecraft leanings of the band would come to full fruition, though, with 2001's *Atlantis Rising*. With that disc they created a concept album that deals with a war between the Old Ones and the Gods of Valhalla. This is a theme at which the song "War In Heaven" from *Out of* the *Abyss* hinted. While many of the cuts on *Atlantis Rising* have no direct link to H.P.L., since they all fit into the Mythos based theme, they will all be addressed here. A fairly lengthy story line is included in the liner notes on the disc setting up the story that the CD documents.

"Megaladon" opens the album. It is a mood piece at first with atmospheric sounds and a spoken processed line of vocals. It bursts into a metal jam with a killer driving bass line and frantic guitar overtop. This feels at times like a more metallic take on early Rush, but as it moves into the song proper it takes on a more standard metal approach, but the Rushish themes do return. This turns into a frantic metal jam later. It features some awesome guitar work later, feeling a bit like the psychedelically-tinged fury of the mid section of Judas Priest's "Sinner." A ballad mode with these sounds dying over top gives way to ocean sounds to end it, "Birth of the Old Ones / First of The Titans / Mastered by no-one, before Poseidon."[34]

The next couple tracks on the disc fall under the heading of "Book I—The Rise (of Atland)." Leading off this duo is "Lemuria." "What we've longed for all these years / Before the world shall soon appear / The Elder Gods have come to free / Lemuria."[35] A keyboard (sounding almost New Age in texture) intro comes over top of the ocean sounds to start this. The composition turns this basis into a ballad segment by placing vocals over the top.

On "Atlantis Rising," the ballad approach of the last one is forgotten. This is a metal stomper that features a meaty guitar riff and vocals that feel a lot like Judas Priest's Rob Halford. This one has no direct Mythos connections. It doesn't wander far musical, but is a very competent and tasty metal track. It ends with the sound of storm

The next segment of the album is entitled "Book II—The Fall (of Atland)." It leads off with "Sea Witch." A guitar driven ballad mode that feels at once like Metallica's "Sanitarium" and Iron Maiden's mellower moments stars this number, and the group build the song up in this manner, "For Cthulhu shall rise / When the witch casts her spells to the King…"[36] As it carries on the following lines come in, "… through her dark incantations / the Old Ones shall appear."[37] The ballad style runs through much of the piece, but the intensity and volume is ramped up later into a stomping recreation of the musical themes.

Since the last track seemed to serve as a summoning, it is appropriate that "Resurrection" follows it. This is heavy and dark with a more raw and extreme metal texture. Some awesome guitar work runs all over the intro to this one. "Resurrection through the Eye of the Sea / As Cthulhu comes alive—Midgard bleeds."[38]

Next up is "Decimation." A cool, slightly off kilter sound starts this, then gives way to a more straightforward dark and very heavy section that is another that calls to mind the more metallic side of Rush. This becomes a very oppressive track filled with metal fury.

"Out of Eye of the Sea / Bringing his demon army / Elder God of blasphemy..."[39] Later lines specify which Elder God is being referenced there, "... Triton defending the well / Falls to Cthulhu's black spell..."[40] "Mankind is brought to its knees / Now Midgard bleeds / Cthulhu's Eyes / Face of Annihilation."[41] "... Unleashed on every shore / comes the Cthulan black horde / Leaving a bloodbath of gore..."[42]

The next segment of the album comes in with the next song. It is entitled "Book III—Bifrost (the Rainbow Bridge)." The first song (of two) in this segment is "Flight of the Ravens." The sound of wind gives way to an acoustic guitar ballad mode. The lyrics on this one have no blatant Lovecraft leaning, but the piece is a powerful ballad.

"March of the Gods" closes out Book III. It is a metal stomper that jumps directly out of the last one. It is quite tasty and features a juicy guitar riff and off kilter bass work. Again there are no specific references to the work of H.P.L. here.

Continuing on with their story line the next step is "Book IV—The Battle (of Midgard)." The track that opens this segment is "Siege of Atlantis," and it is made up of more frantic metal. It includes both some of the most melodic metal on the disc and some very death metal oriented growling in a snarled "siege" that is repeated. It ends in noisy weirdness. "Cthulhu's dark knights doth make their last stand / Valhalla's warriors lay siege to Atland."[43]

"War of the Gods" is the final track both to Book IV and the album. A dramatic hard-edged ballad style makes up the basis of this for most of the song. It turns into a frantic metal jam later, though, then drops back to the balladic style that formed the earlier moments. This time, though, heavy guitars create a mass of sound over the top. A storm ends it. "Holy gods defy the beast of fear / Now the Old One's magik fades / Conjuring their spells the Norns appear / Banishment Cthulhu's fate."[44]

Mark Shelton, the main man behind Manilla Road, shared his insights regarding creating music based on Lovecraft's work. He explained it in the following way:

Actually it is not that difficult. All I have to do is read some Lovecraft and the strange comes out of me automatically. I have always liked haunting sounding music and the trick to making any song that is inspired by Lovecraft is to create lyrics that represent his style of writing or story telling. His work is very atmospheric and so I try to put the same emphasis on the songs that are influenced by his work. You have to not be so obvious in your lyrical content and allow the listener to be able to use their own imagination; so I try not to be too explicit with the lyrical descriptiveness.

In regards to what Lovecraft's work has to offer music, Shelton said, "Very few writers have ever achieved a total style of their own but Lovecraft did and that is what works so well with Lovecraft ideas and Manilla Road music." He further explained the situation in the following way:

Manilla Road has always had a style unlike anyone else and so working with storylines that are of the same unique quality make the songs very interesting and mysterious. Lovecraft, Howard and Poe have been very important in the development of the Manilla Road lyrical approach and so the offering to the music is huge in my mind.

Shelton's introduction to Lovecraft's writing was actually a friend and associate of H.P.L. He said, "Robert E. Howard is what led me to Lovecraft. I was a huge fan of Howard and once I found out that Howard was into Lovecraft I had to check it out." He went onto explain his continuing attention. "What has kept my interest is his ethereal approach to writing and the timeless essence of his stories along with the fact that his works are unique and ethereal." He said that his favorite Lovecraft story is "The Tomb."

Bal-Sagoth is a British band that was formed in the 1980s by a figure known only as "Byron." According to their website it is a "project intended to take the form of a sublimely symphonic black/death metal band swathed in a lyrical concept of dark fantasy & science-fiction, inspired by the celebrated style of the grand pulp horror and fantasy literature of the 1930's [sic], whilst simultaneously being infused with the baroque and arcane mysteries of ages long past and Byron's enduring fascination with ancient mythology and occultism."[45] That, as you might imagine, leads them to fall heavily into Lovecraftian territory. Although only one early track, "Hatheg-Kla" is immediately recognizable as coming from Lovecraft's mythos, Byron reveals this:

In truth I'd say that more or less all our material is in some way or another inspired by Lovecraft and/or his contemporary R.E. Howard. The spirit and thematic essence of the pulp fantasy & horror of the 1930s is something I have tried to infuse our compositions with from the outset. Specifically, the Lovecraftian notions of denied hominid primacy and the existence of pan-galactic entities whose power is so staggering that it can scarcely be perceived or understood by mankind is a concept which permeates the band's lyrics at every level, and has been a key recurring theme which underpins all six Bal-Sagoth albums to date. "Hatheg-Kla," the first track on our debut album, was so named to alert people to the fact that here was a band inspired by the works of Lovecraft.

He further explains that the theme of which he speaks on their albums involves "colossal extra-dimensional fiends which have been trapped within the confines of an empyreal prison following a great war countless aeons ago, and humanity's terrifying realization as to their own true place in the cosmic order of things (and subsequent unwitting attempts to liberate said fiends) which is purely inspired by Lovecraft (and maybe a hint of Marvel Comics too)."

He relates the ways he has incorporated Lovecraftian elements in this way:

... from the creation of my own pantheon of dark star-faring pseudo-gods, some relatively benign, others wholly malefic, and a supporting cast of meddlesome humans who are granted terrifying glimpses of these awesome progenitors of mankind, to the fabrication of a bibliography of apocryphal occult tomes and repositories of forbidden lore full of phonetically un-pronounceable incantations, the tenets of Lovecraft's Cthulhu Mythos were certainly my primary influence in this area of the Bal-Sagoth lyrics. The essence of Lovecraft's literary techniques and stylings can be effectively transposed to the prose/verse hybrid characteristic of the Bal-Sagoth lyrics, and the extensive narrated passages within our songs give ample opportunity to generate a quasi-Lovecraftian atmosphere within the fabric of the soundscapes. Eerie and discordant synthesizers playing cues written to mirror the lyrical content alternate between horrific minor chords and bombastic fanfares, all adding a unique texture to our self styled 'pulp metal.' Bal-Sagoth songs such as "Summoning the Guardians of the Astral Gate" and "The Dreamer In The Catacombs of Ur" effectively showcase this synergy of inspiration and realization.

The aforementioned track, "Hatheg-Kla," is a two-minute instrumental made up of various keyboard tones and layers. The effect is of a dark and mysterious landscape with sounds that hint at hidden horrors. The overall effect is to create a texture which would seem quite appropriate as the backdrop for any number of H.P.L.'s stories. While it certainly does not qualify as heavy metal, it fits nicely into the epic symphonic nature that much European metal calls upon. It is featured on an album entitled *A Black Moon Broods Over Lemuria* and was released in 1995.

As one might guess, Byron is a long-time fan of H.P. Lovecraft; in fact, he did his "third year university special study on the works of Lovecraft, specifically the fusion of literary genres within his stories." He describes the drawing force of Lovecraft's work as follows:

> The scale of Lovecraft's dark vision drew me to his work. Whereas some writers of fantastic and macabre fiction are content to have their threats and dangers to mankind be articulated in purely corporeal and secular terms, Lovecraft's horrors were invariably of such a vast and immeasurable magnitude that not only could the very sight of them sunder a man's mind in an instant, but to even ponder the implications of the existence of such abhorrent fiends would result in severe dementia. Additionally, the masterful engineering of hinted horrors and insidious suggestions of the intrusion of something unnatural into the fabric of normality is one of Lovecraft's most potent literary weapons, the effects of which intensify with successive readings.

Byron lists his favorite Lovecraft stories as, "The Call of Cthulhu," "The Colour Out of Space," *At the Mountains of Madness*, "The Dunwich Horror" and "The Shadow Over Innsmouth."

I tried to reach the band again in regards to their most recent release *The Chthonic Chronicles*, but had no luck. I wasn't even able to get my hands on the lyrics. So, I can't be certain which tracks (if any) have Lovecraftian links. That said, it seems likely (since I believe the term "Chthonic" means related to Cthulhu) that most, if not all of the disc might have ties to Lovecraft's mythos. However, I'll stick here to the songs that where I can make out an explicit link from what information I have.

Assuming my concept of what the term "Cthonic" means, the opener "The Sixth Adulation of His Chthonic Majesty" would be one of those numbers. It begins with keyboards and choral textures building an epic, neo-classical texture. After a time a spoken recitation begins with, "Oh great and luminous one / who came from beyond the stars to slumber serene beneath the Earth."[46] These words, if no others, would seem to indicate that it might be Cthulhu who is referenced here. The verse represents an awakening call and the song reflects this in its musical themes. Dramatic and powerful harder edged sounds (but still with that definite neo-classical texture) emerge to create the motif for the remaining portions of the track. This is built on and reworked in a steady flow of alterations.

Since I'm just including the more blatantly explicit pieces here, the next in line would be the sixth song on the CD, "Shackled to the Trilithon of Kutulu." It is a noisy, metal jam. This is almost pure thrash, but yet there is a spoken recitation at the beginning and some crazy neo-classical instrumentation, feeling like a movie soundtrack all over this. While this track is not for everyone, it is certainly unique. If there is any question about the meaning of this number, it does include the whole "In his kingdom of R'lyeh..." recitation in its closing segments.

The next piece where I find definite Lovecraft leanings is "Unfettering the Hoary Sentinels of Karnak." It is the eighth cut on the album. It has a more straightforward metal approach, but still layers of neo-classical instrumentation skirt around the outside of this motif. The vocals are split between a spoken recitation (similar to that found on some of Rush's early releases) and half snarled, half shouted death metal like sounds. This one is another brutally aggressive piece, but yet they manage to work in an almost playful instrumental break. This again is a bit hard to take at times. Still, when it resolves out into the triumphant sounding, more melodic segment later the song includes some incredible textures.

Entitled "Return to Hatheg-Kla," it's easy to see the closing piece's connection both to the Mythos and to the earlier Bal-Sagoth number. The track begins with weird ambient textures, then other elements join in, but still this doesn't really resemble music, but more dark, mysterious atmosphere. It becomes much more noisy and bombastic, but for almost two minutes it doesn't really develops into anything that could be perceive as a melodic structure. Then a pretty, but rather dark melody plays and operatic, non-lyrical vocals come over the top. They work through a few different incarnations of this theme and the instruments and voices seem to fight for control of the composition. In the end, though, the voices dominate the outro. At roughly three and a half minutes, it's easy to see that this final musical hurrah doesn't last long.

While the bands already discussed have lyrical ties, a few have just the name of the group linking them to the author. Coming out of Spain in the 1980s, metal band Ktulu's only real link to Lovecraft is their name. Another interesting, if passing connection is to Iron Maiden. This band, who started in the '80s, is one of the most literary metal bands, with many of their lyrics drawn from books. However, the only link they have ever had to Lovecraft is in an album cover. Their *Live After Death* disc includes the famous couplet mentioned earlier inscribed on a tombstone.

German band Mekong Delta started in the 1980s and in the course of forging their own breed of thrash oriented progressive metal, also created a good amount of Lovecraft inspired music. While they were absent from the music scene for quite some time, they have recently reformed and have set to take on the music world again with an upcoming new disc. Their album *Music of Eric Zann* is one on which the author has a large impact, as the title would indicate.

The album seems to be a concept disc based fairly loosely around the concept of that Lovecraft tale. It seems to this reviewer that the album equates the songs here to the original story in that the music seems to be a ward against the monsters of the modern world. It opens with "Age of Agony." The track is a metal screamer that combines a classically tinged swirling mass of nearly chaotic music that feels a lot like the cacophony that Lovecraft used to describe Zann's music. Violin soars over the top of much of this music in very appropriate fashion. The metal textures here are both highly tasty and very much in keeping with the concept of the story. The chorus here seems to describe the journey that the listener is about to embark on while at the same time tying it to the theme of the story, "In the dark it began / An irrational ban / Irreversible Curse / I'm the only one left / With the might to fight back / In the battle of sound."[47]

The next several tracks seem to be representative of the "monsters" from which the band is seeking to shield the world. They really don't directly link into the Lovecraftian mythos, except in this symbolic way, so they won't be addressed individually here. Suffice it to say they are more tasty slabs of thrashy metal with a classic sound. The next cut with explicit Lovecraft ties is "Prophecy." However, the track before that, while an instrumental, will certainly be of some interest to Lovecraft fans.

The music on "Interludium (Begging For Mercy)" is very intriguing. It starts with an acoustic classically tinged guitar introduction. This carries forward with increasing levels of complexity for a time, then a classical instrument segment that seems to combine elements of the soundtrack to both "Psycho" and the movie "Reanimator" takes the piece into its next section. These elements merge with metal guitar in a very complex arrangement that again calls to mind the sounds that Zann himself might have created. This one is very classical music dominated, but still has enough metal meat to please fans of the genre. This one is one of the more intriguing marriages of the two styles to be produced. It is exceptionally powerful and more than just a little creepy.

"Prophecy" screams in with more metal fury. It seems to be a call to pull the listener into the work of the group in protective duties. "Before the night is over / You'll be initiated, too / You are elected for the world / You must be prepared when the time will come / Listen to the prophecy now / You're given from the Great Old Ones / The music in your hands is bastion."[48] As the song carries forward more violin is laced over the top of the frantic metal jamming. This is another very tasty heavy metal cut.

While there are more songs before it, the next track that ties fairly directly into Lovecraftian territory is "Epilogue." This piece is really not metal, but more sedate progressive rock. It seems to describe the frustration at the difficulty of the appointed task. It is important to note for those who have not yet read the story, or those who don't remember clearly enough, that the window at which Zann played his protective symphony was located on Rue d'Ausil.

> With tired eyes too sore to rest / I feel so cold inside... Through the old window / From out of space / He must have seen it / Long time ago / I ran away from / The Rue d'Ausil / Where he banned our downfall / In other dimensions / And he gave his life away for the world to live on / What have we learned / Nothing has changed...[49]

In the climax of the story, the narrator does in fact run away as described by this passage, "I plunged wildly away from that glassy-eyed thing in the dark, and from the ghoulish howling of that accursed viol whose fury increased even as I plunged." Another interesting note about the street in question comes in the first sentence of the story, "I have examined maps of the city with the greatest care, yet have never again found the Rue d'Auseil."[50] While the album continues with one more piece, an instrumental, this number truly climaxes the Lovecraftian ties on the disc in a nice way.

The process of creating such music is described by Mekong Delta leader Ralf Hubert in this way:

> We tried to realize it over 2 ways. First we take the story as a metaphor and put it in our time, on the second hand with a special kind of composition, which uses a kind of own harmony room build up out of the so called "Triton" which is split up into intervals of small seconds, and the triton himself, what gives the whole composition a unique sound.

When asked about what Lovecraft has to bring to music, Hubert answered in much more explicit detail than many of the others included here. He said this:

> A lot of inspiration—if you take his typical kind of writing using the "Cognitive Dissonance" you can transfer this into music, do the unexpected, what is done real often on the album. Let's take a real simple example: if you play—let's say E major, than go to the "subdominant" A major followed by the "dominant 7"—H major 7. We are used that the next chord to be done is E again (that's what most of the pop songs are build up like), but why do not go to ES Minor, that is unexpected and strange, as Lovecraft often did in his stories. You can transfer this to nearly every parameter of music, equal if it's rhythm, melody or form. If you listen to the album you will find a lot of examples of Lovecraft's "Cognitive Dissonance" —doing the unexpected.

Listing his favorite H.P.L. stories as "Pickman's Model," "The Music of

Erich Zann" and "The Shadow Over Insmouth," Hubert had the following to say about what drew him to Lovecraft, and what retained him as a fan:

> His special kind of writing and his enormous fantasy—he never really described the abnormous things, but for whatever reason there are suddenly in your head (in my case). This is really unbelievable. And one other thing is also incredible, that he wrote in a way that a lot of things created is out of his fantasy becomes common for a lot people. For example take the *Necronomicon* of the crazy Arab "Abdul Alhazred"; a lot of people in the metal scene believe that this book exists, it's the same like with the "Apocryphs" of Moses. And on top there have been scientists who lived at his time who also thought that he got this book and asked whether they could have a look in it—so many strange things around Lovecraft.

Dream Death is credited by some as America's first death metal band. The band came into existence in 1984 in Pittsburgh, PA and in 1987 joined the ranks of Lovecraft related bands with their first album, *Journey Into Mystery*. That disc included the song "The Elder Race," as their sole Lovecraftian journey. In fact, the disc would be the only release by the group. An altered version of the band, though, would later show up as Penance, but would not produce any more H.P.L. based material.

1985 was the year that the first incarnation of the next band came into existence. Forming under the name Genocide in Flint, Michigan, they would soon be called "Repulsion." Their album *Horrified* was released in 1989, although it was recorded earlier. That disc included the song "The Lurking Fear." The cut bursts in with a meaty, hardcore like riff that calls to mind The Dead Kennedys. The frantic drumming and raw production showcases a song that is one part thrash and one part hardcore punk. This is an exceptionally short song at less than a minute and a half. The lyrics really, though, only seem to share a title with the story, rather telling a tale of a zombified populace after a nuclear war.

Ohio based Necrophagia was formed in 1983. Their sole connection to Lovecraft is a very minor and indirect one. They mention the *Necromonicon* in their song, "Ancient Slumber," but the liner notes state that this was "inspired by the movie 'Evil Dead.'"[51] The lyrics to the song, which appears on their 1987 debut disc Season of the Dead, includes the following lines, "... *Necronomicon*, book bound in flesh / source of all that is evil..."[52] Interestingly enough, though, the closing line, "Ancient Ones rule once more,"[65] could be seen to tie in more closely to the source material.

Formed in Texas in 1983, Rigor Mortis has released one song, "Re-Animator" that is based on Lovecraft territory. While it probably derives its origins from the film rather than the story, this cut is a frantic powerhouse of death metal intensity. The vocals, however, are much easier to understand than the classic death metal growls, and the song includes some intriguing and rather quirky changes. It also features an extended instrumental break. It has few lines of lyrics:

> He seeks fresh bodies in the morgue to test his new creation / Injecting serum in the corpses for the hope of re-animation / He has conquered brain death, welcome back to life! / Re-animator, re-animate me / The human dosage factor is unknown a super charged zombie awakes / Becomes sort of a blood blithering creature everyone's death is at stake / They will give him power, he will give them life! / I'm not insane, I'm dead, but he gave me life![53]

Celtic Frost emerged from the rising star of Switzerland's Hellhammer, taking their place on the metal landscape in 1984. The group were one of the bands responsible for the development of the European style of heavy metal, combining death metal themes and sounds with neo-symphonic arrangements. Later that same year they went into the studio to record the album *Morbid Tales*, which included two Lovecraftian compositions, the only ones the band have done to date.

The first of those tracks, the title song to the disc is based in a fast paced, rough around the edges metal approach, much in the vein of old school thrash. It is essentially one line in the lyrics of this one that ties it to the writings of HPL. While the lyrics seem to literally be a series of glimpses of varying "morbid tales," the following line is an obvious Lovecraft reference, "To Yog Sothoth they moan."[54]

While the other cut, entitled "Nocturnal Fear," again seems to be a series of short lyrical snapshots, only vaguely related to one another, there are more (albeit somewhat vague) Lovecraft links to this one, alongside references to such pieces of Mythology as Tiamat. Only one line is explicitly Lovecraftian ("Azag-thoth howls"[55]) but there are several others that are fairly easy to interpret as being inspired by HPL's mythos. The imagery of "Obscurity hides the plateau / Stars darken at their place"[56] sounds somewhat as if Lovecraft might have imagined it. A possible reference to Cthulhu comes with the line "The sleeping lord awakens."[57] Another line which seems well suited to the Lovecraftian mythos comes toward the end in the form of "The old gods and their tribes."[58] Musically this cut is not that far removed from "Morbid Tales," but does seem to lean a bit more towards what today would be called "hardcore."

Celtic Frost's Martin Eric Ain had this to say about their forays into Lovecraftian territory:

We wanted to create mood pieces that would emulate the inhuman strangeness that Lovecraft had described so often. As one of the earliest extreme metal bands we tried to achieve this by incorporating musical elements considered foreign to the genre. Back in 1984 when we first worked on Lovecraft based themes the heavy metal canon was quite limited and strict. So, for example, we included a multi-layered violin on a track titled "Nocturnal Fear." Said violin was played out of tune and rhythm to what the band had played and this already worked like a charm to evoke a chthonian atmosphere.

Ain went on to say that he felt that Lovecraft appeals to musicians for inspiration because of the following:

I think that his constant threat of an inhumane otherworldliness of monstrous, grotesque and degenerate proportions manifesting itself on our plane of existence, his allusive non-compliance with what he suggests, are what gives his writing the strength to evoke visions, images, smells and sounds that would otherwise be literally unheard of.

Ain revealed that is favorite Lovecraft works are "The entire Arkham-Cycle, or Yog-Sothoth-Cycle as it is also referred to." In speaking of what drew him to Lovecraft's work, and what has kept him as a fan, Ain said that it was this:

The Cthulhu Myth, basically the entire Mythology of the Ancient Ones. *The Necronomicon*, in my opinion it is one of the strongest cases of fiction becoming reality in the history of the occult. His manic, driven, almost hysteric style of writing that had an undeniable urgency to me as a teenager. Any author with the name H.P. Lovecraft that comes up with "characters" that are named Azathoth, Shub Niggurath, Nyarlathotep and the Fungi from Yuggoth has earned my undivided affection.

Formed in 1985, Canadian speed metal group Sacrifice have released two albums with links to Lovecraft, albeit most likely by way of Hollywood. The first of these songs comes with their debut disc *Torment in Fire*. With the title "*Necronomicon*," certainly this song from that album has its ties to H.P.L. However, with lines of lyrics like, "Bound by human flesh / recite the book of the dead"[59] and "rites are read back to hell return the evil dead,"[60] it seems nearly a foregone conclusion that the song refers to the film *The Evil Dead*, rather than to Lovecraft.

The second track, "Re-Animation" is from the group's 1987 *Forward to Termination* disc. The words on this one seem a little less definite about their source, but most likely the Stuart Gordon film is the origin here. "The final curtain has been opened to regain my soul / Blood restores my flesh, ice cold / Awakened, now I break the silence of life / Raging uncontrollably, pummeling with spite."[61]

Texas based band Solitude Aeturnus was formed in 1987. As they developed their metal style their first album *Into* the *Depths of Sorrow* (1991) included the Lovecraft inspired "White Ship." The lyrics seem very much in keeping with that Lovecraftian tale: "I was but a traveler / Floating endless through the sea / On the other side of knowledge / Through the pliancy of dreams / And voices there upon the ship / Spoke of radiant place's splendor / Beautiful shores with sands of gold / Wherein exists no torment or pain."[62] The Lovecraft story "The White Ship" (referenced in Chapter 2) does include the following description of a fabled city, "And the cities of Cathuria are cinctured with golden walls, and their pavements also are of gold."[63] Certainly this comes close to the lines in the song.

Musically this one comes in ploddingly heavy and dark, a bit like Black Sabbath and Candlemass. A killer twisted guitar riff takes it to move the number forward. The vocals have a bit of Eastern tinge to them, as does the song in general. Overlaid backing vocals add some definite depth and a sense of mystery to the tune. They energize the cut later with both more aggression and more speed, and then it shifts into an exceptionally quick paced tune. Then a tasty guitar solo (a bit Eddie Van Halen like) surges overhead to move the piece onward. Then it shifts into a mid-paced Sabbath like groove before launching into a neo-classically influenced jam. This then gives way to the return of the Eastern leaning vocal section. Sound effects seeming to call to mind surf, wind and rain end the composition.

Entombed is a Swedish band that was formed in 1988. With the track "Stranger Aeons," they threw their hat into the Lovecraft ring. The song (from their second album *Clandestine* released in 1991) is basically frantic riffing with death growls over top. It has a few meaty guitar riffs and definitely features an overpoweringly frightening tone. It also includes a tasty guitar solo. A twisted take on the famous couplet that refers to Cthulhu is included in this number—"Stranger Aeons even death may die."[64] Entombed's take on it comes out as "Stranger things that eternal lie / Awaiting beyond the time to die."[65]

What if Spinal Tap were to be a thrash metal band with theatrical overtones like Marilyn Manson or Slipknot? Then consider if they took their lyrical content from the double entendre laden territory where it resides and moved it into the down right raunchy, but still kept the whole sense of doing everything for the joke. The resulting band would more than likely be GWAR. The name GWAR stands for God What an Awful Racket, and the band was formed as marketing experiment at a Richmond, Virginia University. When you consider the group's over the top costumes and characterizations as creatures who have come to earth to destroy mankind Lovecraft would seem a likely candidate for inspiration. They have really only done one song, though, that shows Lovecraft tendencies. That is "Horror of Yig" from their 1990 *Scumdogs of* the *Universe* album. Even with that track, the overall effect of the lyrics is tasteless humor: "I saw Yig. / He's so big. / He smokes cigs. / Eats just like a pig. / Ooooohhhhhh! I saw Yig. I saw Yig. I saw, I saw Yig! ..."[66] They do hint at the type of horror Lovecraft attributes to the Great Old Ones, though in later lines, "... Spreads hate and foul cheer. / The horror, The HORROR! / Where Yig doth tread no man tread tomorrow. / Reeking death harvest of humans in hatred..."[67]

When asked about the song, David Brockie of the group said the following:

> Like a lot of what we have done, I really can't remember the how's and the why's. I do remember reading all the Lovecraft I could get my hands on, and it seemed like a good place to find inspiration. I always liked Lovecraft's monsters the best, especially the way they were described in very vague terms and would send you insane even if you only thought about it... YIG came from the last line of a Lovecraft story I read when I was but a lad—a weird dude moves into an old house and becomes fixated on the steeple of a crumbling church he can see out of his window. The black reveries grow more intense until a demon crawls out of the steeple and flies towards him. This creature he names YIG, but does not describe. The horror of this scene stayed with me. It's best heard in the music in the opening noise jam where you can hear Marlon Brando as Col. Kurtz repeating 'The horror, the horror...' We kind of injected a humorous element to the creature that I'm not sure Lovecraft would approve of. So YIG become for us a hideous, multi-stalked gibbering mess that was a friend of GWAR's but not to be trusted due to his disgusting and treacherous behavior (such as cheating at cards with his multiple tentacles). We even had a straight-up Lovecraft parody demon named "Log-Suckoff." He was a demonic pizza deliveryman.

The track does in fact start with the sound bite that Brockie speaks about, with bagpipes as a backdrop. Then the cut shifts into high gear from here with a frantic heavy metal as frantic attack—not just a musical attack, but rather feeling like a battle in modern warfare. As the vocals kick in they are in a grunting, shouted sort of sound. The music, though, has almost a funky texture, feeling a bit like Primus does Red Hot Chili Peppers. As it carries on, though, a new more solid thrash riff takes it. This one moves through a number of changes, carrying out transformation from one metallic jam to another. This is a high energy and fun extreme metal stomper. The bagpipes and more sounds of war return later amidst this chaos. It is definitely weird, but also a lot of fun.

Brockie also shared his opinion of what makes Lovecraft attractive to musicians.

> If the idea of creating your own world from what comes out of your head appeals to you, you'll find inspiration with H.P. Even a non-horror-phile can see that. If never compromising your vision in the face of extreme disdain sounds admirable, even to the extent of becoming an outcast in "normal" society, then Lovecraft is your man. As far as what it offers to music specifically, if you think of words as notes, and stories as symphonies, you can relate the writing and telling of a story to the arrangement and playing of a song. I don't know if that helps or not but it sounded pretty good.

He spoke of his love of Lovecraft's work in the following way:

> Like many I first became aware of Lovecraft through the pages of old horror mags like *Creepy* and *Eerie*. I was always drawn to horror and anyone who follows a similar course is inevitably confronted with Lovecraft. Unfortunately some very awful films were made in the 60s and 70s that borrowed Lovecraft titles and essentially abandoned the whole story. I wondered how such crappy films could have anything to do with such a supposedly great horror writer. It took a while for me to figure out that it wasn't H.P.'s fault, and that indeed he'd been dead anyway! But finally by early high school I was completely hooked. I re-read my favorites to this day. I suppose that is what keeps me as a fan. I can always find joy in his writings; always imagine new obscenities from his descriptions. He is an endless treasure.

When asked what his favorite Lovecraft tales might be Brockie had this to say:

> My all-time favorite is his longest tale (sometimes it is presented as a novel), "At the Mountains of Madness." Its influence on GWAR is unmistakable—a group of alien beings are frozen in Antarctica, de-thaw, and wreak havoc on an unsuspecting world. Many others come to mind but the titles elude me—lets go with "In the Walls of Eryx" (classic), "The Shadow Over Innsmouth" (fish-people), and "Pickman's Model" (for the painter in me).

Florida based Morbid Angel was one of the original bands that began a death metal movement in the state of Florida. They got their start in the 1980s, and over the years have produced their share of material that touches on the work of Lovecraft. Those H.P.L. tendencies began all the way back with their 1986 demo entitled *Abominations of Desolation* and its track "Azagthoth," a name shared by the band's founding lead guitarist. Musically an odd drum pattern starts this, then gives way to an off-kilter jam that almost feels like a thrash take on modern King Crimson. This one is really odd, but quite interesting. The guitar solo is noisy and raw. They drop it back for a few measures, and then explode out into a new jam that is very meaty. From here the guitar takes another solo. They move into several changes from this point, all in instrumental fashion. At times they even sound like a thrash take on early Rush, but more of the old Metallica elements show up as well.

With 1989's *Altars of Madness*, the band quoted from a Cthulhu chant in the song "Lord of All Fevers and Plagues." "... Ia iak sakkakh ia sakkakth / Ia shaxul / Ia kingu ia cthulu ia azbul / Ia azabua..."[68] The cut pounds in heavy and crunchy, then shifts into a frantic off-kilter thrash that is rather intriguing. The vocals are angry growls. It shifts gears in a clunky turnaround later to a new thrash jam. This feels a lot like early Metallica at times. A great jam transpires after the new thrash mode, this one a noisy guitar solo instrumental progression. Then the fury is pushed to the limit as a scream takes the track into the fastest segment of all. This powers out of the gate all thrusters firing and the frantic vocals just add to the texture.

The 1991 *Blessed Are The Sick* disc included more than one reference to Lovecraft's creations. The first shows up in the song "Unholy Blasphemies." While the majority of the lyrics on this one are anti-Christian rantings, the lines, "Yog Sothoth evil one / Come forth and taste the blood..."[69] do make an appearance. This song is choppy, fast and brutal thrash with death styled vocals. It feels rather raw.

"The Ancient Ones," from the same album, features not only the reference in the title, but also includes the lines "... Come forth ancient ones, Tiamat Kutulu..."[70] and "... Kutulu snaps his jaws."[71] Musically this one comes in fast and very tasty. It includes a meaty instrumental section that's rather quirky and very dynamic. It jumps later to a screaming faster jam. After the last line of vocals another new instrumental section takes it. This is personally one of my favorite songs from the band.

While "Angel of Disease" from 1993's *Covenant* disc includes references to Shub Niggurath and Kutulu, some of the other names that show up, such as Absu and Nammtar show that the most likely source for inspiration was the Simon Edition of the *Necromonicon*. Still, such lines as "Shub Niggurath goat with one thousand young..."[72] and "Abominations of the sky / Kutulu meets in the void / Ancient Ones rule once more...,"[73] while gotten to from an indirect source, are definitely derived from Lovecraft's work nonetheless. The song itself is heavy and frantic metal. It features some extremely strong guitar work. It also has a rather dynamic arrangement and is an especially potent piece of music. It drops to a slower segment with a slight echoey texture that is very effective. The vocals here, while leaning towards a shouted growl, are very easy to understand as opposed to the bulk of songs in that style.

Another track from the same disc that has some Lovecraft references is "Sworn to the Black." This cut thunders in fast and furious with more traditional death metal styled vocals. The enunciation on this is still much clearer than a lot of vocals from this genre. This one is another that is quite strong and it is also very heavy. It also features a very intriguing instrumental break. "Blood of the ancient ones boils / At war—war with the race." [74]

Formulas Fatal to Flesh, the band's 1998 entry includes several songs with Lovecraft ties. The first is "Heaving Earth," which makes mention of "Chthhuhlhu." The song itself is pounding thrash with death growls. It drops to a slower plodding section later and includes a killer guitar solo.

"Prayer of Hatred" opens with the following Lovecraftian declaration, "Blessed Be The Ones / The Most Ancient Ones / Blessed be the Ones / Who were here before and after remain..." [75] This one starts in a mode not unlike the last track, but eventually drops into an almost psychotic sounding off-kilter percussion based section. This gives way to a more melodic instrumental section, but then moves back to the territory from which it came. This is not for everyone, but quite tasty. The more melodic segment, feeling very dark and creepy returns later. The opening section comes back in later, getting quite frantic in its re-creation.

While "Disturbance in The Great Slumber" is an instrumental, it seems to tie into the Mythos both by its title and the fact that it seems to be related to the next cut on the disc, almost serving as the opening segment of it. It starts as a dark but gentle lullaby. Later heavier waves of keyboards carry the melody on. This is a creepy, but enchanting piece. It drops to more sparse elements to end.

"Hellspawn—The Rebirth" feels in many ways like a continuation of the previous number. It starts, though, with plodding metal, then shifts gears to a very brutal and aggressive thrash that makes up the rest of the number. "... Answer the call of the Oldest One..." [76] and "... Forever I dream continual dream / We sleep undisturbed again / Chthhulhu [sic] we dream in peace again..." [77] These lyrics showcase a glance at the sleeping Old One himself, great Cthulhu.

"Covenant of Death" is based on fast paced quirky thrash. It drops to a mellow melodic segment that takes it up to its final noisy conclusion. The only lyrical link to Lovecraft comes in the form of "igi-nu du-a-hur igi-se-zid-gin" [78] While it might not be easily related to Lovecraft, the booklet lists the translation of this line as "Enjoy now this ignorant bliss in which you live / For the awakening soon shall come." [79]

The next track is "Great Invocation of the Living Continuum." Interestingly enough, though, the liner notes include lyrics for this, but the song doesn't show up on the album at all. Those listed words, though, are full of references to H.P.L.'s Mythos.

The following lines, "... That of might shall / Define what is right / For unmatched is the Power / of Chthhulhu [sic] Most High..."[80] show up in the song "Umulamahri." The final words of the track are similar to the invocation of "Prayer of Hatred", "... Ancient Ones rule once more."[81] Musically this one comes in almost stuttering, then shifts to a more brutal frantic riff. This one is a bit weird and nasty and full of brutality. It includes some killer guitar work.

While there has certainly been much heavy metal covered in this chapter, there are many more. This is essentially just the first coming of Lovecraftian metal. Later bands will be addressed in the next chapter.

Chapter 5

MOSHING TO THE MYTHOS:
HEAVY METAL AND LOVECRAFT—PART TWO

Last chapter focused on heavy metal, and this chapter is a continuation of that theme. The difference being that all of the bands featured in Chapter 4 were formed in the 1980s or before, whereas the groups included here are from 1990 to the present day. It is truly proof of Lovecraft's enormous impact on the metal genre that it takes two chapters to showcase that music, but also a lasting tribute that newer bands are picking up the banner and flying it high.

Thergothon started in 1990, and by November of the next year released a four-track demo tape. In addition to showing off the group's own unique blend of doom metal meets death, *Fhtagn-nagh Yog-Sothoth* also presented their intense interest in the writings of H.P. Lovecraft. That recording included four songs, all based on Lovecraft. The numbers were "Elemental," "Evoken," "Yet the Watchers Guard," and "The Twilight Fade."

The first track, "Elemental" features that famous couplet from "The Nameless City," and it is actually attributed to "Abdul Alhazred." That, of course, is the name Lovecraft invented as the author of the infamous *Necronomicon*. This fact is brought home in a letter Lovecraft wrote to Robert E. Howard in 1932.

> I can't quite recall where I did get Abdul Alhazred. There is a dim recollection which associates it with a certain elder—the family lawyer, as it happens, but I can't remember whether I asked him to make up an Arabic name for me, or whether I merely asked him to criticize a choice I had otherwise made.[1]

The song feels a bit like an odd funeral dirge as waves of keys play overtop of a rather slow moving metallic framework. While this one isn't as glacial as much of the rest of the band's music, it is slower than most. The vocals on this one are sung at times, and at other points they come in as incredibly deeply toned groanings. This one is really a strange one, but has some tasty moments. The weird combination of softly sung vocals and growled/snarled words is definitely unusual.

"Evoken" leads of with this verse, "the winds from the abyss of the night / blow out the candles / from beyond the sources of time..."[2] The ending comes in the form of the ominous line, "now the gates are open for Yog-

Sothoth."[3] This track is certainly only for certain listeners. It is slow plodding metal, but only barely heavy metal at that. It is a percussion dominated cut with the guitars seeming to be recorded in a cave. The vocals are decidedly crawling nearly-spoken growling guttural chants. The song is tuned way down to give it a very doom like sound. There are some intriguing guitar lines that come over top at points. It turns more towards traditional crunchy metal later, but is still so low-pitched as to feel as if the recording was slowed down, and the tempo is certainly in keeping with this impression. Odd keyboard strains join in later in the cut to add to the unique texture of the piece.

"Yet The Watchers Guard" is a slab of major plodding stoner metal with death like growls. It is heavier than heavy with a tuned down approach. The vocals are slow and guttural and nearly incomprehensible. The feeling of doom in the piece is oppressive. While this is one more piece covered herein not for everyone, it's certainly interesting. The song begins with these verses, "the towers they stand so tall and proud / at the planes of the planets of madness / the realm of wind and the darkened deities / the black goat of the woods with the thousand young."[4] As it carries forward, we are presented with the following quote, "despite the waste outlook this region is inhabited / the unholy presence of these ancient beings is almost touchable / they can neither see them nor touch them, but you can / feel them present at all the times and you can smell them, smell their foul presence..."[5]

"The Twilight Fade" seems to give images of the Old Ones ending their undersea imprisonment. "From the earth rise winds that chill our old bones / we see through my eyes those statues of frozen life / we hear through my ears the screams fade to the frost / and now as the flames are frozen / we dive to the lake of ice / as the twilight fades away we drown / we drown and we hear the call."[6] The cut thunders in with very raw but Black Sabbath like grinding. It is a short number with mostly spoken vocals. Throughout this section the lyrics are the most easily comprehensible ones of any of the songs. It does shift into more deathlike growls toward the end, and then the cut fades to its conclusion.

Their first (and only) true album, *Stream From the Heavens* (1994) includes two of the songs from that original demo ("Yet the Watchers Guard" and "Elemental") reworked along with four new numbers. Among those new tracks was "The Unknown Kadath in the Cold Waste."

While "The Unknown Kadath in the Cold Waste" is at first similar in many ways to "Yet the Watchers Guard," there is a bit more melody infused and it is considerably shorter. The vocals are echoey, spoken recitations processed to give them a strange distant sound. It is much more ambient in nature. It drops later to a pretty, almost classical sounding, keyboard dominated section that is as melancholy in texture as it is beautiful. This mode doesn't last long, though, shifting gears to more slow paced metal with growling vocals.

Talking about his band's Lovecraft ties, Niko Skorpio said, "We weren't... that Lovecraftian in the beginning, but these elements crept in quite soon and soon dominated the essence of Thergothon." He also explained the creation process as it applies to bringing Lovecraftian textures to the music of the group in the following way:

> My dreams and certain trance states were more or less influential to the process of writing the lyrics. But in general, there were no particular methods I can think of. We just did what we wanted, and it turned out the way you can hear on the records. It just happened.
>
> First, my lyrics played an important part in the creation of the first Lovecraft-inspired songs, so it had a lot to do with the interaction between the lyrics and the music. Also visiting desolate places, certain dreams I used to have... With instrumental tracks I've invoked the particular feel I had when reading some of Lovecraft's stories, and worked under the influence of that. I think making music is magickal work in the sense that you have to put yourself into it, let the thing devour your mind for some time and then it just happens.

When asked if Lovecraft was still an influence on him, Skorpio said, "For me personally, yes, to some extent. I do value the Lovecraftian Gnosis as a useful tool to be employed just as some other magickal system. Kenneth Grant drew some inspiring connections in his books, *Outer Gateways* in particular... As far as the other ex-Thergothon members go, I have no idea but I guess they don't hold any particular interest in Lovecraft's work."

In regards to his interest in Lovecraft he says that what drew him to the author was this:

> ... simply the feeling I got when reading some of his stories. The very same thing keeps me reading. Some time ago I found myself in the position of having to buy myself some of the classic stories again, and re-reading them after a couple of years' break was/is a refreshing experience. I still enjoy them as I did before."

Skorpio's favorite Lovecraft stories are "'Haunter of the Dark,' 'Shadow over Innsmouth,' *The Case of Charles Dexter Ward, At the Mountains of Madness*, 'The Colour Out of Space' and 'Call of Cthulhu' are the first that come to mind... there are many more but let's leave it at that for now."

Swedish band Tiamat came into existence in 1990, releasing their debut album that same year. That disc, *Sumerian Cry*, includes their first Lovecraft

link in the form of "Evilized." That song includes the following lyrics,
"When the stars are right / They will rise from the sea / Creatures from out of
time..."[7] While the Lovecraftian meaning of most of those words should be
clear to anyone who has read along thus far, it should be noted that the first
line refers also directly to the Mythos. Part of the return of the Old Ones
involves the stars being "right," meaning in the proper alignment. Musically
the song jumps right in, pounding out in tasty metallic fury from the time the
light turns green. After a quick paced introduction it slows down just a tad,
then the music kicks back into gear with growled vocals over the top. There
are moments where the fast music and the rhythm on the vocals call to mind
The Dead Kennedys just a bit. Later it drops to an odd sort of jam that almost
has a honky tonk texture (and even includes piano). This turns rather fusion
like in one of the most unusual turns for this type of music. This is quite
tasty, sort of death metal does Booker T. and The M.G.'s. After this interlude
the cut moves back into pounding stripped down metal to carry it through to
its conclusion.

Released the same year, the song "A Winter Shadow" includes these
words, "... A shadow out of time / Hidden between different spheres..."[8] This
suggests a tie to the Lovecraft story "A Shadow Out of Time," with its inter-
dimensionality concept. The music on this one starts with an almost Latin
sounding hard-edged intro that feels like the ending of another track. Then a
crunchy raw riff takes over from there, with acoustic guitar coming over top
to carry the themes from the intro. This runs through for a short time, then a
pounding thrashy segment takes over from there. This main segment of the
cut is rather dynamic and also contains prog metal elements in the form of
keyboard layers. This includes some meaty riffs and a very tasty guitar solo.

The Astral Sleep, which came out in 1991, includes the song "Sumerian
Cry (Part 3)." That one shows Lovecraft references in the form of a few lines
of lyrics. The first couplet is "Calculated ancient knowledge / of Arab's wise
words,"[9] which would seem to refer to the *Necronomicon*, which is
supposedly a collection of knowledge written down by the "mad Arab." One
other set of lines is linked to the works of H.P.L. "Then I saw the Ancient
Ones / Slumbering in their cave / My dreams became nightmares."[10] The
references here seem fairly obvious. The song is a pounding aggressive
thrashy slab of metal with growled vocals. The instrumental break on this has
a great melodic texture and includes both tasty guitar solos and some nice
keyboard elements. They drop it into a different, slower segment later in this
segment. In my opinion this is the best part of the track. It moves back to the
earlier modes of to carry forward. Then the tune drops to just guitar for a
fairly short burst to end it.

Yet another band to get started in the year 1990, Seance were a Swedish death metal band. They made one journey into Lovecraftian territory with their 1992 album *Forever Laid To Rest* and the song "*Necronomicon.*"

Vader was formed in Poland in 1986. They have had several Lovecraft references in their music over the years, some direct, some by way of the Simon Edition of the *Necronomicon*. Their 1990 demo included the first two of those Lovecraft linked songs. The first was "From Beyond." The second, "Breath of Centuries," would appear on their first full disc. "From Beyond" is simply a pretty, if a bit mysterious and creepy keyboard instrumental. It is brief, lasting just over a minute.

Their first full album would be *The Ultimate Incantation* (1992), and in addition to the aforementioned song, it included two other tracks with Lovecraft elements the first of these was "Dark Age." This is frantic, but not overly brutal thrash with growling vocals. While some of this one is not directly tied to the Mythos, the vague references warrant inclusion here. This has a very intriguing riff later and some exceptionally tasty guitar textures. "Strange vision dreams in my mind / When I am walking through the night / Each time I see the visage of the moon / Dead cities amongst the sands / under the black abyss of the seas / the Elder Race / From beyond the stars..."[11] "... Sample a dark universe / Domain of the strange races / With the angry gods / Best forgotten and left undisturbed / You know, of course / I'll be back from the dead, Blessing the blackness in glory / of billions of years / On collapsed stars / The rituals of the Ancient Race..."[12]

The song "Testimony" from the same album includes several quotes from the Simon *Necronomicon* and other elements that call to mind H.P.L.'s works, "Creatures dreaming in the dark / Remember the time before the dark / They're still waiting at the gates / Find the Wisdom in the Starlight!..."[13] A later segment contains these words—a summoning chant: "... Call the Ancient Ones / Ia! Khtulu Zi Kur!"[14] This comes in fast and furious, then drops just a bit to a killer fast groove. Growling screamed vocals deliver the lyrics. An instrumental section later is brief, but very tasty. This one is fairly dynamic and very strong, moving through a number of changes, each section being quite powerful.

As previously mentioned, the recording also included "Breath of Centuries" which has quite a few Lovecraft references. "Black cities hidden in the dark / Among the waters beneath the seas / Horrible thoughts destroy the minds / Through the endless nights..."[15] Those words seem to indicate both Cthulhu's R'lyeh (this is the sunken city where Cthulhu awaits his rebirth) waiting under the water, but the way that ancient one comes to people in dreams. In H.P.L.'s Mythos certain people are influenced by

Cthulhu to work on his behalf through their dreams. Those themes are continued in the following lines, "... Buried in the frozen seas / Tombs of forgotten gods / Who came forth from blackened stars / A breath of centuries here..."[16] Even the famous couplet is paraphrased in the song, "...This is not death—which can eternal die / But with the strange eons—even death may die..."[17]

Musically this one comes in with lots of metal crunch. A tolling bell comes over top, and then a dark, mysterious tone takes it. The growling vocals spit out their words. This is heavy, aggressive and potent. Screaming guitars on top take it mid song as some of the intro sounds return. A waling guitar moves it alone at the end of the music and the sounds of wind join to finish the track off.

The band's album *Sothis* from 1994 includes an instrumental entitled "R'lyeh." Their 1995 disc *De Profundis* features lyrics that, according to the liner notes, were drawn extensively from the Simon *Necronomicon*.

Hailing from Slovakia, the band Azathoth has more than just the name to tie them into the Lovecraft Mythos. While their first demo was released in 1992, it wasn't until another six years had passed that their connection to the author in the form of song emerged. It came from their *Artless Puppet Show* collection, and in the form of "The Haunter of the Dark."

Sweden's Therion is a death metal band that was formed in the late 1980's. They released their first disc in 1990, but their first foray into Lovecraft based territory was not to come until 1991. They made that journey with a song entitled "Ctulhu" that appeared on the album *Beyond Sanctorum*. The cut is extremely heavy and rather Sabbath-like in its early modes. As the death growls enter the music turns to frantic thrash. Eventually, though a more classic metal sound gives way to a dark, somewhat more sedate sparse arrangement. This eventually moves back into the thrash to carry forward. This is turned later into an exceptionally tasty instrumental excursion that goes through a number of changes in terms of arrangement, then gives way to more of the verse type thrash. Noise eventually ends it.

2004's *Lemuria/Sirius B* was to be the next time the works of H.P.L. would show up in the band's music. This time the entry came in the form of "Call of Dagon." The track included these lyrics, "Call of Dagon! / The Deep One is calling you / Call of Dagon! / Hear the night sky sing."[18] *The Encyclopedia Cthulhiana* describes Dagon as, "minor being who leads the deep ones and in turn serves Cthulhu."[19] The deep ones, according to the same book, are, "fish-like humanoid beings who worship Dagon, Hydra and Cthulhu, though this title may also be applied to other aquatic creatures who worship the Great Old Ones."[20] The origins for this come from Lovecraft's story "Dagon."

The musical change between the two tracks is purely unbelievable. This one comes in with almost progressive rock like ballad structures. As it moves forward the themes, feeling to me a bit like the theme song to "Gilligan's Island" take on progressive metal formats with strong symphonic textures. Operatic female singing, at times in many layers, makes up the vocal arrangement here. This one is extremely powerful and epic in its approach. It includes an exceptionally tasty epic metal progression for its mid-section.

Therion's Christofer Johnsson shared some of his views with me on this subject. He said that the music on their Lovecraftian songs was "inspired by the pictures I got in my head from reading" Lovecraft's work. He said that Lovecraft's appeal as inspiration for music, "for particularly metal music, I'd say they can be a huge source of inspirations—horror lyrics." When asked about his favorite Lovecraft works, Johnsson revealed that, "'The Nameless City,' 'The Colour Out of Space'—and 'The Dunwich Horror' would be among my top ones. And, of course, 'The Call of Cthulhu.'"

He spoke of becoming a Lovecraft fan (and what keeps him as a fan) in the following way:

> I don't know how I first came in contact with his books, I guess he's so famous in Sweden that it's pretty much common knowledge (in educated families) that he exists and what style he writes—a bit like Edgar Allan Poe, I suppose.
>
> What really attracted me with Lovecraft, is the language he used when describing environments, extremely few authors can make me feel so present at the places he describes. What really made me stick to him is the timeless stories, I am to be 34 and they are just as actual reading as when I was a school boy. It's really something for everyone that appreciates quality literature and enjoys horror stories and probably the only author that both me and my grandfather could read without the feeling of him reading a book of his time and me reading something old. Lovecraft will definitely be one of the few authors of the 20th century that will survive this century too.

Not to be confused with either German band whose names, other than the capitalization of the final "n," is the same as this one, NecronomicoN is a Canadian band whose describes their music as "spiritual occult death metal." The band formed in 1991 (technically they were together earlier, but under a different name) and released their first demo, *Morbid Ritual* (which included several Lovecraftian songs—in fact all but one) that same year. According to the member of the group who goes by the name of Rob the Witch, H.P.L. was part of the concept of the band at their formation. He puts it this way:

> Well actually we started the band in 1988 and at that time we were really into H.P.L. I was reading a lot of his books, watching related movies and of course playing the R.P.G. "The Call of Cthulhu."

Like most bands, when we began, we were not really serious and were playing music just for fun. That was way before thinking about getting seriously in business. At the time our band name was Cataclysm (not to be confused with the actual Kataklysm, it was way before them) but after a while we changed our name to NecronomicoN because the meaning of the name reflected more what we would speak about in the lyrics; first, the fact that we were having fun with H.P.L. and secondly, the future themes that we were to focus on: reincarnation and life after death.

Focusing on the recording of the *Morbid Ritual* demo (1990/91) we worked on a total H.P.L. concept. All of our show posters from that time were with a creature from the H.P.L. mythos drawn specially for the occasions and the demo itself was explaining some situations and creatures as well.

He also described the concepts of the songs from the demo one by one. According to him "Morbid Ritual" describes, "an extreme ritual where deranged people are calling Azatoth." He added that, "This song had a part 2, "Rise Azatoth," which has never been recorded. It talked about the devastation resulting from Azatoth descending."

Regarding "Dark Young of Shub-Nygurath" [sic] he said that it relates this dark story. "Among the trees of a dark forest, Shub Nygurath, [sic] the black goat of the wood gave birth to her monstrous babies who are hidins, waiting for human and animal bait to pass by. Her children will be fed."

Speaking about the song "Fear," Rob the Witch said the following:

This song was one of a series of short songs that lasted only a few seconds, the time to play a few notes rapidly and scream the title. At the time grindcore bands were doing that kind of stuff. The title was chosen to explain the simple emotion that most of the narrators of the H.P.L. stories were living. This song was played live followed by "Horror and Terror," which were in the same vein.

The final cut on the demo was "Cursed." Here is what Rob the Witch had to say about that number:

This song really showed the next step in the bands musical evolution. Lyric-wise, "The Curse of Cthulhu" was the biggest inspiration, as well as physical transformation, self-reflection and of course, nightmarish revelations—such as Cthulhu speaking to the character, who dreams of becoming one of his prophetic children to prepare his upcoming rising.

Their first actual CD, *The Silver Key* from 1996, included a number of Lovecraft linked songs. Those songs were the title track, a rerecording of "Morbid Ritual," "The Asylum," "Hunting Horror" and "Cthonians". Rob the Witch describes the release in this way, "This mini LP's concept was based on the past and future through the eyes of the H.P.L. mythos. It offered some songs from NecronomicoN's ending era and the new musical direction with the album's title track."

That title track is a slab of fast paced tasty riffing with guttural, death metal type vocals over top. This is super high energy and includes some great moments. The vocals however are very hard to understand. There are also some intriguing moments where more operatic vocals over the top of everything lend a dramatic science fiction film type of sound. Rob the Witch speaks of this track in the following way:

> The lyrics and theme of this song were getting more spiritual, preparing the future concept of the band (reincarnation and life after death), but using the All in One, terms related to Yog Sothoth. It is easy to see the bubbly form of Yog Sothoth coming through a time vortex on the album cover as described in many H.P.L. mythos references. The spheres of Yog Sothoth were supposed to represent the possible universe in which this dark god is able to travel at his will.

Of the newer version of "Morbid Ritual" Rob the Witch said, "Due to the success of this song, we decided to rerecord it with better production, but the over all concept stayed the same." This plods in slowly, but with a very tasty main riff. It wanders through in a rather psychotic sort of metallic romp. After a time, though, it shifts to a stalking sort of musical texture and death metal growls emerge over the top of this. This one is quite meaty, and moves out into a frantic sort of oddly timed segment for a time. There are textures here that even feel a little like the Dead Kennedy's at times—that is, if the DK's were slower and more metal. Later a very meaty guitar solo comes in over the top of one of the most intriguing musical segments on show here. The bass guitar even throws in some frantic jamming in the backdrop of some of the latter segments of this. It jumps straight into the next one.

Rob the Witch went on to describe that next track, "The Asylum" in this way, "more or less an intro to the next song. We tried to recreate the atmosphere inside the Arkham asylum with all of the screaming, crying, and of course an insane ritualist locked away in a cell but still incanting the great ones." It is much more frantic and quite tasty. The vocals are fairly unintelligible death growls. As strong as the music is on this short piece, though, who cares if you can understand the words or not.

In reference to the next track, "The Haunting Horror," this is what he said:

> I can't remember clearly from which story I was inspired, but it was related to an old church, and its spire a Haunting Horror was lurking in the dark. That creature was protecting an ancient knowledge, if I remember, and was hunting

down those who were fool enough to try to reach that knowledge or too curious about the spire. So, the song was the narration of someone haunted by a cult and offered in sacrifice to the Haunting Horror, the keeper of certain wisdom related to the great old ones.

The cut starts with odd atmospheric elements that carry it until a pounding death metal thrash takes it through the main song structure. This one has some very meaty guitar work amongst its musical elements. It really has an off-kilter, almost psychotic texture to it.

The final track from the disc is "Cthonians." Rob the Witch had this to say about that piece:

> This song puts us in the context that tremors and earthquakes were related to wormy creatures who were living in the ground. It was explained that this reality was written in the oldest forbidden books. A part of the song lyrics were in the Pnakotic language. The really famous sentence, "Ph'nglui mglw'nafh chtulhu r'lyeh mgah'nagl fhtagn," was incorporated into the song giving it a real doom sense.

Perhaps the tastiest sound of all, feeling like a cross between old Black Sabbath and Candlemass, starts this one off in fine style. As this grind kicks into gear they turn it into a faster paced slab of death metal that is very effective. Then they drop it back to a different structure later with a pounding sort of rhythmic texture and a psychotic texture to the guitar lines. The number is definitely a powerhouse and quite dynamic. It is also not for the faint of heart as it is probably the most extreme metal piece on show here. I personally really like the Sabbath-like riff the best, but they pack a lot of wallop into one track here.

When asked about how they used their music to create a Lovecraftian type soundscape, here is what he had to say:

> Well at the time we were really not thinking about creating sounds and ambience related to that. It was more about the text itself. Our music was our music and the texts were the text; it was as simple as that. Now it would be really different. We would probably try to create a more suitable atmosphere to the H.P.L. concept with more keyboards gloomy and deep sounds and wavy space stuff. I'm saying that, but at the same time we recreated in "The Asylum," the atmosphere of this place.... I think we were about to go in that way, though.

He said that he feels Lovecraft's writing brings to music, "simply, a lot of dark themes and background for pure dark, black, goth (whatever category). For a band that can recreate that atmosphere it's just the perfect inspiration for that kind of music—maybe in some electro dark stuff too, I think."

Rob the Witch also revealed what drew him to H.P. Lovecraft's work in the first place. This is what he said about that subject:

> Well, at the time I was playing role-playing games like AD&D [Advanced Dungeons and Dragons], but the thrill of being scared while playing was something in at the time. So, we started to play the Call of Cthulhu RPG, which was well known to be scary as hell. We would play by candlelight, in a cabin on a lake during a stormy night. It was really cool but we hit the real stuff when after a while every guy on our team knew more about the myth, having been into the H.P.L. books, which boosted the games' atmosphere. Today I went back into some H.P.L. because of your book (need to have the feeling again), but other than that I haven't been into H.P.L. for at least a decade, if not more.

He also shared his favorite Lovecraft tales with me. He lists them as "Dagon," "The Call of Cthulhu" and *The Case of Charles Dexter Ward*. Of "Dagon" he says that it "is real doom." As to that list of favorites, he adds, "unfortunately, I can't say more, because I've read these novels in French, so I don't know the original English titles."

Another band with Lovecraft connections also came into being in 1991. That group is Blood Ritual. While the main core of the band's output centers around satanic endeavors, their debut disc was entitled *At the Mountains of Madness*.

While Deicide's "Dead By Dawn" was originally released on one of the group's two demos that were recorded under the name Amon, it is one of two songs they have done with Lovecraft references. This Florida based death metal outfit was formed in 1989 under that other name, but became Deicide upon signing to Roadrunner Records in 1990. That was the year they released their self-titled disc, which included the aforementioned "Dead By Dawn" as a reissue of their original demos.

The song is an intriguing one. Frantically fast riffing with some killer guitar sounds form the basis. The vocals are a combination of hardcore, death metal and thrash. The band manage to create a sound that is uniquely alien. It's definitely not for everyone with its extreme nature, but does a fairly good job of capturing a dark and scary tone that fits Lovecraft. This is some very tasty guitar work reminiscent of Judas Priest's *Sad Wings of Destiny* era. It does mention the *Necronomicon*, but from looking at the lyrics, and the title, it seems pretty obvious that this points to the *Evil Dead* movies rather than Lovecraft directly: "Book of the dead, pages bound in human flesh."[21]

When they released their second album, *Legion* in 1992, it included the track "Dead But Dreaming." This one seems more likely to be drawn from Lovecraft's work directly, but that does not seem to be the exclusive source for the lyrics. "The house of death is opening / Hanging from their primal sleep / Forbidden to be seen / Spirit of the elder gods / Are dead but must live on / Still to life and yet they breath / Dead but dreaming... / Lords of the world within the space between."[22] Musically this one doesn't stray far from the path of the other piece, but is a bit less creepy and more straightforward. Once again, it is a fast paced number that is based on some strong riffing. The vocals here fall more fully into a death mode, though.

Florida-style death metal by way of Sweden came about when Peter Tagtren, inspired by a trip to that southern state, formed the band Hypocrisy in 1990. Three years later, with the release of their second album, *Obsculum Obscenum* put forth the cut "Necronomicon," to date their only song with Lovecraft ties. That piece showcases a guitar and bass combination that delivers a decidedly turbo charged Black Sabbath sound. The drums take it in another direction with their frantic delivery, and the growling vocals make certain that this is not confused with any style of music but death metal. It does include a more aggressive thrash like segment later. It is fairly dynamic, and features both tasty guitar chording and a killer solo. Other than the admittedly vague line "Summon the Gods."[23] and the title, this one seems more an ode to Satan worship than any link to H.P. Lovecraft, though.

While absolutes are always suspect (paradox intended), Electric Wizard has been called "the heaviest band ever." I will not weigh in on that moniker, as I have not heard every group that has ever existed, but I will say that they are heavy. The outfit hails from England and was formed in the early 1990s. After playing under a couple different names for brief periods, they settled on Electric Wizard in time to release the single "Demon Lung" in 1993.

Their first full album came out the next year in the form of an eponymously titled disc, but it wouldn't be until 1998 when they released the EP *Supercoven* that the band would show their Lovecraft influences in the form of song. The title track includes a serious homage to Lovecraft's mythos, and one of the most blatant ones they have released to date. The first three verses of the track contain these lyrics, whose origins are quite obvious.

> Black sun master / Under starless sky / Black stone altar / They pray to the sign
> The old ones were / And they shall be again / Yog Sothoth is the gate /
> Planetary alignment predicts their reign / Supercoven / Have awakened the
> Ancient Ones / Mindless slaves to the black god / Moan dark hymns to the sun
> To the sun [24]

The song comes in with odd, atmospheric sounds that feel as if they would be quite at home in a horror film. As what sounds like an incantation is spoken over this, waves of keyboard like textures also emerge. Then it begins to modulate out into a feedback laden, echoey sort of space sound with major psychedelic elements. Slowly this is worked and reworked into main plodding, Black Sabbath-like song structure. It doesn't seem likely that anyone would ever accuse this of being fast, but it does become extremely heavy in an old Black Sabbath sort of way. It is almost four and a half minutes into this 13 plus minute opus before any vocals enter. They are sort of screamed, but not fiercely, in an almost punk rock sneering tone. It's not until almost half way through that there is any sort of change. This comes in the form of a more melodic, albeit noisy, raw punkish take on plodding metal themes. In this new section the cut really feels very poorly produced. Distortion is all over this, but still the garage band sort of approach works well for these guys. There is some great retro guitar soloing later in the track, feeling a bit like a cross between Cream and the MC-5. After the ten-minute mark another change out occurs, pulling the band into another plodding jam that feels like a raw Black Sabbath. Unfortunately the guitar soloing on this segment is not as tasty as the sounds that preceded it. This ends with a spoken loop that seems like someone in an asylum repeating the title over and over with no music to back it up.

The third full album from the band, *Dopethrone* included two forays into Lovecraftian territory. On the first track these links are not extremely blatant. That song, "Vinum Sabbathi," leads of the track and begins with a spoken sample that could be argued to be Lovecraft related. The voice says, "When you get into one of these groups, there's only a couple of ways you can get out. One, is death; the other, is mental institutions."[25] Those are the two situations in which most characters in Lovecraft's tales end, so the possibility is there. If that were the only link here, though, it would be a tenuous one at best. This song pounds in a psychedelic sounding grind that is quite effective. At less than four minutes, this is also one of the band's more brief cuts. Lyrically it is not explicitly tied to the author, but certainly the theme of dark arts revealing themselves too late to be a trap has Lovecraft tendencies. The lyrics contain this verse which shows that concept, "Now I'm a slave to the black drug / Forced to serve this black god / I thought myself a master of the arts / This dimension of misery is my penance."[26]

The next track from *Dopethrone* to show Lovecraftian ties is even more blatant than "Supercoven," though. The cut was a three-part, fifteen plus minute, magnum opus entitled "Weird Tales." Within the track the sections each have their own names in the form of "Electric Frost," "Golgotha," and "Altar of Melektaus." From the very first line, "From ancient Yuggoth, black rays emit,"[27] links to H.P.L. are apparent. While that is the only real reference in the first verse, the second stanza is even more explicit in its usage. "What man has seen unknown Kadath / Whose dreamy angles, confused and trapped / Beyond the frozen waste you will find / Hyperborean continent entombed from time."[28]

These words are certainly tied to Lovecraft's story *The Dream-Quest of Unknown Kadath*. It is quite simple to see how they echo these words from the story. "Carter resolved to go with bold entreaty whither no man had gone before, and dare the icy deserts through the dark to where unknown Kadath, veiled in cloud and crowned with unimagined stars, holds secret and nocturnal the onyx castle of the Great Ones."[29]

The cut comes in faster than most songs by the group, but still not what anyone would consider scorchingly fast. It launches straight into a stomping Sabbath-like jam that carries it for a couple minutes with little variation. Then it drops to a considerably slower, but very heavy and powerful new musical journey. After a verse, the song nearly stops, but then it moves to more textural jamming for a short period before bursting back up to the powerhouse that came before. Another verse comes across and then gives way to a noisy instrumental progression that is extremely tasty. They work through in a very early Sabbath oriented journey before a crescendo takes it to more atmospheric sounds. Then the music begins to gradually rise back up from this respite, feeling as slow as a lumbering dinosaur climbing from the tar pit. Then it explodes out into an extremely slow, but also very meaty and heavy new musical movement. This moves through several variations on the theme, never speeding up, but definitely taking an inspired approach to the music. As it carries forward, though, there are spacey elements beginning to emerge over the top. These eventually take control of the piece, with the band's jamming falling further and further behind these pieces of odd atmosphere until little is left but the odd sounds. Then a new element begins to emerge amidst this backdrop. But instead of rising back up, the track seems content to play about with these themes for a while. Once again the rest of the group drops completely away after a time, and only the strange textures remain. This slow moving sonic sludge takes the composition onward for several minutes until eventually ending it.

With their next album, 2002's *Let Us Prey*, the band added another Lovecraft notch to their belt. It came in the form of the song "The Outsider." The cut comes in ultra heavy with more of that Black Sabbath oriented texture. It trudges slowly down the path for around three minutes before the vocals ever enter. When they do, they are short phrases tied fairly directly to the story. They are sort of chanted in a very understated, barely audible manner. The group moves this jam after the vocals into a noisy, swirling sort of progression that is pretty cool—and full of wah guitar sounds. Then it wanders into more of a space rock jam with both Sabbath elements and textures that call to mind early Hawkwind just a bit. They carry it on by moving back into the vocal segment later. This is actually one of the group's tasty Lovecraftian morsels in terms of music and weighs in at a bit over nine minutes.

The most recent Electric Wizard entries into the land of Lovecraft are from their fifth full album, *We Live* that was released in 2004. The first such link comes with the song "Eko Eko Azarak" That song's entry is a barely only, though, with just one phrase vaguely linking into the mythos. It comes in the form of this line, "Ancient race seed this cursed place."[30] Noisy feedback starts this one and continues it for a while with only slight musical elements emerging amidst this chaos. It is nearly a minute in before the first real "music" hits, coming in the form of another slow plodding Sabbath like jam. After the first few lines of vocals the band launch into an exceptionally meaty guitar solo driven instrumental segment. Then they plod back to where they came from for the next lyrics. After some more vocals the number shows hints of moving in a new direction, but instead sludges forward in the same manner. Eventually it drops back a bit to a very doom oriented transitionary segment, then pound it back out. It's not until nearly six and a half minutes in that the song changes in any appreciable way, turning a corner into another slow moving instrumental segment that explores new musical ground. This eventually is transformed into a killer, classic rock Sabbath oriented musical voyage that has a lot of character and instrumental virtuosity. It explodes out later into a chugging sort of riff driven take on this theme to move onward. After a time this gives way to just percussion to take the track to its conclusion.

With the other Lovecraftian number on show on the disc, "The Sun Has Turned to Black," the inspiration is much more explicit in the lyrics. The first indication appears in the second verse with the line, "They hide amongst the stars and wait..."[31] If that was too vague for you, however, the final line of the track cinches it with "the old ones rule supreme." A super low sounding crunch starts this one off and it carries out from there in a rather feedback laden, slowly morphing manner. At a little past the forty-second mark, the cut bursts out into the first real riff on show here. This is, as you might guess also very much in the style of old Black Sabbath. As far as song structure this one doesn't wander far, but they work some serious magic with what they have going. It is also worth noting that at less than six and a half minutes, this is one of the shortest tracks from the band to be covered here.

Regarding his band's Lovecraft usage, Electric Wizard vocalist/guitarist Justin (Jus) Oborn said, "a lot of Electric Wizard songs have been influenced by Lovecraft, directly or indirectly." He added that, "I think the whole Weird Tales gang have had a huge influence." He also explained how the group create a Lovecraftian texture in the music in the following way:

> Well, I'm always drawn to what Lovecraft was trying to say in his essay on supernatural fiction, basically saying that true weird fiction should create a feeling of otherworldliness, a kind of disembodiment from reality. He believed that true weird art must have that certain frisson, not just chilling but truly disturbing because you feel that your ties to the accepted reality have been severely shaken and in some cases actually severed... almost in the same sense as a drug trip. I think Lovecraft was struggling a little to get his point across but I think most Lovecraft devotees understand completely this feeling he is describing... and this is the feeling we are trying to recreate in Electric Wizard. We try to use strange longing type melodies and we try to alter time perception within the riffs by slowing down and bending time in certain places—in fact any way we can to try and break down people's perceptions of traditional song structures. But we start using a traditional song structure then pervert and twist it until people become, hopefully, disorientated and eventually enveloped. People have said that when they hear us play they feel they have taken drugs when they haven't. I think this is just their way of rationalizing their experience. Really we have dislocated them from reality and that makes them feel weird—this is the effect that Lovecraft's writing has on people too.

Regarding the contribution of Lovecraft's writing to music, Oborn had this to say:

> I think that a lot of the concepts within his work can be very inspirational, especially his idea that sorcery and magic can be effected by music, art and mathematics rather than the traditional use of banal incantations, etc., "Dreams in the Witch House" and "Music of Erich Zann" especially. These concepts especially influenced my writing—the idea that certain angles and sound frequencies could actually bend reality and maybe gain us entry to different dimensions and realities, and the more frightening thought that it could open gateways for other things to enter our reality.

Asked about how he first became interested in Lovecraft's work and what has kept him as a fan, Oborn had quite a bit to say.

> I got into Lovecraft when I was quite young, maybe 13 or 14, and to someone that age he was very inspirational. I remember finding the *Dagon* collection in the school library and it was as if I had found some secret dusty relic in the hidden recesses of the library, much like finding the *Necronomicon*. The idea that you could find these old secret grimoires in old bookshops was very exciting and led me on a pilgrimage to all the old bookshops. Of course, I never found the *Necronomicon* but I did find more Lovecraft, Clark Ashton Smith,

Robert E. Howard etc and these in a very real sense were my *Necronomicon*s. I mean to a 14 year old that such books were written in the '20s and '30s was incredible. It was my secret. Everyone else was reading Shaun Hutson or James Herbert.

As I got older i really got more into it and the stories really started to effect me mentally, I felt genuinely disturbed with strange thoughts, dreams and even hallucinations. What with the LSD I was ingesting I felt like the mad Arab himself. I think at one point I felt I was becoming possessed by Lovecraft. I started getting a lot of those "did aliens visit earth in ancient times?" type of paperbacks and started doing my own research into prehistory and of course became very paranoid and disturbed that Lovecraft might be right and Cthulhu was rising. I mean the time is right! And what about the tsunami? Was it the seal of R'lyeh being broken? I'm sure a lot of Lovecraft fans are losing sleep over this right now.

Bethzaida is a dark metal band from Norway that was formed in 1993. With their first full album, *Nine Worlds*, Bethzaida made their way into the annals of Lovecraftian music by including the song "The Outsider," which is definitely drawn from the story of the same name. The quest begins with shadows of horror in attendance: "... Following the road to a castle in the night / People there are screaming, going insane with fright / What could it be there that scares them so / Well... I hope that I'll never know..."[32] As the song nears its conclusion, the truth is finally revealed. "... Finding a river he sees his mirror image in it / The thing he sees, he knows it is himself / 'This is too hard to live with', he cries in desperate tears..."[33] I really have no interest in spoiling the surprise (for those who haven't already read the story), as this conclusion is one of Lovecraft's better horrors, so suffice it to say that these lyrics do a nice job of capturing the essence of the tale.

A doom metal band from England, Eterne was just two musicians, David Dando and Martyn Lear. The group's demo *The Endless*, released in 1983, was their first foray into Lovecraft inspired territory. It included the song, "The Crawling Chaos." The next year their first full album was put out, and it included, in addition to the previous track, one other Lovecraftian tune called "Still Dreaming."

Kindred Idol was formed in 1989, and released one album *Conscious in the Mudvein*. That release from 1994 included two H.P. Lovecraft related tracks, "Sea of Gthey" and "By Erich Zahn." According to band founder Scott Kesler, "The name of the band came from the story 'The Call of Cthulhu' and was a description of the base relief found by Carter. The whole imagery of Kindred Idol was based on the melancholy feel of the world Lovecraft created and the way he tried to tell every day type stories in an imaginative form."

Regarding the first mentioned track, Kesler had the following to say, "'Sea of Gthey' is about the story 'A Shadow over Innsmouth' directly. The song itself has a rolling feel to it that is very hypnotic and menacing. It tells the complete story in an abstract style to get all of the story into such a short song."

Kesler also revealed that, "I started reading Lovecraft around the 8th grade. I fell in love with his style of macabre writing." Speaking in more detail about this topic, Kesler continued, "I read a Stephen King book in the seventh grade, and he mentioned H.P. Lovecraft. So like a rabid dog, I sniffed out his books, which was not easy, and began devouring his work."

"What kept me as a fan, was him. His life story which I have searched out and found out a lot about him from Donovan Loches. I think that is the spelling. Anyways, it is possible to be eternal when you are shunned and distant from the norm, no matter what a person may feel, or told." Kesler also said that "The Tomb" was his all time favorite Lovecraft Story. He was quick to add, though, "'The Colour Out of Space,' 'The Rats in The Walls,' 'Pickmans Model,' 'The Music of Erich Zann,' damn, I could go on and on. All of those are tops—well, plus *At the Mountains of Madness*, which holds a special place in my heart since it was the first one I read. 'The Call of Cthulhu,' 'Azathoth,' any ways, you get the hint. I am a Lovecraft junkie."

It must be mentioned that while the Argentina based metal outfit Lovecraft (formed in 1992) bears the author's name, that seems to be the only real connection. So no need for further discussion of them seems needed.

Coming out of Holland in the mid-1980s, death metal band Pestilence released one album that had Lovecraft ties. That disc was 1991's *Testimony of* the *Ancients*. While the disc's links to the author are not blatant, there are numerous lines that could be seen as vaguely coming from a Lovecraftian source. Still, this could easily be passed over, were it not for the flowing in the thanks on the CD booklet, "The Ancient Ones and The Elder Gods for the balance of good and evil."[34] Since none of the songs are explicitly based on Lovecraft, I won't address any of them in detail, but rather discuss the album overall. The band's name suggests a death metal outfit, but that would certainly be an unfair description of this disc. While some of the material on the CD has both death and thrash elements, it is really quite a dynamic and varied collection from some considerably talented musicians. The band manage to include a number of musical excursions and elements that fall closely into a progressive rock vein. The result is something that probably lands most fully into the category of prog metal. Even then, this is a bit more raw than that at points, so that classification only fits so well. Needless to say, this is a very creative and powerful album that is hard to pigeonhole.

Formed in Switzerland in the late 1980's Samael is metal band that has moved from standard dark metal into the vein of more creative and less restrictive heavy metal over the years. Their foray into Lovecraft inspired music came with their first full-length album, *Worship Him*, that was released in 1991. The song that they offer up is "Rite of Cthulhu," which is a roughly two-minute instrumental. It starts with a creepy effects-driven guitar solo that truly feels worthy of the Old One. As the band joins in it takes on a more straightforward metal approach, but that guitar still drives it in decidedly Lovecraftian ways.

Vorph from that band had this to say about Lovecraft's influence on the act:

> I don't know to what extent Lovecraft has been an inspiration to our music. We had an instrumental song called "Rite of Cthulhu" on our debut album, which was of course named after one of Lovecraft's entities. If I remember it well "Cthulhu" was the closest thing to a black hole and it impress me at the time by its powerful force of destruction. We could almost compare it with Hinduist divinity "Kali" but the fact that Lovecraft descriptions are often vague makes it even more dramatic and menacing.

Regarding his thoughts on what Lovecraft's writing has to offer to music, Vorph said this, "His pandemonium is rich and it leaves a large place for imagination. He had sent arrows through some of the darkest place of the mind and what words can no longer explain music can express. Lovecraft's universe is stimulating alternative creations..."

He also said that what drew him to H.P.L. was "I first become familiar with his name while reading *The Necronicon*. He added that the lasting appeal of H.P.L. is that, "the core of his stories where written but they radiated far away into our subconscious, that make his work timeless "

Part of the Florida death metal movement, Massacre first made their mark on the genre with the album *From Beyond* released in 1991. It featured Lovecraft references in its title track and several others.

The connections start with the opening track of the disc, "Dawn of Eternity." The sounds of a storm start it, then a cymbal enters and this gives way to a plodding heavy and powerful dirge. A more frantic guitar progression emerges from this. Then the cut turns into a fast-paced thrash styled jam with death metal growls overtop. This includes a rather weird chaotic noisy guitar solo. "...The fall of man is now at hand / Awakened from an ancient slumber / The immortal ones return / The Earth is theirs once again."[35]

The title track is the next one with ties to Lovecraft. While the lyrics don't seem to fully address the story, they come much closer to the content of H.P.L.'s original writing than they do to the Stuart Gordon film that bears its name. "... Simultaneously they appear / Repulsive animated beings / In a kaleidoscopic void of light / Creatures of inept creations / Foreign alien monstrosities / Devouring and fusing together / Forms of infinite madness / Ripping at my mind..."[36] The Lovecraft story "From Beyond" tells of horrors that exist all around us, but in a sort of alternate reality that can only cross over when certain factors are brought into play. Musically this one doesn't differ in terms of style, but is based on a different set of riffs. Later, though, there is a section that feels like a metal science fiction theme. This doesn't remain in play for long, though. Instead the track reverts to its more standard death/thrash pattern.

The final cut which ties into Lovecraft's themes comes in the form of "Symbolic Immortality." This one musically is raw and frantic death based thrash that doesn't differ much from the other tracks. While the lyrics here have no blatant links to H.P.L., the overall theme seems to have his ideas keyed in. "Beyond the walls of sleep / Lies the secret to immortality..."[37] "... Inverted turth / False tale of Madness / Jest of the Elders / It's all a fool's game."[38]

The Finnish metal band Sentenced formed in 1989, and with their second album *North From Here*, released in 1993, they joined the ranks of artists who have touched their music to the writings of HPL. While its lyrics are not explicitly tied to the story from which the title is taken, "Beyond the Wall of Sleep" presents themes that are certainly connected to Lovecraft's Dream Cycle. "Fade into dream... / Deep into a dormant pseudo-life / Drown into night... / Pass through the gate of sleep"[39] ... "To live a life asleep... / is to master mortality / I wander between these worlds / On a quest to find a key."[40] Dark and creepy, this one is a very fast track, and the growled vocals add much to the fright texture. At times the music on this one feels a lot like Black Sabbath played at double or triple speed. The twin guitar attack occasionally calls to mind Iron Maiden. The number is quite dynamic, moving through many changes.

Danish band Mercyful Fate creates a unique style of metal. Meshing vocalist King Diamond's unusual vocal pyrotechnics and nearly incomparable range with crunchy metal guitar and arrangements that teeter between solid heavy metal, extreme progressive rock changes and neo-classical movements, their sound is unmistakable and unmatched. It is certainly not for everyone, but any fan of solid musicianship should be able to appreciate the talent of the group. Currently on their second incarnation (they broke up in the 1980s and reformed in 1993), two Lovecraftian tracks have appeared from them during this new life.

1994's *Time* saw the release of the track, "The Mad Arab (Part One: The Vision)". One need really look no further than the title to see the reference to Lovecraft's fictional alter-ego, Alhazred, the author the *Necronomicon*. However, the lyrics certainly confirm the connection: "The son of a shepherd, Abdul Alhazred / Traveling in the mountains, the mountains to the east."[41] While this is the only specific Lovecraft link in the lyrics, it is obvious that the words present the story of this anti-hero. Musically, this one is quite an adventure. Eastern sounds set to a smoking metal theme creates the main basis of the track. A dynamic and creative arrangement paints this one as a dramatic and thematic number. The guitar solo segment is exceptionally tasty and leads to a full on instrumental break that, while short, is great. This turns to a neoclassical movie theme sound to end.

With *Into the Unknown*, released two years later, the band not only continued the promise of that song, but also re-established their Lovecraft ties. The follow-up second part of the piece was entitled "Kutulu (The Mad Arab Part Two)", and had even more explicit lyrical references to Lovecraft's works. When the previous installment ended, Alhazred was running from evil clerics. With this song it seems he escaped into the desert, but his escape has not come without a price. "... Feeling colder.../ I see, I see, I see the amulet of Evil Gods... / Evil Gods / Can you hear the voices in my head... / Can you hear the voices in my head / Can you hear the voices, what they say? / Kutulu... Kutulu... Kutulu... Kutulu..."[42] As the track continues we find that he has been, "Traveling for years to believe in the sign / And I know them well now, all of the Ancient Ones.."[43] The narrator mentions the writing of the book in his telling of the tale. "Hear me as Kutulu raises his evil head / Drooling for my soul / I must finish this book tonight / Tomorrow... I might be of the dead / I'm burning up...I'm burning up / I wish for you... the gods will be merciful."[44] Musically this one carries on the same Eastern tinged themes. It is both more straightforward, but also creepier than its predecessor. It drops to a mellower balladic segment that is simply awesome, and then jumps back to its earlier elements. It includes a screaming guitar solo that gets quite dynamic and twisted and serves as the closing of the piece.

Begun in 1994, Dutch metal band Orphanage have produced two Lovecraft influenced tracks. The first was "The Case of Charles Dexter Ward" from 1995's *Oblivion*. Given that title, one expects a track laden with Lovecraft elements, and the lyrics do not let the listener down. The first lines foretell the story before us, "A magician with powers so strange resurrected from the past / He changed dust into flesh so not to rest eternally..."[45] and the rest of the song delivers. There is even a direct reference to another of the characters of Lovecraft's story, Joseph Curwen. I say another of the characters, although the two are actually tied to one another in a unique way. Again, too much information on that aspect would spoil the story.

Musically this starts in a progressive metal manner, but switches to a death metal growling thrash for the opening verse. The alternating segments are more prog oriented with melodic vocal lines. A progressive rock like instrumental break gives way to a mellow segment, and then it jumps back up until another laid back section takes it. This is a very dynamic track with something for everyone.

The second track, also taken from *Oblivion*, also bears the title of a Lovecraft story, and this one is "At The Mountains of Madness." The first lines set the scene, "...the lavas that restlessly roll / Their sulphurous currents down Yaanek / In the ultimate climes of the pole / That groan as they roll down Mount Yaanek / In the realms of the boreal pole..."[46] As the track continues, the lyrics paint a strong image of the story:

> ... thinking back, remembering, my tale seems so unreal / I'm closed up but the time has come to reveal / anxious, also ignorant, my investigative mind had led me there and led me to be so blind / haunted are the mountains, I plead for your restraint / or hope for men's survival will be faint / all my days are nightmares and memories haunt my brain / my former mind of knowledge has gone insane...[47]

This one starts off in a very progressive rock type format, with a dark sort of progression that is dominated by piano. This gives way to a crunchier take on these themes. Then it drops to just atmospheric keys and a mellow operatic female voice. From there, though, it jumps to a pounding metallic jam with growled vocals. This has some meaty riffing and a great multi-layered vocal arrangement later. The prog metal elements return with a keyboard dominated instrumental break, then they drop it back to the movement based on the operatic singing before bursting back up to the segment that came before and starting the whole progression all over again. A thrash-like instrumental break with some scorching guitar work comes in as it carries forward, then the band launch into a frantic, aggressive movement. They still manage to thrown in the more prog metal segment with the layered vocals again, though despite the ferocity of this section. Then a new keyboard laden break takes it, feeling more like Dream Theater than any metal band. A very deep spoken word section (over the top of a very heavy crunch guitar fest) takes it next and then the band move back up to furious territory to carry on. After this, though, they drop it back to just keys and the opera like vocals to end it. It is one heck of a ride.

Lex Vogelaar, the member of the group who was responsible for these two pieces, spoke of their genesis in this way:

> I had written the music and figured the atmosphere of H.P.L. would fit very well to the music. At the time I had been reading a lot of his work, and it was only a matter of time before I would use his work in one of my lyrics. I think Orphanage's style lends itself perfectly for H.P.L.'s atmospheres. Most of the songs would be suitable for a H.P.L. lyric. The music of Orphanage has basically a dark mood, with the occasional moment of brightness, just like a lot of H.P.L.'s stories. Also Orphanage's songs work towards a climax. Each repetition of a musical part has a little extra added to it. That would correspond to H.P.L.'s cumulative horror style of writing.

Vogelaar also said that he felt what Lovecraft's influence brings to music is, "basically the mood and atmosphere." He explains further that, "after (or even during) reading one of his stories I felt a peak in my inspiration levels which led to the creation of some of my finest compositions. I'm sure some Orphanage songs with non H.P.L. lyrics were (partly) written under this condition, but don't ask me which ones, because it has been too long."

Vogelaar describes his being drawn to the work of Lovecraft in the following way:

> I've had a period in my life (from 17 to 22-ish years old) that I was very much into horror. I came into contact with a guy called Ralph [Ralf] Hubert [of Mekong Delta] who pointed me towards H.P.L.'s work. In the years following I tracked down and read most of H.P.L.'s work. One of the most intriguing aspects is the consistency of his Cthulhu Mythos universe. There are so many cross-references between his stories that this could probably justify university research. Also H.P.L. wrote in a way that his stories seemed like true stories instead of fiction. That was also one of the reasons I was really sucked into his work.

He revealed that his favorite Lovecraft stories, off the top of his head, are "The Music of Erich Zann," "The Call of Cthulhu," "The Shadow Over Innsmouth," *The Case of Charles Dexter Ward* and *At the Mountains of Madness.*

Darklands are a side project of the band Left Hand Solution. Formed in 1992, their 1996 *Chronicles* release finds them turning their gothic doom metal sound to Lovecraft inspired material with "Dead But Not Dreaming." However, a reference to "The Absu" makes it seem very likely that this influence comes by way of the Simon *Necronomicon,* rather than the source material itself. Still, such lines as this opening segment, "Death reigns—even in solitude / Spawn of such raging hate / In the city doth asleep / Underneath the sand and stones / R'lyeh—the place of my dreams / Sunken so long ago"[48] hold enough of a link to make this one of definite interest to those drawn to it from H.P.L.

Twin Obscenity was formed in Norway in 1991, and in 1997, with the release of their first full-length album, made their way into the realm of Lovecraft by including the track "Revelations of Glaaki."

While death metal's Disincarnate only has one song with a Lovecraftian reference, considering that the group only ever released one album gives that song a bit more significance in their catalog. The group's entry is the song "Entranced" from the album, *Dreams of the Carrion Kind*, which was released in 1993. Although musically the song doesn't really feel very Lovecraftian, it is exceptionally meaty and should please fans of good crunchy metal. It has a lot of elements of early Sabbath, but still manages to incorporate the faster paced thrashy textures. The vocals are the growled death variety.

The lyrics are very distinctly drawn from Lovecraft's story, "The Tomb." "Ancestral home in the twilight deeps / Beckons to me with unseen fingers / Forefathers haunt / Calling to me from this dark charnel house / Corrupted through lifelong seclusion / Driven by an unnatural force / Drawn to this vault / Declivity where the light reaches not / Enigmatic crypt of my bloodline / Place of ancestral remains / Temple of my fascination / Possessing me..."[49]

Of the tomb referenced by the title, Lovecraft's story says this in describing it.

... Close by my home there lies a singular wooded hollow, in whose twilight deeps I spent most of my time; reading, thinking, and dreaming. Down its moss-covered slopes my first steps of infancy were taken, and around its grotesquely gnarled oak trees my first fancies of boyhood were woven. Well did I come to know the presiding dryads of those trees, and often have I watched their wild dances in the struggling beams of a waning moon but of these things I must not now speak. I will tell only of the lone tomb in the darkest of the hillside thickets [note that this is in fact the origin of the name of the band Darkest of the Hillside Thickets—to be covered in a later chapter]; the deserted tomb of the Hydes, an old and exalted family whose last direct descendant had been laid within its black recesses many decades before my birth.

The vault to which I refer is of ancient granite, weathered and discolored by the mists and dampness of generations. Excavated back into the hillside, the structure is visible only at the entrance. The door, a ponderous and forbidding slab of stone, hangs upon rusted iron hinges, and is fastened ajar in a queerly sinister way by means of heavy iron chains and padlocks, according to a gruesome fashion of half a century ago. The abode of the race whose scions are here inurned had once crowned the declivity which holds the tomb, but had long since fallen victim to the flames which sprang up from a stroke of lightning. Of the midnight storm which destroyed this gloomy mansion, the older inhabitants of the region sometimes speak in hushed and uneasy voices; alluding to what they call 'divine wrath' in a manner that in later years vaguely increased the always strong fascination which I had felt for the forest-darkened sepulcher. One man only had perished in the fire. When the last of the Hydes was buried in this place of shade and stillness, the sad urnful of ashes had come from a distant land, to which the family had repaired when the mansion burned down. No one remains to lay flowers before the granite portal, and few care to brave the depressing shadows which seem to linger strangely about the water-worn stones...[50]

As the song continues far more links to the story surface. "Familiar far beyond the tenancy / of the body which I now possess / Eyes affixed upon the dank portal / Alone I lie entranced / Echoes of my forgotten lives / Summoning me to the gothic retreat / Here I belong / My casket awaits, my heritage calls / Sinister flashes of supersight / Penetrate the veils of empiricism / Sanity wanes / I witness my lineage perish in flames... Though but twenty-one winters have / Chilled my bodily frame / Blasphemy pours in torrents from my lips."[51] For those who have not yet had the pleasure of reading the story, I will refrain from showing the parallels. Those who have a familiarity with the source material will, no doubt, spot them for themselves.

British doom metal band Solstice was formed in the early 1990s. Their 1998 *New Dark Age* album included the opening paragraph to "The Call of Cthulhu" in the title track.

Richard M. Walker of that band had this to say about how he created a Lovecraftian texture to the music, "Through the use of dissonant chords, chord inversions, morbid and grandiose harmony parts, and finally the lyrical approach that pays homage to the Cthulhu mythos."

He also included the lyrics to the song "New Dark Age II" as an example of those ties via the words.

Beyond these mountains lay vistas of dread / Black sea of infinity herein they drift / Devolved as one atrophied architects / Cyclopean forms askew in the midst / (Of) seraphic decay, an unbeheld might / The arcane majesty a conqueror awaits / Captors of millennia cloaked in confusion / Cast ever out to the tides of time / Gathered in silent peripheral empires / (Of) dust choked oceans who sing their last / Vanquished voyagers of revelation / A brooding enigma yet still to pass / Sinistral gulfs yet may be crossed / To ophidian cowering citadels / Raptoral judgement upon all our sins / This placid island of ignorance[52]

Looking at these lyrics it is definitely possible to discern indirect links to the Lovecraftian mythos, but nothing really calls out as being explicit. Still, that might well be the most effective way to present H.P.L. links as many point to his more vague approach of describing horrors as one of the strengths of his work.

When asked about what he feels Lovecraft's work has to offer music in general Walker said this:

> That is not easy to answer. I could only say what Lovecraft's writings offered me, and how they inspired my music. Everyone interprets his work in a different way, I chose to draw on his feelings of suffocating horror and unnamable dread and present them both musically and lyrically in the best way I could. He was simply a master of his art, with a command of the English Language unparalleled and an imagination that has yet to be matched.

Walker revealed that what he finds to be the true draw to Lovecraft's work is "the absolute bleakness and feeling of ultimate doom of his tales, and again his use of language." He listed his favorite H.P.L. stories to be *At the Mountains of Madness*, *The Strange* [sic] *Case of Charles Dexter Ward*, "The Colour Out of Space" and "The Shadow Over Innsmouth."

There are types of metal music called "GrindCore," "Hardcore" and others, but I'll bet few out there have heard of EduCore. That's what the members of BloodHag call their style of the genre. The band, who were formed in 1995, coined this term because one of the goals of the outfit was to educate the metal listening public to the debt that the genre owed to the writings of science fiction and horror masters. In fact, the core of the group at the time was two published science fiction writers (and two educators at that) Professor J.B. Stratton and Dr. J.M. McNulty. With credentials like that it would seem pre-destined that the group would wind up touching on Lovecraftian territory, and they certainly have.

They did so in style with the song "H.P. Lovecraft." Actually they have a whole series of tracks named after the various authors. The lyrics begin with these lines, "He was little known until he died / 'Cuz the real demons were behind his eyes."[53] I find some more words worth repeating in these lyrics, "And then I heard Cthulhu's Call / Other writers jumped on your boat / Even you weren't scared of what you wrote / You told of monters lurking in the mist."[54] The track, as one might guess, tries to both encapsulate H.P.L.'s life and also to capture the lure of his writing both in personal terms and in regards to the influence his work has had. Even Metallica's contributions to Lovecraftian music are mentioned with this line, "At least one song by Metallica."[55]

Formed in 1996, Non Serviam recorded one song which includes a number of Lovecraft references. That track, "Which Eternal Lie" comes from their 1998 *Necrotical* disc. The track begins with a Lovecraft styled incantation, "Ph'nglui Mglw'nafh Cthulhu R'lyeh Wgah'nagl Fhtagn, Lä! Lä! / N'ghaa, N'n'ghai! Lä! Lä! Y-hah, Y-nyah, Y-nyah! / N'ghaa, N'n'ghai, Vaf'l Fthaghn—Yog-Sothoth! Yog-Sothoth..."[56] As it carries on both the famous Cthulhu couplet and a call to the Old One are issued, "... That is not dead which can eternal lie / And with strange aeons even death may die / Call of Cthulhu..."[57] Later a scene which seems straight from one of the Mythos tales emerges, "... and as the fire dies, the man lies on the ground / Evil has struck his mind, too powerful to hold / In the centre of the sign a figure is taking form / The portal is open the circle is closed, as the old ones told / Yog-Sothoth arrives from his wicked domain / From far beyond the stars..."[58] The end result is spelled out later, "Raging inferno, as the old ones return / Returning and claiming their earth / Slaughtering all that come in their way / So long they've awaited this day / All that is human, extirpated / All that man has built, devasted..."[59]

Greensberg, South Carolina was the birthplace of Nile (the band, not the river). Formed in 1993, they have had several tracks whose inspiration comes, either directly or by way of the Simon edition of the *Necronomicon*, from Lovecraft. Two of the songs are included on their *Amongst* the *Catacombs of Nephren-Ka* album, which was released in 1998.

The first of those songs is "Barra Edinazzu" whose lyrics come directly from the aforementioned *Necronomicon*. None of the piece is in English, rather coming in the form of a mystical spell.

The second number has its origins in the Lovecraft tale "The Outsider." While the majority of the lyrics to that one ("Beneath Eternal Oceans of Sand") are borrowed from that story, there is also mention of "Nephren-Ka" and "The Valley of Hadoth," "Yet underneath endless oceans of sand / I have not forgotten / Those who had betrayed me. / Silent and unmovable, / I am not sorry / For I had hated the light. / Now I ride with the undead / Across the night-sky / And play by day Amongst the catacombs of Nephren-Ka / In the sealed and unknown / Valley of Hadoth by the Nile."[60]

2000's *Black Seeds of Vengeance* included one more track that seems to have Lovecraftian ties—that one being "The Nameless City of The Accursed." This track is a brutal, pounding fast paced one with death scream/growls. It is not very long, but the CD booklet clearly states that is based on H.P.L.'s story.

Destiny's End was formed in 1997, and with their first album, *Breathe Deep The Dark* (1998), began a flirtation with Lovecraft related material (at least indirectly). That album included a few pieces which fall into the Lovecraftian territory. First up was the title track, which draws its story line (at least a bit) from "The Outsider." Frantic drumming starts it, then a very tasty guitar riff enters to carry the track into its opening verse. This one is fast paced, rather epic sounding heavy metal. A slower, slightly sparser segment later is quite powerful and leads into a short instrumental break. A Rob Halford like scream later is worth mentioning as are the stellar bridge and instrumental section that follow. Some of the guitar soloing here, with its Eastern tinges, is just plain awesome. This whole track is a definite winner. One really needs to only look to the first verse to see the links that this one has to the story. "I'm Obscure, the shadow black / Alone I walk on the shunned path / Centuries mine, reveal the past / The unknown yawning black..."[61]

Also worth mentioning is the two part song "Idle City/The Fortress Unvanquishable," which Perry Grayson (who was the group's guitarist) says was based on the story "The Fortress Unvanquishable Save for Sacnoth" by Lord Dunsany—a writer who was probably as big an influence on H.P.L. as Poe. It is for that reason, and the request of Grayson, that I mention it here. It also goes to the concept of the foundation from which their other Lovecraftian material came.

The first of the two tracks, "Idle City" starts with keyboards and as guitar enters the number takes on a ballad-like style. This has a dark and mysterious texture, feeling quite a bit like Iron Maiden's dark ballad-like pieces. It shifts gear to a fast paced, old world dominated metal structure that again brings up visions of Maiden. This has a galloping sort of texture in its melodic metallic themes. It runs through a number of intriguing changes. "The Fortress Unvanquishable" continues the themes, both musically and lyrically. While in many ways it doesn't feel different than its predecessor it does move those musical concepts further along the road. This one feels a bit like King Diamond at times. They do pull it down to a killer metallic grind later to good effect. Together both tracks represent a very powerful and creative old school metal journey.

With the follow up disc, 2000's *Transition*, one more cut was added to this list. That number was "Vanished," which again has some influences, but certainly far from a full on homage, from "The Outsider." A pretty, but rather dark, acoustic guitar ballad approach begins the cut and it rises upward ever slowly in this manner. This one is extremely evocative and powerful and the layered vocal arrangement is a nice touch. The whole structure of this song has a lot of elements of progressive rock, and it's quite an interesting piece of music. It turns heavier later, but is really one heck of a dramatic ride. They shift it out eventually into a fairly frantic, almost thrashy jam that quite meaty. This instrumental segment includes some very tasty guitar soloing.

After a while, though, they move it back down to the more balladic song structures to carry it onward. Honestly, I hear quite a bit of the progressive metal school of sound here—think bands like Fates Warning. This sampling of the lyrics shows a good segment of the link between them and the story: "… Arrogant world of beings unlike me / In solitude forever / Against dreary nights and long days / Beneath these stars, yet still I live…"[62]

Of the process of creating music befitting Lovecraft oriented themes, Grayson had the following to say:

> I guess the main thing was to try to keep the music and lyrics as dark as most of the stories Lovecraft wrote. These aren't tunes about frolicking around in the sunlight. Most of the stuff I wrote with a Lovecraftian bent to it tends to have something in common with "The Outsider." Dwelling on things that the "world of men" tends to ignore or shun. That goes for the deeper material I've written, but not as much for what I'm doing with Falcon [his current group]. With Falcon I haven't written too much that's fantasy inspired, aside from a Thin Lizzy and Dunsany-inspired song called "Elfland's Daughter." Most of my Falcon tunes deal more with reality. I'm cutting loose lyrically a lot more these days. The lyrics I contributed to Destiny's End were a lot more austere. With Artisan I dealt more with the real world too, except in the case of a set of lyrics called "The Ultimate Question," which was never used. I can't forget Lord Dunsany, who was a huge influence on my writing "Idle City/The Fortress Unvanquishable" (a two part song) on *Breathe Deep the Dark* (the 1st Destiny's End album). "The Fortress Unvanquishable Save for Sacnoth" is the story that I drew on. Since Dunsany made an enormous impact on Lovecraft, I think it's worth mentioning.

When asked what he thought Lovecraft's writing had to offer music, Grayson said this:

> Although H.P.L. didn't play music himself, it's obvious that it had some kind of influence on him. He did write "The Music of Erich Zann" after all! Though he wasn't a musician or a dabbler in psychedelic drugs (no acid for me, thanks!), Lovecraft obviously has a lot to offer bands and musicians with open minds. The bleak imagery in H.P.L.'s stories tend to fit well with metal and the more Dunsanian and dreamy Lovecraft stuff lends itself to music that's more psychedelic or progressive. Metal has a lot in common with horror, so it only makes sense that someone like H.P.L. would have a big effect on metal bands. The rather heavy mysteries of life, death and man's ultimate place in the universe (in H.P.L.'s opinion a rather minute one at best!) make good fuel for lyrics—not to mention the fact that horror just for entertainment's sake plays a big role in the metal scene. As far as the psychedelic side of things goes, obviously I think musicians could really be inspired (and have been) by the sublime otherworldly beauty H.P.L. described in stories like *The Dream-Quest of Unknown Kadath*, "The Other Gods," "The White Ship," "The Quest of Iranon," etc.

When asked about the attraction of Lovecraft's writing to himself, he put it this way:

> H.P.L. went beyond the typical conventions of horror. His work makes you think beyond yourself and question reality and man's seemingly insignificant place in the universe. H.P.L.'s stuff entertains as well as provokes the reader. Although I do dig the tried and true horror elements (vampires, lycanthropes, gothic madmen, witches, etc.), there was just something so much more unique about Lovecraft that grabbed me the first time I read one of his stories.

Grayson lists *The Dream-Quest of Unknown Kadath*, "The Whisperer in Darkness," *At the Mountains of Madness*, "The Shadow Out of Time" and "The Outsider" as his favorite Lovecraft stories.

Another metal band who have touched heavily onto Lovecraftian ground is Chton. This Norwegian outfit was formed in 1999, and their first real album, *Cthonian Lifecode*, would not be released until 2004. According to guitarist Torstein, "we have moved from very 'occult horror'-inspired lyrics to more anti-religious lyrics with our newer stuff, but we still hold Lovecraft, the *Necronomicon* and things related very high."

That first disc included three songs that have Lovecraft as an inspiration. They are "Enemie," "Book of Black Earth" and "Crawling Chaos." While that first one is considered by Torstein to have Lovecraft elements present, I could see little except one verse, "Wretched Demon of my Dreams / Unspeakable your name / Yet I call you!"[63]

The song "Book of Black Earth" has more definite links to Lovecraft's core mythos, seeming as if it might be a summoning for the Old Ones. "Rise from the pits of the ancient / Rise from the abyss of old."[64] As it continues, so do these links. "I emerge / descendant of damnation / yet old among the elders / fire, water, wind and earth / gather for my 2nd birth."[65] Musically, this one is a pounding slab of extreme heavy metal with death growls, groans over the top. There is one bridge that feels just a bit like a heavier Black Sabbath. The screamed vocals over this section are exceptionally potent.

"Crawling Chaos" comes in, appropriately chaotic with a texture like a more metallic modern King Crimson. This is frantic and tasty with more character than the previous piece covered here. It feels almost like a heavy metal hammering. The vocals are still in the extreme death metal mode. The bridge here has some exceptionally tasty guitar soloing. This gives way to a drop down, seeming almost like a false ending, then a new jam emerges from there, pounding up in directions not heard previously in the track.

Torstein described the influence of Lovecraft on their music in this way, "it's song-lyrics first and foremost, and they are never meant to 'stand alone' without the music as works of literature. The Lovecraft-inspiration may be found in content more so than in texture." He also explained that, "The world and mythos of Lovecraft holds imagery that translates very well into the music of Chton, at least." In regards to metal in general, Torstein stated, "I think the writings of Lovecraft functions mainly as inspiration for many metal musicians as horror goes hand in hand with most forms of metal. I guess I'm far from alone writing song-lyrics inspired by his twisted world of the disturbed mind."

Referring to his personal relationship with the works of H.P.L., Torstein said, "I can't remember what initially drew me to Lovecraft, but I think it was a Norwegian translation of 'The Rats in the Wall' that I read at an early age. What has kept me as a fan is rather obvious: once infected you can never get cured." As to his favorite Lovecraft tales, "There are many, but the one I remember from the top of my head right now is the 'Polaris' story and also 'From Beyond.'"

One of the newer bands to partake of the Lovecraftian fruits in their musical creation is the Finnish band Aarni. Formed in 1998, the band plays a type of metal that incorporates folk, progressive rock and ambient into the mix. The group have released several songs that have their basis in the worlds of H.P.L. The first of these was released in 2001.

If the title to that song ("The Black Keys (of R'lyeh)")did not let you know that it is based on Lovecraft's work, certainly the chorus would. "The Black Keys of R'lyeh and Cthulhu arise / bring about your glory and our imminent demise."[66] Feedback starts this one, then the band launch into a raw, bouncy jam that has elements of classic rock and heavy metal combined into one stylistic mix. As the vocals enter this drops back to a ballad like texture. Those sung words come in like a deep, echoey chanting texture. The chorus pounds back out, but still the singing remains essentially the same. The first two lines of the verse that follows the first chorus certainly hold many more Lovecraft references. "Now thou art dead, yet I live forevermore / I became the shoggoth-master and Deep Ones hold me in awe." As this carries on through the rocking segment of the cut there is some exceptionally tasty guitar work. They eventually drop it back to just odd keys and then a spoken, processed vocal takes the lyrics forward. After this, though, they power it up to a fast paced, thrash like segment and death metal growls emerge over the top of this motif. Eventually just bass guitar remains and then it moves back towards the more mainstream rock textures. This cut without question is more accessible than some of the latter Lovecraft based songs they would produce. It would not be until the next year that the group would again release any similar inspired music.

"Ubbo-Sathla" is one of these songs. The lyrics to this one are drawn from the fictional *Book of Eibon*. This is sort of a roundabout reference, in that, while Lovecraft has mentioned the book (both in his letters and in a co-written story) it has truly come to life in the works of others that have been drawn on his universe. It should be noted that while these lyrics are listed as belonging to the cut, I can't really hear them unless they are hidden in the more strange sections of noise related music. The song starts very slowly and deliberately with dark understated tones slowly rising up from the abyss. Then a new melody with a mysterious, rather Eastern tone emerges from the guitar that moves its way upward. This then gives way after a time to a slow moving sparse arrangement based on guitar feedback. It is after this that the true chaos enters in the form of noisy freeform sounds that are rather frightening. This then leads into something that feels like free form jazz gone horribly wrong. The droning heavy sounds return after this section. This cut is definitely not something that everyone will enjoy, but it is without question very creative.

"Reaching Azathoth," released at the same time, starts with keyboards working their way through spacey weird textures. After this sort of atmospheric introduction more keyboard sounds begin to come on board and weave waves of symphonic like musical structures. This is at times pretty and at other points rather abrasive. Percussion eventually shows up in the background and becomes more and more prominent as time goes on. It then drops back once more to just strange keyboard sounds, then an extremely heavy bass guitar dominated jam takes over from there, plodding along in a definite doom mode. After a time noisy lines of guitar create a climbing pattern over this backdrop. The feedback oriented bass guitar jam continues on after these sounds have left. The vocals come in with a distorted, extremely processed whispered approach. The lyrics to this one are taken directly from, and attributed to, H.P. Lovecraft's own words. This moves along this way for some time, but uncanny keyboard textures emerge over the top of it later. It alternates late between the keyboard textures and more of the doom thudding. It seems at times that the music is attempting to simulate this description from the words to the cut, "amidst the muffled, maddening beating of vile drums and the thin monotonous whine of accursed flutes."[68] This one is certainly more accessible than the previous number, but nonetheless still for only a select audience. At almost twelve minutes in length it is also considerably longer than the previous piece.

The band's latest Lovecraftian number was recorded in 2006 for a new compilation, but has yet to be released. The title is "Lovecraft Knew." While all the lyrics have meanings that tie to H.P.L.'s literary legacy, perhaps the most telling ones are these:

> Under the rule of the Great Old Ones
> Their titanic masses tip our planet's axis
> Cyclopean storms and monstrous waves come crashing.
> Under the rule of the Great Old Ones
> At last tectonic convulsions mark the end of terrene life.
> Under the rule of the Great Old Ones.[69]

The music on the cut starts with strange, otherworldly atmosphere and builds on that for a time. After about thirty seconds crunchy guitar sounds enter and begin swirling in weird, slow moving patterns. Then other sonic elements rise and begin to fight for control and the cut becomes quite dissonant and disquieting. This grows until the lyrics come in, very far in the backdrop of the seemingly random pattern of sounds. They are slowed down and very hard to recognize as words. As this carries on there are more spoken, almost normal patterns that occasionally show up, but still far too distant in the mix to be easily discerned. At nearly six minutes in the cut shifts to a very sparse arrangement. Then it eventually moves upward into the first real heavy metal textures of the disc, a driving rhythmic jam. As keys come over the top of this it takes on almost a prog metal approach. This actually becomes almost progressive rock in texture for a time, then shifts again to more unique music with a freeform sort of feel to it. It plods along in a dissonant movement and the most straightforward vocals, still processed, but further up in the mix, enter.

Master Warjomaa of the group shared some of his insights on Lovecraft, music and his band's creation of music within the Mythos. His views on the process of creating music that reflects Lovecraftian textures are as follows:

> As Lovecraft's stories revolve around cosmic horror and alienation, I think the music should seek to reflect and convey those themes and feelings in the listener. Some of the musical elements I've chosen to employ in Aarni's past and especially future material include disharmony, arhythmicality and unnatural sounds in general. Anything to evoke an unnerving and unsettling atmosphere, really. Traditional Western diatonic music is so rigid, regular and well defined that stepping outside is relatively easy in my opinion. Creating unresolved tension with unconventional "out there" melodic/chordal patterns seems to work well. To give a slightly more concrete example, in Aarni's HPL-inspired stuff I have often used the mandatory cacophonic flutes, unusually tuned and untuned guitars, obscure synth sounds and whatnot.

Warjomaa (who lists his favorite H.P.L. works as "The Hound," "The White Ship," "The Outsider," "The Call of Cthulhu," *Dream-Quest of Unknown*

Kadath, "The Horror In The Museum" and "The Quest of Iranon") also had quite a bit to say about what he feels Lovecraft's work can bring to music.

> Well, I consider good music as an escape from banality—the goal of quality writing as well. To me, Tolkien for example is much more banal than H.P.L.'s cosmic, fatalistic horror fiction. So Lovecraft's literary creations lend themselves nicely to the more unconventional auditory realm. You can enter an altered state of reality both by literature and music. Yet I don't see much point in creating some sort of soundtrack to reading H.P.L.; in my opinion each art form should be enjoyed on its own.
>
> I consider Lovecraft's writings a good source of inspiration because there's a sense of profoundness in them; so to speak they strike a deep chord in one's psyche and that is something I always consider a key factor in what makes an inspiration for composing music.

If his responses to the previous questions were interesting, perhaps the most intriguing response came when I asked him what drew him to Lovecraft and has kept him as a fan.

> Curiously enough, my introduction to the gent from Providence seems like something out of his own writings: in 1987 my occultist and sci-fi enthusiast grandfather (following a certain esoteric tradition introduced by his own sea captain grandfather) lent me a collection of H.P.L.'s stories printed in the 1940s (which I've since inherited along with the rest of his library).
>
> I first read the novel "The Call of Cthulhu" and was instantly hooked. After that I began to game master the Call of Cthulhu role-playing game by Chaosium and even wrote a couple of puerile Cthulhu stories myself. Since then I've collected H.P.L.'s entire works, including the ghostwritten novels and the Cthulhoid writings of Clark Ashton Smith, Robert E. Howard and other authors of Lovecraft's circle.
>
> I suspect my fascination has been kept alive by the sheer dreamlike genius of H.P.L.'s creations. In my opinion, what he lacks in literary style he more than makes up in originality and atmosphere. The influences of Lord Dunsany, Poe and others on Lovecraft's work seem insignificant to me, I consider him an original thanks largely to his creative unbalanced mind...

Catacombs hails from Arizona and have been around since early in the 2000s. The mastermind behind this project is Xathagorra Mlandroth, and he had been working in the fields of doom and death metal since 1989, but this particular incarnation was not unearthed until much more recently. While Mlandroth is definitely a fan of Lovecraft, he has only released one track that has ties to H.P.L. That one is the title song to the *In the Depths of R'lyeh* CD, which was released in 2006.

When asked about his favorite Lovecraft stories, Mlandroth said this:

> Just to name a few... "What the Moon Brings," *At the Mountains of Madness*, "Dagon," "The Doom That Came to Sarnath," "The Other Gods," "The Tomb," "Beyond the Wall of Sleep," "Nyarlathotep," "From Beyond," "The Crawling Chaos," "The Festival," "The Nameless City," "Imprisoned With the Pharaohs," "The Shadow Over Innsmouth," "The Lurking Fear," "The Statement of Randolph Carter"... and some others which are personal to me, but that list is long enough.

In regards to the origins of his interest in H.P.L. and the continuation of that interest, Mlandroth had quite a bit to say:

> *Lovecraft's writings are, uncannily, very similar to my own, and many of his literary works touch on concepts, and especially essences and atmospheres, which have always been a part of who I am, since long before I ever read his works. His writings evoke things which I've always felt, and certain concepts that "play on" personal beliefs and/or creations out of my own being. Hence, these are the reasons why, even 20 years later, I still re-read Lovecraft on a regular basis, as it just continues to "feed" me on many levels and in many ways. On a last note, my literary style has always been, again... uncannily, very similar to his. He leaves much up to the imagination, through not only leaving things "open-ended" and up to interpretation, but does so through the atmospheres he evokes as well as what he does or does not "explain" directly in his stories. My personal feeling is that he is the greatest writer who every lived, as his literary works exude qualities that are simply unmatched by any other author to date. He is able to create worlds in just a few pages of writing, due to the fact that, intrinsically, in some other almost unexplainable way, his writings pull you in and make your consciousness automatically "expand" upon what you've read. It's really very interesting, at least to me, from both a psychological, creative and energetic perspective. But of course, I may be the only one on the planet who experiences this effect for all I know, so that's just my "take" on his works and what make them a permanent and personal part of my life.*

When he speaks of his writing bearing similarities to those of Lovecraft one need look no further than to the song addressed by this book to see that connection. Indeed, in many ways it seems as if Lovecraft himself could have written the words. "He who sleeps, ageless, out of time / awakens now from restless sleep / stirring in the depths of his aqueous tomb / at the sound of the gathering / of the neophytes of doom / chants in unknown tongues / echo through accursed halls / the great eyes open..."[70]

A creepy sort of guitar riff starts and becomes the main emphasis of this cut early on. It is joined by almost orchestral bursts of power that are based entirely on metal instrumentation, but gain their classical textures from the usage and arrangement. The cut builds incredibly slowly from this point and eventually a death metal growl comes over the top as the cut plods along. At about 2 minutes in it drops back to a more sparse arrangement and the guitar takes on textures that remind me a bit of early Judas Priest. It turns heavier again in a while and runs through several variants of an incredibly slowly moving wall of sound. Eventually those death growls emerge again and the cut has an exceptionally scary and otherworldly texture to it. It moves along in basically the same ways (the varying segments returning and being reworked) for all of its eleven plus minutes, in a heavy, atmospheric jam that is slow moving, but very hot, much like a flow of magma coming in the aftermath of a volcanic eruption. This definitely isn't for everyone, but fans of doom metal will have to hunt far and wide to find something that moves this slowly and is more atmospherically metallic than this one.

Of the creative process for this song as it relates to Lovecraftian music in general, Mlandroth had the following to say:

> With the one song on the Catacombs album "In the Depths of R'lyeh." which is the only song that is Lovecraft-related, it's not something that I had to intentionally "try" to create. Those essences and atmospheres are a natural part of how I write music in general. However, with that particular song, I did want it to be as haunting, under worldly and other worldly as possible, and with a true feeling of doom (in terms of the meaning of the word, not the style of music) and a palpable "cavernous" feel. Hence, as with everything else it had to be brutally heavy in terms of sound, timings and delivery, but slightly different and unique in its incredibly haunting, mysterious, and unsettling atmospheres... and that's what I created.

Mlandroth also had quite a bit to say about what he sees Lovecraft's work bringing to the general musical table:

> Generally speaking, you have to have a great amount of personal depth and evolvement to really get something from Lovecraft's works on a deeper level. I think for those few who are on that level, Lovecraft's writings can offer worlds of inspiration in terms of a miasma of atmospheres and essences, and even inspire many concepts which to integrate into one's music or even their personal lives. If you're able to connect on a deeper, personal and energetic level to the atmospheres and essences he created and it's a part of who you are, his writings can inspire you to write music that is truly dark and disturbing, haunting and macabre, that truly leaves a lasting impression and creates worlds, just as his writings have.

The German band Philosopher was formed in 2002, and are self proclaimed as "Lovecraftian Death Metal." To date they have an EP, *What Dwells Beyond*, and one album out, 2004's *Thoughts*.

The group's guitarist, Alex "Snakes" Pohl, described the process of trying to create Lovecraftian music like this:

> Music wise we just try to catch the certain atmosphere that catches you when you read one of H.P.L.'s stories or his poetry, you know? We're trying to create kind of a musical analogy to the mood rather than the stories. In my opinion, everything H.P.L. ever wrote (including those many long letters) is part of one whole concept and we're exploring that given our music. That's about the trip we'd like to take the listener on.

> Besides we're very interested in the occult and philosophical themes (as the band-name might indicate) and it's again thanks to H.P.L., since he brought me onto this. To me his work was really a gateway. Though he always claimed to be anti-occult, he could still be of big influence anyway. H.P.L. even knew how to create the occult (the sinister, the unknown) itself sometimes, if you want to see it that way. Just think of all the stuff that's been written on the subject of the *Necronomicon*, and all those magical hoaxes about that. And does it really exist? Not bad for a declared non-occultist, is it?

When asked what he felt Lovecraft's body of work had to offer to music in general, Pohl said this:

> Quite a lot, to us his writings and the writings of the circle and of all the people who were influenced by the circle are, amongst other works really like the basement of our musical inspiration. Whenever I want to get in the mood for that certain, creepy, apocalyptic atmosphere I just read Lovecraft. In my opinion he's still unbeaten as a writer of the supernatural. I mean, as time goes by, who is scared of Dracula or the mummy still? But Lovecraft's "creations" and just to think of that there could be something to it, a reality just a blink from our own? —hard to beat that.

Lovecraft is so ingrained in him that Pohl was hard pressed to remember how he first got interested in the author. In fact when asked about that and what has been the enduring quality of H.P.L., this is what he had to say:

> I don't know anymore how I might have been stumbled over his work, maybe a friend lent me a book once or so. But since my first H.P.L. story "The Rats in the Wall" I've read all I could get. To me he's the typical genius, the absolute creative, since his stories combine root elements of fiction (Science Fiction, Horror, Fantasy) to create something far bigger than just the sum of the parts. In just telling us some tiny bits he created an immense universe of fear that grows still. He's the true father of supernatural horror and its absolute master still.

As one might expect of a person so influenced by the author's work, even just asking Pohl about his favorite Lovecraft stories got more of answer than a simply listing.

> "Rats In the Wall," of course, and "The Outsider," "The Dunwich Horror," and "The Music of Erich Zann" since that helped a lot to define my way of making the guitar sound during the leads. You know just like all squealing and ripping the veil of reality, opening gates, that's what it's about—gates in the mind. And there are so many more, I like almost all of his stories and I strongly recommend to read as much of it as you could ever get, even try some fake *Necronomicon*'s once in a while—they're very amusing at least.

Looking first to that 2003 EP, we find that it contains four tracks. The first of these is "Within Aeons." It opens with a fast paced riff that is very meaty. They run through in a thrash like manner for a while. They move it through a few variants before the death growls enter to carry the vocals. It drops later to a more sparse arrangement that is very rhythmic in texture. They carry this through a few changes and then slow it down a bit in a stuttering sort of rhythmic pattern. It speeds back up later. The cut stays relatively stable for a time, then drops into a killer instrumental jam. At first this is slowed down a bit, but extremely meaty. Then it bursts out with an extremely tasty guitar solo segment where lines of sound swirl around each other in a fairly awesome sonic tapestry. This works its way through, and then moves back into the song proper to carry it forward. In a complete change of pace, a crescendo gives way to what sounds like a tolling bell and then the band move the track out into atmospheric, textural wanderings for the last minute or so of the piece. It's a nice way to end a solid number. The final verse of the lyrics (presented below) shows the most blatant example of the Lovecraft connection to the song.

> Once again is the symbol drawn / The stars are right! They long for human blood, again they rise! / So weeps the sycamore, there's no more light! / Stepping out of their catacombs to rule their heir another time! / Exist through aeons the walls of time /Resisting the eye of the gods behind / Closing the circle, blood drawn in line to rule again—forever in time![71]

Next up is "Nephren Ka." This one also shows up on the album, so I'll address the lyrics when discussing the album. Percussion brings this one in with a fast paced rhythmic pattern. Then an extremely heavy progression enters and the number is off. This one is at times slow and plodding, but reminds me quite a bit (albeit with death growls for the vocals) of the sort of sound that Metallica did on *Ride The Lightning*. This one has a very strong metal texture. They slow it down even more later, but continue to produce a strong metal texture. After running through like this for a time, though, it speeds back up to carry forward. As it moves out later into a more melodic jam, I find it to be one of the best musical passages the band have created. They then turn the corner into a more dynamic sort of jam with varying segments of guitar dominated musical themes and percussive breaks. After another burst of vocals they switch it up with a killer epic metal sort of jam that has neo-classical leanings. Between this section and the section that preceded this last vocal movement, this one is a far stronger song than the one that preceded—and truth be told that one was good, too. They throw in some exceptionally powerful metallic instrumental work on this section, and then drop it to piano—yes, I said piano, to carry it through to its conclusion.

"Dweller in Ruins" shares lyrics (and is really the same song) with the track "What Dwells Beyond" from the full album. So, we'll examine the lyrics when we get to that segment. It is a lot more Metallica-like than its predecessor. In fact, they jump in here with a minute and a half jam that has a killer series of changes all based on a proto-thrash style. That said, the sound is a bit more stripped down and has moments where you can hear hints of 1980s metal in the guitar over layers. Later they turn the corner into an incredible jam with Eastern tinges. This movement is extended and extremely powerful. Overall, this cut is not as dynamic as "Nephren Ka," but somewhat easier to catch hold of and fall into the jam.

While the final cut on the EP doesn't have a distinctly Lovecraftian title, and it is an instrumental (therefore it has no lyrics to tie it to the Mythos), I'm going to discuss it simply because it is not distinctly excluded from Lovecraft connections, and it is the only other track on show here, anyway. "Incantation of Vendiggo (Instrumental Outro)" starts with the sounds of a gentle storm. The music comes in tentatively at first, and based on an almost progressive rock or new age texture. As it carries forward more dark and ominous textures emerge in the arrangement, but still the overall tone doesn't change. The sound becomes more lush and bit higher in volume, but then there is a subtle shift for a short time with waves of nearly frightening sound beginning to coalesce at the top of this motif. This doesn't remain long, though and when it leaves the only thing still there is what sounds like a plucked acoustic guitar (but is actually an ancient Turkish instrument known as a Ut)—which has been in the mix throughout most of the track. This eventually stops playing and just the sound of the storm, seemingly heavier by this point remains to finally end the track after working alone for a while.

With their first full-length album *Thoughts*, released the following year, they continued on with Lovecraftian themes in a big way. The disc opens with "700 Steps of Deeper Slumber," and the lyrics to that track (while there aren't many) show off hints of H.P.L. right off the bat. "Behold Careful Dreamer! / Descending from the cavern of flame those stairs lead to the Enchanted Wood of the Dreamlands."[72] It is fairly obvious from looking at these lyrics that they refer to *The Dream-Quest of Unknown Kadath*.

It begins with atmosphere, much like the instrumental that ended the EP. Then sound begins to build in a pretty, almost new age approach that has elements of Celtic music within. They build this up into a pretty yet, brief instrumental. The vocals play along on this one, but so indistinctly and far back in the mix (almost dream-like) that you might (as I did) mistake it for an instrumental. It is possible, though, as you really can't hear the words, that this is an instrumental, with simply non-lyrical vocal lines. Several other tracks on show here include lyrics, but yet no vocals on the song. So, it is not outside the realm of possibilities, and I really can't tell for sure.

With the next number, "Awakening Senses," these guys waste no time getting to the frantic hard-edged jamming. This one pounds in frantic and furious straight out of the gate. The band again show off Metallica (the early years) leanings, but also a bit of those epic metal textures. The vocals, though are pure death metal. This one is very tasty and rather dynamic. It also includes some strong guitar work. I particularly like they way they slow it down on the short, but cool outro. The lyrics here don't seem distinctly Lovecraft based, but there is a vague sense of textures that are in line with H.P.L.'s Mythos. It's enough of a connection for me to include this one here, but not enough to warrant examples from the texts.

With the next number, though, the Lovecraft based ideas are more definite. While still not seeming to speak to one particular story, they are far easier to discern. Looking to the first several lines of "Beyond Darkness" we can see both references to the old gods and also the idea of the truth of existence driving a person insane.

> Truth is not to be portrayed by the Mentally Sane / Behind the brightly lit surface / where the shadows force out every beam of light / where faith into vital life crushes / by the rotten stench of a silenced past / between the ruins of forgotten ages / beyond the darkness lost creatures of the old gods survived / beyond darkness clandestine / Look through my eyes and see with me / what ages try to hide for eternity 'til now you were blind.[73]

Once again they jump right in with this one is a slightly oddly timed frantic excursion. They fire through an instrumental intro for quite some time before the vocals enter. This is another hard as nails, heavy as iron, death jam. It then slows down to something that feels a lot like doom metal with a heavy, plodding arrangement. That segment doesn't remain long, though, the band powering it back up to more of what came before. Then comes a new fast paced jam with a little less of a heavy texture, more reminiscent of the epic metal sound, to carry it onward. From here eventually an exceptionally tasty guitar solo segment emerges. After this, the band rework this into something closer to the textures that preceded it before twisting the motif around again for the next vocal mode. The extremely slow plodding section returns for the chorus. Another strong guitar solo comes in later. This song is very dynamic shifting almost constantly. The outro is back to the slow paced sound with just a short movement that even calls to mind Black Sabbath a bit.

The next number is "Elysia," and although it is an instrumental, the liner notes include a description of the concepts of the song. It's only one line, but that line is quite Lovecraftian: "Home of the Elder Beings and Center of Forces yet unknown to mankind."[74] of course, when you figure that the track is less than four minutes in length, this small number of words seems appropriate. Musically this one is a major change of pace. It is a pretty instrumental that is both melancholy in texture and very regal sounding. The predominant instrument is piano.

Next is "What Dwells Beyond." In addition to sharing a title with the EP, this track is the one that also has the same lyrics as two songs from that outing. So tied to Lovecraft are the words to this one, and also considering that they are actually used for two different songs, I am going to include the entire text here.

> Beware of the olden ritual Tomes! / For the only truth they offer is Eternal Madness. / So come now proceed the ritual and open the gates / So come now and the elder ones will have you for prey / Sacrifice your journeys so thoughtful lead into the unknown kingdom amongst old Kadath! / Nothing will ever reach beyond a wisdom of deadly soulside / Thou dreamest a deadly vision / Thou dwellst beyond the dark. / Unholy intervention a god but dead thou art / So come and hate is ours in endless pain we rule! / So come and this world is yours into damnation of another species' sacrifice! / And so you rise! / So now proceeded is the ritual and opened the gates / So I face the elder ones they have me for prey suicide! / My journey has ended now leads into unknown one with the old Kadath / Nothing will ever be able to touch my deadly wisdom suicide! / This stands to be forever withstands the force of time![75]

Anyone familiar with Lovecraft's work (or, for that matter, who has read this far into this book) should have little trouble spotting the H.P.L. ties on this one. It is evidently not taken directly from any one story, yet it should seem quite obvious that the lyrics are directly related to Howard Phillip's work. This is another which pounds in feeling a lot like *Ride the Lightning* era

Metallica. The band work through several incarnations of the themes on the introduction. This intro includes some the most tasty guitar soloing on the whole disc, and it's about a minute before any vocals emerge. While a large chunk of the track is fairly monolithic in its approach, after a time they shift gears into a very meaty instrumental progression with strong Eastern tones. This section of the song works through several variations and truly saves this one from getting "over done" in terms of staying in one place too long. While this is not the strongest cut on the disc, that instrumental break, along with a very brief Eastern segment that sounds like flute or recorder at the end, save this one from becoming too typical. While this is basically the same song as "Dweller In Ruins," there are differences. I like them both for different reasons.

"Wounds" is next, musically this one is a frantically quick and heavy death metal jam that pounds pretty much throughout its length. This track is another which suffers just a little from sameness, but once again the instrumental segment with its meaty sounds pulls it up from the brink of potential disaster. The lyrics speak of the old gods and also of lies. I believe that the "lies" referred to address the concept of our vision of reality being a falsehood and that the truth is a universe in which The Old Ones are the once and future rulers of this world.

Another short atmospheric instrumental, "47° 5_ S, 126° 49_ W" is pretty, but also mysterious. The title refers to the coordinates that Lovecraft cited for the location of Cthulhu's city of R'lyeh.

The next track also appeared on the EP. Here "Nephren Ka" is about half a minute shorter. It doesn't differ much from the earlier rendition significantly, other than the shortened length. Most of the alterations seem to be in the form of some added layers of sound here. Granted, those layers really do a nice job of infusing a sense of the weird, which is appropriate, but overall this one is basically the same track. The lyrics refer to Lovecraft's story "Under the Pyramids" which is also known as "Imprisoned with the Pharaohs," which Lovecraft wrote with/for Harry Houdini. Still, the closing segment here really has a great atmosphere of weirdness woven into it. It is a nice touch.

"Dreamside" comes next on the disc. The lyrics seem to speak, without an extreme explicitness, of the varying themes of dream that are common to Lovecraftian works. While overall this one is another frantic slab of death metal fury, there are odd changes throughout. One such element is an unusual drop back to a weird little almost world music percussion segment. Another is a keyboard layer that shows up over the top to lend an otherworldly texture at points. There is also a rather odd sounding, but very tasty, distant guitar solo section later with more of those Eastern tinged sounds. It seems that even when these guys create a work of music that is fairly generic, they throw enough curve balls into the mix to make it something special. There is even a section here that almost feels like a jazz take on death metal.

The lyrics to the next track ("World In Rapture") could almost go by you without spotting the Lovecraftian textures. At first glance I mistook it for an anti-Christianity number, but when you check out the last few lines, it is obvious that the references to that real religion refer back to the universal lie concept that recurs throughout this release. "They eternal lie dreaming there and waiting for the day / Your Gods'll be falling down to pray / R'lyeh is what you fear deep in your soul / you bleed can't hide your tears you know that there is more than the eternal lie and you are no longer blind."[76]

Musically this one falls into a very Black Sabbath like territory. In fact, as I'm a big fan of that sound, this is probably my favorite piece on the album. It's overall a fairly slow paced grind with an old school metal sound, but the growling death metal vocals keep you from forgetting the musical style. Still, the jam has enough of that Black Sabbath sound—even in some of the chordal progressions and changes—to please fans of that band. It is a nice change of pace, and with some extremely tasty moments.

The closer, "I Am Providence," is another instrumental. This one bears the dedication, "In memory of the immortal genius (1890-1937)."[77] The first minute plus of this is a pretty and intricate, rather classical piano solo. Then it shifts out into an atmospheric, and frightening sounding mix that feels like it could be an otherworldly ritual for one of the Old Ones. The title is also the inscription that is actually on Lovecraft's head stone. It's a classy way, both musically and in terms of the dedication, to end the disc.

A one-man "band," Fireaxe is the heavy metal outlet for Brian Voth. Under that moniker he has released one Lovecraft based album, aptly entitled, *Lovecraftian Nightmares*. The songs are poems that were written by H.P.L. set to music. Of his writing process in creating the album, Voth had this to say:

> I would start by reading the poems with the intent of setting them to music. The meter and the tone of the lines would provoke a melody in the creative part of my brain that would match both. After the melody was established it was a matter of adding accompaniments which underlined the mood and harmonized with the melody. As I was writing the songs I realized that they were a significant departure from what listeners have grown to expect from popular music. Lovecraft's lines are much longer than typical lyrical lines and lacked a strong chorus, but then he never intended them to become pop songs. Rather than make changes or additions to the poems to fit them into the modern musical style I decided to let the poems dictate how the music needed to be in

order to correctly capture the meter and mood. That was a major challenge. Further complicating that approach was that the mood would often change several times throughout the poem, so I couldn't just come up one or two musical ideas and repeat them throughout the song. So the music had to keep a consistent style to hold the song together while changing to match the moods throughout. For each song I worked hard to accomplish that, and the result are songs which take you on a journey in much the same way the poems do. The songs are longer, and go through many passages, much like classical music or the rare ballad. The process of writing such songs changed the way that I approach music. In the past I used to write songs in the popular style: verse-chorus-repeat. Now my aim is to craft a complete song based around a story or theme much like the operatic tradition. I feel that I have grown greatly as an artist as a result.

Voth revealed that for him, "Lovecraft has an intellectual appeal, since the characters in his stories often make their discoveries in the pursuit of knowledge." He continued by adding the following to this statement:

> I've had a number of revelations in my life which occurred while I was reading a book and experienced that moment where my calm, orderly reality was turned on its head. The darker themes appeal to my atheistic side. Lovecraft left Christianity out of his stories and his characters never made appeals to any god to save them. To me it seemed as if he was saying in his stories "Your god doesn't exist. These are the real gods, and they aren't going to save your soul, they're going to devour it."

Voth revealed that his favorite Lovecraft tales are *At the Mountains of Madness* and *The Dream-Quest of Unknown Kadath*. He also gave the following insight:

> It's interesting to compare Lovecraft's "mythos" with any other religion. Whereas all the religions in the world are uplifting and focus on salvation, Lovecraft's is just the opposite, stating that the best that humans can hope for is to live a quiet life in ignorance and not catch the attention of the gods. I think that if you've ever worked in or dealt with a bureaucracy that you can relate to that concept. Why would the universe of afterlife be any different?

Looking to Voth's album, while the sound of Fireaxe certain falls into heavy metal, there are other elements present as well. The music here runs across a fairly wide gamut, but Iron Maiden and King Diamond type sounds are the most prevalent. This is an interesting album only marred by two things. First, the production on the disc is a bit flat and convoluted. Secondly, Voth's vocals can at times be quite rough around the edges. Still, the material on show is definitely interesting enough to make this one well worth the time to get through it.

Starting off the CD is "Beyond Zimbabwe." Appropriately an odd, tribal segment starts it, and then a metal stomp takes the cut. The intro to this features some very tasty soloing. The vocals on the cut feel a bit awkward, but the meaty main riff more than makes up for it, and Voth's frantic guitar soloing certainly doesn't hurt either.

"Nightmare Lake" comes next. Voth's falsetto at the start of this is a bit rough, but the balladic segment that comes in then is quite effective. After a verse in this mode it bursts out into a strong and dramatic metallic fury that calls to mind King Diamond just a bit. It drops to acapella later, then a reprise of the balladic segment returns. It pulls down from there to just a spoken voice, then bursts back up to the King Diamond-like territory. This one is very heavy and quite dynamic, eventually making its way back to the ballad style. Spoken words end this.

The next number is "The Ancient Track." This one, again quite aptly, starts with an olde world acapella segment starts. Voth jumps in with a balladic guitar melody. A guitar solo wanders over the top before his vocals enter here, this feeling a bit like old Rush. It gets rather heavy, but never wanders far.

Coming in heavy, dramatic and dark, the intro to "The Outpost" feels like prog metal. It shifts gear to a frantic speed metal approach, though. Although Voth's vocals are nowhere near as potent as Bruce Dickinson's, musically this cut feels a bit like Iron Maiden. This is another fairly dynamic number and eventually drops to a strummed slower segment. It jumps back up later to the Maidenesque jam with a vengeance. A false ending leads to a reprise of this same section.

A garagey early Rush mode starts "Despair," and a nice vocal harmony arrangement marred only by some weakness in Voth's performance, is a nice touch. Heavy flourishes punctuate the verse segments here. A heavier bridge with non-lyrical vocals is an effective change of pace. This ends in a slightly rough acapella section.

The next cut on show is "Whispers In the Night." A great balladic mode with dark and mysterious tones, aided by (again Voth shows his gift for being appropriate) whispered vocals starts this. The cut gradually builds as the actual vocals enter. This mode runs through the first two and a half or so minutes until it finally bursts forth in metallic fury, again feeling a bit like Maiden. Voth's singing is stronger here and he has some very tasty guitar fills. This wanders into a more plodding metallic zone later, very heavy and doom like.

Percussion with weird vocals start "Hounds of Tindalos," then frantic jamming again feeling like both Maiden and King Diamond takes the piece.

This is very dynamic and just a little hard to follow.

Next in line is "Nemesis." Based on a keyboard line, the vocals come in with a dark but mellow mood. It runs through in this style for a time until a new hard-edged segment jumps in again a bit like Iron Maiden. It eventually drops back to the mellower mode for a time before leaping back up to the fury. It repeats this pattern one more time before it ends.

Starting in a sound that is kind of a cross between a weird progressive rock and Judas Priest's "Dreamer Deceiver", "Festival" builds very gradually. It doesn't wander far, though, instead remaining a mellow, but somewhat spooky cut.

Voth closes out the album with "Nathicana." A Mike Oldfield-type sound starts this and runs through for a time, bouncy and echoey. Voth eventually builds on this and creates a balladic experience from this basis. His falsetto comes across a little harsh at times. This balladic section combined with that Oldfield-like section makes up the first five and a half minutes of the piece. Eventually a guitar solo comes across the top, heralding a movement in new directions. This mode is a flanged sounding prog rock type sound, with the solo continuing its run over top. After a minute and a half or so, this gives way to a crunchy take on the earlier modes, essentially the same song, just turned more metal. After another several minutes of building a new guitar solo enters, this one quite noisy, but still meaty. It then shifts to a new melodic movement built on waves of flanged noisy guitar, feeling a bit like a garagey take on early Rush. It drops to the mellower first verse section later to carry the song to its conclusion. This epic piece is by far the longest on the album.

Voth has also been featured on two more Lovecraft related albums. These are Famlende Forsøk's *One Night I Had a Frightful Dream* and various artists' release *Strange Aeons*. Both of these will be covered in later chapters.

These words draw to a close the book's look at heavy metal. It seems certain that more Lovecraftian metal music will come in the future, but next the attention will be turned to punk rock.

Chapter 6

SAFETY PINS AND YOG-SOTHOTH: PUNK ROCK TAKES ON LOVECRAFT

Punk rock is a form of music that originated in the mid 1970s as a response to overproduced disco, arena rock and other types of music. It was meant to be a raw, back to basics approach to music and often featured a lot of angst. It was not uncommon (honestly or not) for band members to brag about their inability to play. It was also associated with a type of dress that included torn clothing, safety pins and black leather. Early bands in the genre included The Sex Pistols, The Clash, The Dead Boys and The Ramones. New Wave (a more pop oriented/synthesizer dominated style) came out of the punk rock movement and the current wave of emo bands (modern pop-oriented punk rock) are direct descendants from the early punkers. Another type of music called "hardcore" also had its roots in punk, with bands like The Dead Kennedys pioneering the sound by playing a musical style that combine punk rock's raw nature and snotty, angry attitude with thrash metal's speed and precision.

The first punk incursion into the mythos of H.P.L. was made by a band called "Rudimentary Peni." The band's first EP was released in 1981, but it wouldn't be until the 1989 release *Cacophony* that the band would journey into Lovecraftian territory—and in a big way. The entire album is based in one way or another on H.P.L.'s life or work. It varies from song to song, but it's there.

The disc opens with "Nightgaunts," a track whose title alone shows the Lovecraft ties. The lyrics (much like all the lyrics of the band) represent a sort of stream of consciousness hodgepodge of ideas and images given the form of words with the most commonly repeated term being the title. An odd sort of musical texture starts this, then weird fast paced spoken word section takes over until the band launch into a hard edged, fast paced jam. The main vocals enter and carry through over this backdrop with the spoken word stuff (just the title now) also running at the same time, sort of punctuating the lines. This ends with a scream and a clumsy sounding crescendo. The entire track lasts less than a minute.

They follow it up with "The Horrors In the Museum." While there is no major variation on the style of the lyrical content, no one would mistake the words of one song for the other. Musically a quick sound bite saying, "oh, sonny, I'm sure you know…" serves to start this one. The cut is a bouncing, fast paced jam that is quite entertaining. The vocals are delivered with a typical sneer. There are points in the track where the vocals tend to imitate the sound of a theremin—and this is an extremely nice touch. This eventually wanders into weird noise based chaos as it carries toward its conclusion.

The next cut on the disc is "The Only Child." It is certainly one which refers more to H.P.L.'s life than to his work, as he was, in fact, an "only child." Bass guitar starts this by itself and carries it for a time. Then the band launch into a bouncing sort of rather psychedelic punk rock jam with slightly sneering vocals. It ends with noisy weirdness.

While it has certainly been written (and repeated here) that every song on this album has some tie to Lovecraft, one would be hard pressed to find the connection with the next song to be included. That cut is "Architectonic And Dominant" and includes only two words, "flamelike sunset,"[1] for its lyrics. I'm certain there is a link to H.P.L., but I can't tell you what it is. This one comes in rather like heavy metal, and the whole introduction is in that format. As it kicks into the next segment, though, the frantic punk rock textures take over. This runs through to that verse, then it drops to a segment that's a bit like a twisted Gregorian chant to eventually end.

The next track, "The Evil Clergyman" is much more closely tied to H.P.L.'s work. I saw the title to be speaking of the Cultists and dark priests that often show up in Lovecraft's stories. However, S. T. Joshi told me that it, "refers to a fragmentary story by H.P.L." This piece is a crunchy, high-energy punk rocker rather in the mode of bands like The Dead Boys. This is one of the Rudimentary Peni songs that I like more than the rest. It is a fast paced stomper, that while an instrumental seems to be based on H.P.L. both by the title and the fact that it is on this album. It ends with a fast paced monologue of seeming gibberish, or at least unconnected ideas.

"Brown Jenkin," of course, takes its title from the Lovecraftian character with the same name. A whistling in the background of this pounding dark punk opus leads one to think at first that it's a live recording. That whistling sound, though remains throughout in a rather annoying pattern and the semblance of a live performance goes away. This one is essentially a hard-edged tasty punk rock instrumental with some retro rock and roll textures. Some of the frantic spoken recitation ends it.

Another whose link is easy to see is "Crazed Couplet," of course, referring fairly directly to H.P.L.'s famous lines that are often given a similar name. In fact, the song has few lyrics and all of them are drawn from or a variation on that source. "That is not dead which can eternal lie / And with strange aeons even death may die, / Dead death, dead death, death dead! /

Death dead!"[2] Musically this one is frantic punk with a slowed down sounding spoken vocal of the couplet. Then during the later points of the cut the "dead death" part is sung over the top of this. This ends with a spoken word recitation.

The next song in line is "Sarcophogus." One need look no further than the first line of the song, which is actually the title of a Lovecraft story, "Imprisoned with the pharaohs,"[3] to see the obvious ties that bind this one to the Lovecraft mythos. For me this one was a little hard to take in the first modes. A rather disharmonic guitar pattern is good, but the vocals add to it in a very unappealing way. This one is just plain weird and a bit too abrasive for my tastes.

"Lovecraft Baby" is another where the links to H.P.L. should be obvious just from the title. This one is bouncy and fun with a bit of Elvis mixed in with the band's usual punk rock textures. It's obvious that they played this one for the fun of it.

They follow that cut with "Dream City." This is one of the more accessible numbers on the disc with a bouncing punk rock / classic rock theme serving as the backdrop for the unusual, but cool, falsetto vocals. A short segment with an almost prog rock texture takes it to just spoken vocals that serve as the eventual conclusion.

Next up is "C12 H22 O11." While I'm not sure about the Lovecraftian connection on this song, the title is actually the chemical composition of refined sucrose. This is another that has a fairly standard punk rock mode to the music, at least at first. It then shifts to a weird, dark spacey jam, then more of the spoken babble sounding atmosphere of which these guys seem extremely fond.

"Zenophobia" is the next track on the disc. The cut is a plodding sort of jam with groaned, screamed vocals in its early section. This part feels like one portion Dave Clark Five and one piece AC/DC done by a garage band. It definitely has a solid chunk of psychedelia, but in a very raw, crunchy arrangement. It then drops to an atmospheric sound with a sort of clerical ministration spoken over the top of lines of guitar. Then it becomes a tongue in cheek conversation. Sound effects take it out from there.

Next in line is the song "Sunset for the Lords of Venus." The piece is at first a straightforward jam. This section is purely instrumental, but then it ends and some spoken word madness concludes it.

That one is followed by "Beyond the Tanarian Hills." The track has almost whiney vocals, but in a sneering sort of way. It also has one of the most meaty riffs powering it of any the band have done. Interestingly enough, this one feels a bit like Led Zeppelin's form of classic rock at times, but twisted around into an odd sort of version of itself.

"Imps of the Perverse" is next in line. The vast majority of this cut is a fast paced spoken rant (done with a tongue in cheek accent) of a critic of H.P.L. As it carries on some hints of music are brought in for a short time. Then it goes back to the stream of consciousness trashing of Lovecraft. Eventually, though, the band launch into a frantic, progression that is pretty interesting. I'd say the most intriguing part of this one is how fast and long the guy can rant without a break.

That one is followed by "The Loved Dead." While the lyrics certainly speak of H.P.L., I'd say it would serve them best to present them here without comment and let the reader draw their own conclusion. "They've taken Lovecraft's lantern jaw off and are embalming him / his pale complexion feigns an aura more lifelike than when he lived the adoration of dead personalities safe fantasia / immortality of the unobtainable."[4] Those lines represent the entire lyrical content of the song. The cut starts with a fast paced bass line, then it jumps into a frantic jam that feels a bit like Hawkwind. Breathy, almost hiccupped lines of vocals come over the top. The bass guitar truly powers this cut, moving furious lines ever upward. It ends with another spoken segment and is one of my favorite cuts on the disc.

"Periwig Power" is next up on the CD. This launches in with a fast paced riff and the cut is fairly "normal," save for the odd vocals, mostly delivered in the spoken, shouted seemingly humorous vein as most of the singing on this disc. Gasping and coughing ends this number.

"Kappa Alpha Tau" comes in next in sequence on the album. On this one the links to Lovecraft are somewhat unclear. Other than the title—H.P.L. wrote a poem called "The Anthem of Kappa Alpha Tau"—I can see only a few minor hints. There is a reference to a cat and these words that have a vague H.P.L. texture, "artifacts of the aether / specks of the universe."[5] There is also a reference to "noble aloof,"[6] which might be someone's interpretation of Mr. Lovecraft himself. I have been informed by S. T. Joshi that the band could not have read "The Anthem of Kappa Alpha Tau" before writing this song, as it had not been published until Joshi himself resurrected it in 2001. He was, however, able to shed light on the origins of this song. According to Joshi, "'Kappa Alpha Tau' (the Greek letters KAT) is the name H.P.L. gave to a group of cats next door to his house at 66 College St. in Providence, where he lived from 1933 till his death in 1937." It is also possible that the song is somehow inspired by Lovecraft's essay, "Cats and Dogs" from 1926. I have not been able to verify it. In any case, this comes in with a metallic segment with a burst of crunch and a snarling, evil sounding vocal. It stomps through for a short time in this mode, after which it drops back to what sounds like some kind of a creature either purring or snoring.

If anyone who knows anything about Lovecraft's personality and life misses the link in the next song's title, he or she should probably start over. That title is a long one, "American Anglophile in the World Turned Upside-Down." This is a bouncing sort of punk rock jam with more of those frantically fast and most unintelligible spoken voices, this time in multiple layers, set over the top.

They follow that song up with "Memento Mori," and frankly, I would say that this one really is not Lovecraft based at all. The only lyrics are "Die, bugger, die."[7] This is an angry frantic punk rock powerhouse. The only link to H.P.L. that I can find comes during a section at the end that is just a swirling of words spoken. It includes the name "Theobold," which is a nickname of Lovecraft's.

Next in line is "Better Not Born." The cut starts with more spoken word, fast paced and a bit more "normal" than the other such work here. This is shortly accompanied by a tasty mid-paced jam that is one of the more meaty ones on show here. Weird spoken distorted sound bites in a very brief showing end this. This one is another that feels a bit like Hawkwind. It is also my favorite cut on the disc. I have been unable to track down the lyrics to this one, but I believe they may be taken directly from Lovecraft's writings.

"Arkham Hearse" is the next track to show up here. If you have read the title to the song, you have also seen every word in the lyrics. I suppose just the usage of Arkham puts this one into Lovecraftian territory. That said, though, you would have to include any Batman comic books in the same category as the Asylum in that magazine is called "Arkham." The cut stomps in feeling a bit like Ted Nugent meets AC/DC, but after a while shifts towards the more strange. This one is good, but not amongst the best on show. It ends with a short spoken sound bite.

While the next one, "The Old Man Is Not So Terribly Misanthropic" is almost certainly about H.P.L., it seems like the lyrics would be hard for most people to figure out. Still, just the title seems likely to give away the identity of the "old man." If that's the case, then the opening line certainly pays tribute to the author with "You do not realize how much I appreciate you."[8] This is one of the more pure punk showings here, feeling a lot like The Dead Boys, with perhaps a bit of Hawkwind thrown into the mix. Another spoken bit ends it. Joshi said of the lyrics to this one, "The line 'You do not realize how much I appreciate you' is a reference to Sonia (Greene) Davis's [Lovecraft's wife] memoir of H.P.L., in which she says that he would say something like this to her—he could never bring himself to say 'I love you.'"

The next cut to show up on the CD is "Gentlemen Prefer Blood." This track feels like a twisted take on 1950s rock and even the Grease Soundtrack. It is somewhat plodding and definitely strange, but rather fun.

With their next song, the group seem specifically to turn their attention to Lovecraft's wife Sonia (Greene). While again the lyrics are most certainly obtuse, there are definite signs pointing in the direction that she was the "Sonia" whose name the song shares. "I've made up my mind to steal you my dear / Never the initiator / head of the house is humbled / who is Phillips, Phillips."[9] While this is a subject that is probably best addressed elsewhere, in terms of lovemaking, Sonia Lovecraft said that H.P.L. did not initiate the process. Musically this track has a sort of psychedelic psychosis sound. It's almost like a 1960's romp, but twisted around into something far stranger and less accessible.

Another title which will be crystal clear to anyone with a good knowledge of Lovecraft's life, the next track is entitled, "The Day the Universe Ceased (March 15th 1937)." That date is the day that the author died, and certainly one could perceive that his universe might have ceased on that day. Of course, there have been far too many people carrying on his legacy for that to be true, but the title makes a nice tribute nonetheless. While the lyrics don't present such a lasting and beautiful homage, they do make it clear that the song is in fact about that particular significance of the date. I have to say that Lovecraft probably would not have approved of the form of verbiage, but I suppose it's the sentiment that counts.

Next up is "The Crime of the Century." I must confess that while this is one of the more odd pieces on the disc, it is also very intriguing. It is a quick paced, fairly interesting musical excursion with barely intelligible spoken bits over the top of it. Joshi told me that the title "is a reference to a rather racist essay that H.P.L. wrote in 1915, referring to World War I."

"Musick In Diabola" comes next on the disc. It is yet another frantically paced punk rock jam in the early modes, and then it shifts gear towards an odd space rock sort of movement. The spoken words come in later and run over the top of this spacey jam. I suspect that many of the words here are lifted directly from Lovecraftian text, but since some of them I can't make out, nor get my hands on the lyrics, I can't be sure. At over two minutes, this is one of the longest tracks on show here.

Lyrically, "Shard" is probably the most brilliant piece on the album, and I'd have to say the most in keeping with Lovecraft's style of storytelling. The lyrics seem to work best as a whole, so here I present them as such—certainly the comparisons to something from one of H.P.L.'s stories should be obvious.

Call of Cthulhu / As I'm recording here in this studio this shard will surely reach someone / Someone who'll know but all these messages have been in vain from the little glass bottle to the unfilmable such things just should not be writ / so please destroy this if you wish to live / 'tis better in ignorance to dwell than to go screaming into the abyss worse than hell / But all these messages have been in vain from the little glass bottle to the Call of Cthulhu.[10]

A very odd falsetto serves as the vocals over the top of a slow punk grind. Then after this short, twenty seconds or so, introduction, the vocals come in with a more "normal" texture, but the falsetto still returns at points. This is another of the stronger cuts on the disc, assuming you can get by that somewhat whiny falsetto. The music here is dark, mysterious and very meaty. The song is also one of the few that top the two-minute mark. It ends with a throaty groaning sound.

The album is closed out with "Black on Gold." The cut is less than thirty seconds and feels a bit like the theme to the 1960s Batman TV series, but with different vocals. This one is intriguing, but I can't make out the lyrics enough to find the Lovecraft connection.

The Vaselines were a Scottish quartet whose biggest claim to fame was the fact that Kurt Cobain of Nirvana was a big fan. Despite their relative obscurity and only having released one album (a second compilation was put out after their demise) this outfit, formed in 1987, has a good cult following. With their track entitled "Lovecraft," they created a fast-paced punk tune that has psychedelic leanings. Although the band has said that this song is a tribute to the author, the lyrics seem to give little credence to that fact. Rather than focus on horror they seem preoccupied with kinky sex and violence.

Coming from a town named "Sunnymead" doesn't seem to make a band a likely candidate to wander into the dark and frightening world of Lovecraftian tales and music, but that is exactly the birthplace of the California outfit White Flag. This skate / hardcore punk group was formed in 1982, and 1996's *Step Back 10* album includes three Lovecraftian tracks (which were released previously on separate recordings), "Cthulu [sic] Calling," "At the Mountains of Madness" and "Wake Up Screaming."

While the chorus is just the title, the middle verse of "Cthulu [sic] Calling" makes some definite references to the Great Old One.

Anger in his empty soul
An evil thrust out of control
Monolith of ancient time
Something scared sends the sign
Awakened from its ancient sleep

Cthulu calling from the deep
Returning to reclaim his spawn
Holding back the golden rays of dawn[11]

The verse that comes next, though, even brings in a reference to *At the Mountains of Madness*.

Madness at a mountain's peak
Skies dissolve in burning heat
Space collapses in his path
Beckoning I call his wrath[12]

A tolling bell starts this one off, then they launch into a fast and raw old school punk jam. This one is quite effective, but the band show that they are not content to stay in one place. They run through in this main song structure until the chorus after that mid-verse, then drop it back to a slower paced, but very tasty instrumental bridge. This runs through for a little while, to give way to the segment that came before it to finish out the track.

"At the Mountains of Madness" comes across as pretty typical punk rock. A nice layered group of nearly shouted vocals is a nice touch, though, as is an echoey guitar solo.

The lyrics to "Wake Up Screaming" contain just quick references in sort of a random off-handed way to the Lovecraft mythos—a line here and there. These lines are the two references that I spot. "In shrouded pain I watch the skies / For colors out of space and time."[13] "I sit alone in my shuttered room."[14]

A fast paced percussion begins this track and as the rest of the band enter it is in the form of a rather Dead Kennedy's like riff. This one is angry and very tasty old school punk. There is an intriguing ascending section that leads into the bridge. That bridge is a short period of chaos. There is another segment later that is almost all percussion with just some bass guitar. That portion leads to an anarchic sort of power-up cacophony that serves as the outro. This one is actually one of my favorites from the band, a real classic sounding punk rock tune.

According to band member Pat Fear, the group used various techniques on the songs to achieve a Lovecraft type texture.

On "Cthulu [sic] Calling" we put some scary sounds in it, I am a bit embarrassed our singer pronounced it "CTH" instead of "KT" as in "KTULU," the correct pronunciation. "At the Mountains of Madness" isn't really about anything in the story, it's mostly horrifying images like dying and being buried alive etc—not specific to the actual story. "Wake Up Screaming" has H.P.L. in lyrical references like "The Color out of Space" is mentioned, etc. All the songs were written to be chilling and unpleasant; lots of dismal minor chords. "Wake up Screaming" has some very odd time signatures and lots of sounds of someone in agony.

Fear also revealed that the band has written one other Lovecraft based song, "Within the Walls of Eryx," but they have yet to record it. He also said that, "reading things like H.P.L. and Philip K Dick and Ray Bradbury (other authors we reference) and watching shows like the original *Outer Limits* helps people think outside the lines and allows them to be more imaginative, in areas they may have never thought to explore before."

Regarding his interest in Lovecraft, Fear says that good writing and interesting topics drew him to the author and have kept him a fan. He explained, "I discovered him by accident with no prompting from others or any background knowledge." The first story he read by HPL was "the Houdini one 'Imprisoned with the Pharaohs.'" Continuing on, Fear had the following to add, "I had seen 'The Shuttered Room' movie and thought it was OK, but it certainly isn't the HPL story; it's more Robert Bloch I guess. I'd seen 'The Haunted Palace' but didn't know it was based on an HPL story." His favorite Lovecraft tales are "'Within the Walls of Eryx' (His only Sci Fi story...), 'Imprisoned with the Pharaohs,' 'The Color out of Space,' 'The Dunwich Horror' and 'The Shadow over Innsmouth.'"

With a name like "Lurking Fear," it's hard to imagine a band playing anything but Lovecraft based songs. (that is, after all, the title of an H.P. Lovecraft story.) However, this punk outfit has only done two explicitly Lovecraftian numbers. The first is "Innsmouth Bay—Edge of Identity." As the band describes the two songs, "'Innsmouth Bay' is based loosely on H.P. Lovecraft's 'The Shadow Over Innsmouth.' After the hapless narrator's discovery of his dark personal secret, he wanders the world in search of who he used to be. That's the 'Edge of Identity.'" The cut is energetic and fun, but while the sound of the instruments rather resembles old school punk rock, the vocals are more in the neighborhood of somewhat amateurish emo.

Band member Dan Ross says the following of the song:

> It is more in a Lovecraftian style with a narrator who is going through a journey of discovery, finding out the secret horrors of his heritage. There is a steady buildup with bits of hinted horror sprinkled in that leads to a terrifying revelation about himself. 'Edge of Identity' is even more scary, I think, because it deals with the same fears all of us deal with, especially as young adults, when trying to figure out how to get by in a cold, unpleasant and insane world.

Looking to the lyrics of the track, at least the "Innsmouth Bay" part of the song, we find this verse: "Coming home after a long time / Investigating the family line / See my past come to life/ Stories told about our history."[15] This relates to the story fairly well, as much of the horror revolves around a realization about the narrator's family history. The chorus of the track brings in additional Lovecraftian elements. "In Innsmouth Bay the secret stays / of a time long ago when the Old Gods played / Gods of the ocean and sons of Man / Mixed together to form an alternate plan."[16]

Their other Lovecraftian track is "Something in The Basement," and the group's description of this one is, "based very loosely on Lovecraft's 'The Shunned House' and also on the band's house at the time." Musically this one is not all that different than the other one, but in the opinion of this reviewer it is the stronger of the two. Of the song Ross says:

"Something in the Basement" does not really have a Lovecraftian build up to a mind-shattering revelation type of structure, it's more of a party song that mixes some Lovecraftian ideas from "The Shunned House" with what was going on in the basement of the house we lived in. That was quite a horrible and even Lovecraftian place and definitely inspired the song.

Of the connection to Lovecraft's work and music, Ross had this insight:

It's great fodder for death-rock (or as we proclaimed ourselves, "un-dead rock"), punk-rock, folk and whatever else type music where the interest is less in love songs and more into dark story-telling. If not adapting an actual story, there's always the creatures and tomes. Lurking Fear's drummer (and bass player on the CD) Tim Ayanardi, was playing bass in another band at the time called Three-Legged Dog and he was inspired to write a song for them called "Necronomicon."

He went on to say that:

Honestly what drew me to my first Lovecraft encounter was Michael Whelan's cover to The Tomb collection. I was 11 or so and I found Lovecraft's imagery to be this crazy over the top stuff, full of the type of monsters I'd scribble on the borders of my homework. That kept me hooked for a long time, the monsters, deities and gods of his pantheon. Later I grew to appreciate his complex and skillful sculpting of a story that can grab you from the start and bring you to a whopper of a conclusion. Rarely does even a good detective story successfully start with the protagonist in jail/nut house/other planet/brain case and keep a dramatic tension from there.

His favorite Lovecraft stories are "The Rats in the Walls," "The Shunned House," "Dreams in the Witch House," "The Call of Cthulhu" and The Case of Charles Dexter Ward. He adds, "and others change places in the ranks depending on my mood. I love At the Mountains of Madness, but really have to be in the right mood and situation to read it."

Natives of Vancouver, BC, Dayglo Abortions are rather infamous having had numerous obscenity charges aimed at them for album covers and lyrics. They utilized their particular blend of heavy metal and punk to create one Lovecraft related number, "Spawn of Yog-Sothoth." The song was released on their *Here Today Guano Tomorrow* disc that was released in 1988. The only real connection here is the title of the song, and, more specifically, the name "Yog-Sothoth." *The Encyclopedia Cthulhiana* describes Yog-Sothoth as "Outer God also known by the title Lurker at the Threshold."[17] Since certain versions of the game Dungeons and Dragons include the Lovecraftian Mythos, the following lines would seem to indicate that the game might well be the source of the song more than Lovecraft's work itself. "The beast 400 hit points / The beast strength 25 / The beast charisma -7 if you meet his eye you'll die."[18] In the game the term "hit points" refers to something that might be considered life energy in that once that much damage is done to the being it dies. Strength and charisma are also attributes that all characters and monsters in that game possess.

Musically this one comes in noisy and fairly quick paced, with "warming up" sort of feel. A backwards, distorted, spoken vocal comes over the top. Then this sort of crescendo like movement gives way to a pounding, but slower heavy jam that runs through for short time without vocals. Then a fast paced percussion line takes the song and it begins to work through this quicker texture to make up the main song structure. The vocals are shouted over the top and there are some tasty riffs on the cut. As is expected with punk rock, this one doesn't have a lot of changes, but does feature some meaty guitar soloing. There are points where it reminds me of The Dead Boys and other times when I hear bands like Black Flag and still other moments where Suicidal Tendencies come to mind.

Babyland is a self-described "electronic junk punk" band that was formed in 1989. While the group has only one song based on the works of H.P.L., "Arthur Jermyn," band member Smith, who wrote the lyrics to the track is very well versed and inspired by the writer. Of that specific song, Smith says:

> We came up with the song "Arthur Jermyn" in 1992, and yes—the title and subject matter is definitely related to the H.P.L. weird tale. It was a great song to do live at the time because it was obviously a great opportunity to light things on fire (lighting things on fire here in LA was very popular in 1992). The song appeared on our first full-length release, *You Suck Crap*. Musically, it is pretty dark and noisy, with a slow marching beat and long, falling bass notes that just dive into the abyss. The back half is dominated by an overwhelming screeching sound that kind of punctuates the terror inherent in the overall idea (reality's sharp

edge, perhaps?), and the very end is just a sort of audio smoldering of the ashes.

The point of the song is related to the meaning that we derive from the story itself, which is that racist beliefs result in devastating self-destruction and insecurity. The character's problem is not that he is a "white ape," nor is it that he "looked in the box." His problem is that he was so wrapped up in the identity of being a superior being that when he saw the truth he could no longer survive. In other words, what white supremacy boils down to is that, at best, "white people" came from "white apes"—but apes nonetheless. The tragic part, like a lot of H.P.L. protagonists, is that the character isn't actually a bad guy himself—he has just inherited the condition and must pay the price because he is just curious enough to want to know the truth, but not such an evil sociopath that he can actually live with it. I grant that this might be a debatable interpretation of whatever H.P.L.'s intentions might have been with the story, but that's how we see it.

That being said—the idea is one that I think stands: When the rational mind considers the totally insubstantial nature of platforms like racial or religious superiority, there is really nothing at all to stand on—and those who have grown dependent upon these concepts for their own philosophical/psychological health end up falling pretty hard when they really look at reality for what it is and not just what their mythologies told them it was. I think that fatalist skepticism like this is a theme that comes up again and again in the works of H.P.L., and it's a topic that we are totally drawn to as artists.

The cut comes in with keys and percussion in a very psychotic fast paced pattern. Waves of (for lack of a better term) "race car sounding" keyboards weave over the top of this. The vocals are angry, but still quite easy to understand. This one is very odd, but also quite tasty. It drops to just keys with a sort of strange breathing over top after a while, and then jumps back up to a more energized take on the section that preceded it. The vocals here become horrified screams. With an out of breath respiration, the keys wind their way down to end the piece. While it is safe to say that the song does tend to capture the main themes of the story, I feel that Smith's descriptions are sufficient to explain the connections. To use more of Lovecraft's work in this manner would tend to take away from the power of the story for those who have yet to read it.

Smith states that, "I have been a giant H.P.L. fan since high school (mid '80s), and I rarely leave town without something he wrote (usually an exceptionally beat up copy of the Del Rey reissue of "The Doom That Came to Sarnath") stashed in my bags somewhere."

With an official description that begins with the following lines, it's obvious that the next outfit has a lot of footing heavily in Lovecraftian territory:

In a dark, ancient graveyard, overgrown with strange vines and forgotten by
man, a hideous chorus of chimes erupts, heralding the arrival of Hour 13...
Bathed in an eerie ultraviolet light, the air charged with the smell of ozone, the
Tri-Lobed Burning eye forces its way into our world once more, and infuses a
long dead man with unholy cosmic energy. And a mission—To open the way
for the Old Ones to enter into our dimension once more, so that they might
wreak havoc and bring chaos and degradation to the worlds that were once
theirs. [19]

While the Virginia based group started off in the late 1990s under the name
"The Von Dooms," by this point in time they have been re-christened
"Ghosts Run Wild." Since their bandleader Jim Destro (who in all honesty is
the band, as he currently is the only one producing that music—yes, he's
talented) considers it to be the same project—and essentially always known
by the new name—I will refer to it that way here. Considering the
description above, and the fact that Destro lists H.P.L. (along with several of
his cohorts) as influences, it should be no surprise that he has recorded songs
based on Lovecraft's mythos.

Starting with the very first release, a cassette entitled *From Beyond* (a
trend is certainly visible already), there were Lovecraftian pieces to be had.
The first cut with such links is "The Stars Are Right." One only needs to look
as far as the first two lines of the song to see the Lovecraftian links, but
personally I prefer the variation on those lines that is used in the second
verse. "The stars are right tonight tonight / Great old ones sleep and shun the
light."[20]

The lyrics to "Coffin Rock" do not refer to a new type of the musical
genre, but rather to a location that feels as if it might have come from one of
Lovecraft's tales. Certainly the lyrics bring in to play the Old Ones and other
of Lovecraft's unholy creations. The first verse is made up of the following
lines: "Left behind by those of old / That evil piece of primal stone / Should
have left it alone / Seized up by what crept through the gate / Now it's a little
too late / A massing up of tendrils and eyes / That crawls and slides."[21]

This has a raw sort of sound that is quite typical of punk rock. The guitar
riff that drives this reminds me a bit of The Dead Kennedys or Circle Jerks.
The echoey sound on the bridge lends a 1950s horror film texture to it. This
one is energetic and fun.

With a title like "The Shadow Out of Time" there should be little doubt
as to the next song's Lovecraft ties. While that name lends one to consider
the link, the lyrics fulfill the promise. This excerpt from the final verse shows
off the Lovecraftian tendencies quite well. "Minds are rearranging / Mines
shattered and broken."[22] Those who remember the story whose title this song
shares, or the glances at it that this book has already provided, will know that

both mines and the concept of minds being stolen and moved are key elements in this story.

The next track that ties into Lovecraft's work has a more humorous, less serious connection, but a solid one, nonetheless. That song is "Miskatonic Massacre," and with this chorus, "Miskatonic alma mater / Students here just cannon fodder / No escape why even bother / So raise a pint of Arkham lager," the link (while not explicit to H.P.L.'s stories or characters) is definite.

With the next release, the CD *Demos From the Dead*, the Lovecraft banner was again raised. The first song on show here to feature the themes of H.P.L. is "Crawling Chaos." The cut includes references to a number of Lovecraftian creations. Certainly the line "Tentacles flying all over the place"[23] could be seen to be a reference to Cthulhu, but honestly there are a number of other entities from Lovecraft's fiction that have similar features. Hastur seems to be mentioned with the words, "Naming names you musn't hear."[24]

This cut is faster paced and has a texture that seems to encompass the sounds of The Cramps with a bit of The Plasmatics and The Dead Boys thrown into the mix. That said, though, there are some slight elements of Motorhead alongside the earlier mentioned sounds and even a little bit of The Ramones on the chorus. The vocals on this one are more easily understood and this is an extremely fun track.

The aforementioned "Miskatonic Massacre" is also on this disc, and so is "Tri-Lobed Burning Eye." On this one the links are not explicit (other than the name Yog Sothoth), but they are definite. "Hell blurred titan flying in on death's wing / I'm an ugly ugly ugly unnamable thing / Yeah yeah yeah, he was left to rot / Straight from the belly of Yog Sothoth."[25]

The next CD to be cut loose from this project was *I'll Be Lurking For You*. While the title track is really not Lovecraftian, it does include the lines "The stars are right / Each night up above."

That same disc includes the song "De Vermis Mysterium." The title refers to a fictional book from Lovecraft's Mythos whose name translates to "The Mystery of the Worm." This book was first mentioned in the story "Haunter of The Dark," but has reappeared in Mythos based works ever since. Musically this one is a raw, but extremely meaty punk jam that again shows musical tendencies that fall in along the lines of The Dead Kennedys. As before, though, the vocals are not in line with that band's style at all.

"Crawling Chaos" shows up once more on this disc, and closes out the Lovecraft basis for the album. In fact, this is the last Lovecraft reference to date for Ghosts Run Wild. It seems likely that they will raise the flag of

H.P.L. again, though. When asked about what he feels Lovecraft's writing has to offer music, Destro says, "I guess it offers different things to everybody. It seems like more and more bands are popping up who are drawing from him. Personally, I'm drawn to the idea of man being small and meaningless in the universe."

He also described his particular method of incorporating Lovecraftian elements into his music.

> I try to infuse as many strange sounds and effects as possible while still keeping it a punk rock song—also a lot of echos on the vocals... anything to to make a song sound more mysterious. Rock really isn't the best way to express H.P.L.'s ideas, but listening to a lot of crazy meaningless noise (Erich Zann style) probably wouldn't sound too great to most humans.

While Destro revealed that when it comes to favorite Lovecraft stories, "'The Rats in the Walls' and 'The Outsider' are tied for number one," he also shared the details of his discovery of Lovecraft and what has kept him coming back.

> I first came across Lovecraft through reading the Conan stories and comic books. People writing into the Conan comics' letter pages would often bring him up. The *Necronomicon* sounded very cool and interesting to me, and I wanted to know more about it. I think I've stayed a fan, because I come across something I hadn't noticed before every time I re-read his stories. Also, he's just so much better than every other horror writer; it just seems like a waste of time reading their stuff after you've been exposed to H.P.L.

Another musical style that can be seen as coming, at least indirectly, from punk rock is Goth. That genre will be the topic of the next chapter.

Chapter 7

DARK DREAMS:
H.P.L.'S INFLUENCE ON GOTHIC MUSIC

While Goth music's beginnings can be traced to the punk movement of the late 1970s, it wasn't until the early '80s that it became a separate and distinct genre label. Led by bands like Bauhaus the sound was decidedly dark and has as much in common with horror cinema as it does with music. Literary and philosophical elements are also prevalent with the overall texture leaning to the melancholy and sometimes frightening. This would seem fertile ground for Lovecraftian elements, and there are certainly a number of examples of groups that have sown their artistic crops in this field.

The trio Cassandra Complex was formed in 1980, although originally as a duo. They joined the ranks of Lovecraft inspired artists when they released the album *Satan, Bugs Bunny and Me* in 1989, adding it to their catalog of goth discs. The song "E.O.D (Esoteric Order of Dagon)" was the one that brought them into the fold.

Goth rockers Fields of the Nephilim were formed in England in 1984, and contributed four Lovecraft oriented tracks within their catalog. The band's music was a unique combination of sounds that frequently crossed over into progressive rock territory. The lyrical content, dark musical textures and guttural vocal approach of Carl McCoy, though, always kept them firmly rooted in their gothic base.

The first Lovecraftian reference appears on their first full-length album, *Dawnrazor*, which was released in 1987. It comes in the form of the song "Reanimator." While the title certainly calls to mind HPL's "Herbert West—Reanimator," the lyrics would seem to have little to do with the story. Interestingly enough, they seem to not explicitly address the movie, either (which is in most ways a completely different work). "Pain, we are transforming / With your daughters underground / Pain, we look like sisters / Caught up in a landslide / Falling down / Too far you can't feel it / Too far you can't reach it / Too far / Reanimator / Reanimator now."[1] Musically this song starts in a fast paced modern Rush like arrangement, but the dark low pitched hard rocking vocals will definitely not let anyone believe the track is by them. It is a pretty basic hard rock track, but still is a bit off-kilter. Perhaps a good analogy would be a combination of Led Zeppelin, Rush, Danzig, The Cure and The Misfits—if one can picture that. It twists later into a more progressive rock oriented mode, but the dark tone and guttural vocals remain, although non-lyrical at this point. This segment serves to end the piece.

Their second disc, *The Nephilim*, released the following year, included two songs which mention Cthulhu, although in the alternate spelling of "Kthulhu." The first of the tracks, "The Watchman" is a piece which essentially is made up of three musical sections. The first segment is a dramatic ballad type section. It builds quite slowly, based primarily on mellower guitar stylings and overtones lend an eerie texture. A false ending gives way to more crunchy guitar, then a new faster paced melody takes it again, feeling a bit like The Cure, but with more deep guttural vocals. A bridge moves it back to more textural tones before it jumps back up. It ends in cinematic noise related sounds. The lyrics on this one, while not seeming totally to be derived from Lovecraft, do have some elements that appear to be explicitly tied to the mythos. "You sleep, you sleep, follow me / It's just another day, remember I am calling you / Just another day, remember she's calling for you / Just another day, Kthulhu I am calling for you / Just another day, An empire has fallen from view."[2]

With "Last Exit For the Lost," the other track from *The Nephilim* to include references to Kthulhu, the group created a song that is over nine and a half minutes in length. It is another that is essentially constructed in three sections. A dark, ambient tone starts it and acoustic guitar creates the melody that takes over. The group build this up with dark deep vocals that are at once a bit reminiscent of both Robert Smith (The Cure) and David Bowie. Overtones achieve a spooky sound that works well. As this moves forward into the next segment, the arrangement turns to a lush and dark progressive rock style. Again, echoes of The Cure show up, but with a more prog style. The third section speeds the track up and feels rather like a spooky progressive rock merging of The Cure and The Doors. As they develop this it begins to swirl around like a whirling dervish. The lyrics, other than the line "Closer and closer Kthulhu calls,"[3] seem to have little to do with Lovecraft's work.

The final Fields of the Nephilim piece that shows connections to the work of Lovecraft is "Intro (Dead But Dreaming)" from 1990's *Earth Inferno* disc. As an instrumental, surely only the title ties to the author directly. Although becoming fairly developed as it carries on, this one starts in ambient tones and sonic weirdness. It turns dark and ominous very quickly. At times one is reminded of the keyboard oriented, spooky interludes that show up on a King Diamond album.

Garden of Delight was founded in 1991 in Germany. The gothic band has had a number of tracks that show connections to Lovecraft, although many come through the Simon Edition of the *Necronomicon*. These ties begin with their *ENKI'S Temple* album released in 1992. The disc included three songs that have connections to H.P.L., "Ancient God (but never gone), "Inanna", "Sumerian Haze" and "ENKI'S Temple and the Gates of UR." With *Epitaph*, released the same year, they added another track to the list. This time out it was "The Epic of the Sumer Ziusudra." 1992's *Shared Creation* included the obviously Lovecraftian, "Shared Creation (The Lovecraft Mix)." Their next album was *Necromanteion IV* (1994) and included the tracks "Spirit Invocation—Black Book Version", "Downwards to A Sea" and "Watchers Out of Time." With 1996's *Scheoul* they produced "The Colour Out of Time."

Formed in 1992, Morphine Angel released one Lovecraft based cut, in the form of "Breakfast With Cthulu" from their *Project ISA* disc. As the title gives reason to believe, the lyrics include many references to Lovecraft's Mythos, but with an oddly humorous twist. In fact, so entwined are the Lovecraft themes here, that I feel it is appropriate to include the entire song's lyrics.

Open up the gates
And have a little taste
You know you can't be late
The ones who dream won't wait
The shining stars go mad
I grab another butter pat
Breakfast with Cthulu

Potato cakes and cheese
Would Sub-Nigurath please?
Or a bowl of Corn Flakes
Blackest house of pancakes
Black Goat of the Woods
Consuming tasty foods
Breakfast with Cthulu

Cthulu, take my soul
To Village Inn we'll go
Your insanity
With eggs over easy
An omelet severed upon
The Trapezohedron
A treat I can't resist
Scrambled egg abyss

[Indecipherable Yoggothic Ramblings][4]

The track comes in with a hard-edged, echoey sound, quite punk rock in texture. It runs through like this for a time, then shifts into more an otherworldly, slightly chaotic mix with definite psychedelic leanings. This one is part punk, part metal, but still all Goth rock. As it moves into the "ramblings" part the cut takes on an even more echoey, spacey feedback dominated texture that is just a tiny bit like some of the spacey meanderings that Jimi Hendrix occasionally took off on. A short segment of atmospheric textures ends it. It's an intriguing song both lyrically and musically. Interestingly enough, the gent who penned the track (Paul Fredric) is now with an outfit called Asmodeus X. That band's forthcoming disc has another Lovecraftian piece which will be addressed in a later chapter. The vast majority of his comments will be used there, but here is what he had to say in regards to the creation of this particular track:

> Now, my own process of trying to do the "Lovecraft Sound" begins in Chicago, circa 1994. I had long held an interest in the so-called Black Arts, and my quest for hidden knowledge had led me to interaction with several initiates of an esoteric order known as the "Yankee Rose Lodge." This clandestine group was led by an individual known as "Sir Cthulu," and much of their work centered around concepts from the mythos. Sir Cthulu had gone so far even as to construct his own Trapezohedron, and a Yuggothic language. This individual indeed somehow managed to manifest at certain times a genuine otherworldly and thoroughly creepy presence. After a night of conducting certain unspeakable operations and forbidden rites, Sir Cthulu and I went to breakfast at a local Denny's.

> Driving home that afternoon, I thought to myself "Wow... I just had breakfast with Cthulu." I couldn't help but chuckle at the preposterous notion, and so what would later become one of the most endearing Morphine Angel songs was born. From the first moment I knew that "Breakfast with Cthulu" was destined to follow the humorous "Road to Yuggoth," and I made no attempt to divert this. The music is bouncy, the sound effects cheesy, and the lyrics border on the ludicrous.

> "Breakfast with Cthulu" may have been entertaining, but left me wanting in the way of that non-natural and other-worldly sensation that seemed so much the essence of H.P.L.'s writings. Again, creating a non-natural sensation using conventional instrumentation is challenging to the point of confounding, and so it was several years before I made another serious attempt at it.

Cradle of Filth, a gothic metal band, saw the light of day in 1991 in the UK. While the group's cinematic approach and horror movie aesthetic might make them seem an obvious choice for delving into Lovecraftian territory for material, only one song, "Cthulhu Dawn" from 2000's *Midian* disc has fallen into that literary area. It should be mentioned, though, that they also released a compilation album called *Lovecraft and Witch Hearts*, but the title was the only H.P.L. link there.

A weird neo-symphonic intro gives way to a frantic neo-classical musical excursion to start that piece. The band twist that backdrop into a dark and dynamic musical progression. The cut is musically perplexing in its seemingly unrelated segments. This creates a texture that manages to make it feel alien, much like contact with one of the Old Ones would.

Unfortunately, other than the repeated chorus of "Cthulhu Dawn" and a vague theme of the end of mankind's existence, the lyrics seem to bear little tie to the works of Lovecraft. Indeed, they are filled instead with images of dead rising from the grave, anti-Christian symbols and references and visions of satanic icons. Therefore, this one has only a passing tie to H.P.L.'s work.

This brings us to the conclusion of the coverage of varied genres of music. It does not take us to the end of the line, though. There are quite a few artists out there whose connection to the Lovecraftian Mythos is so strong that coverage of them warranted a full chapter. Those musicians will be addressed in the upcoming chapters.

Chapter 8

OLIVER TARANCZEWSKI: ELECTRONIC GOTHIC ELDER GOD

Starting as a duo in 1992, Evil's Toy became a trio when Oliver Taranczewski was added to the lineup of Volker Lutz and Thorsten Brenda in 1997. Along with the addition of another musician, Taranczewski also brought his love of H.P. Lovecraft with him. Eventually this band would morph into the T.O.Y., and those Lovecraftian influences remained in that group, too.

According to Taranczewski many of the lyrics he has written for both Evil's Toy and T.O.Y. have been influenced by the writings of Lovecraft. He says the following:

> I came across Lovecraft when I was like 14 or 15 years old and used to read Stephen King. A friend of mine introduced me to Lovecraft. And *The Case of Charles Dexter Ward* was the first story by Lovecraft I ever read. I was really fascinated by this strange, old fashioned, dark setting. A horror story in the 1920, I never read anything like that before. And to be honest, I could not imagine a Lovecraft story taking place in the present. When I read the books, all the settings, the protagonists and antagonists, which I formed in my head where always in black and white like in old silent movies. Strange, isn't it?

Taranczewski's favorite Lovecraft stories include "The Horror in the Museum," "The Music of Erich Zann" and "The Call of Cthulhu."

In describing part of his usage of Lovecraft in his music, Taranczewski says:

> Some of Lovecraft's writings dealt with dreams, and I often picked up this concept like in the song "Dream Operator" for my new project Yavin 4 which will be released in the states in January [2005] by Negative Gain, Chicago. Basically phrases, concepts or images of the Lovecraft stories I read are somewhere hidden in a secret drawer in the backside of my mind and appear sometimes when it comes to writing lyrics. I never sat down and said: "OK, now you have to write a Lovecraft text, or something ..." The depth and the darkness in his stories and his wide variety of works, the dark moods of his protagonists cause dark and weird lyrics, which need dark and weird music. So, the Evil's Toy sound always fit to the Lovecraft inspired lyrics. Maybe the soft synthpop sound of T.O.Y. is one reason, why I rarely write darker lyrics nowadays. I just started doing darker lyrics again for Yavin 4.

The first of those Lovecraft oriented lyrics for Evil's Toy appear on the disc *Illusion*. That album included the track "Prevision." of the track Taranczewski reveals that it is only "partly inspired by Lovecraft's story 'In the Walls of Eryx.'" The majority of the inspiration he said came from a "futuristic RPG [role playing game] which deals with Lovecraftian scenarios." Musically, this one is an electronic, bouncing nearly techno dance type of number. It has a mysterious texture behind its somewhat cheery musical texture. The vocals to the number have a dark, spoken, snarled approach. This one feels a bit like a less heavy version of "Du Hast" by Rammstein. Picture that sound with the metallic sound stripped away, and you have a decent idea of what this one sounds like.

With 1998's *Angels Only* disc, Evil's Toy added three more Lovecraft oriented cuts to their catalog. They were "Back on Earth", "From Above Comes Sleep" and "Colours Out of Space." Of the first of those, the lyricist had this to say, "'Back on Earth' is about one of the Great Old Ones." He describes it as "an attempt of a vague description of one unnatural alien being who ruled the Earth before humanity formed." Musically it starts with just keyboards, but rather quickly changes to a fairly typical dance number with techno overtones. It would be pretty easy to see this track serving as the musical impetus at a European dance club. That seems a bit ironic considering the lyrical themes that it contains. I like the chorus segment in the later portions of the track. The vocal arrangement here is quite potent.

"From Above Comes Sleep," according to its author, is written as a description of the city of R'lyeh. "Exploited cultures of civilisations / on decline / Extinguished and erased / surviving in everlasting sleep / protected imaginations of non-human figures / Geometrical buildings / of incredible unearthly dimensions."[1] The keyboard textures that begin it have a lot of dramatic power. It runs through in an intriguing introduction, but then drops to a more dark techno/dance arrangement to move it forward. I'd have to say that this is one of my favorites from Evil's Toy. It is just about perfect for its style of music and has a lot of character and depth. The keyboard solo later is a nice addition to the number.

Of the final Lovecraft inspired song from that album, Taranczewski says, "'Colours Out of Space' is the most obvious Lovecraft inspired text, which is funny, because I didn't like the story that much." He says that although the story is in his opinion among the weaker of Lovecraft's work, he loved the title, so he wrote a song about it. Electronic keyboards and percussive textures start this. A couple sound bites come over top before the song proper hits. This one has a somewhat dark groove and snarled vocals. The chorus takes on a lot of power and majesty while still maintaining the overall texture of the rest of the piece. An interlude later includes more sound bites over the techno backdrop. It moves back into the chorus eventually, and the final sound bite says, "I'm switching off now—bye bye"[2]—a nice touch.

The single of "Transparent Frequencies," released that same year, included another song with Lovecraftian lyrics, "Motionless." The author of the song refers to it in this way, "I was aware of that fact that I wrote some mixture of *The Dream-Quest for Unknown Kadath* and 'Dreams in the Witch-House'... about a person, who slowly becomes insane." The song comes in with an even more dance oriented bouncy groove, but still has strong elements of the dark in its mood. It later drops to just textural keys for a short break. After another verse, keyboard waves wash over top in a solo—one of the most effective parts of the cut. Later (after another verse) the percussive textures drop away and pretty, but sad keys take the number in atmospheric tones. Then the main themes return to carry the composition forward again, but this time without vocals in a more lush arrangement. This gives way in time to a drop back in the construction that serves to end the piece.

The next Evil's Toy album included the track "Timeless" in which Taranczewski refers to Cthulhu with the line "... when wrong is right and right is wrong the sleeper awakes ..."[3]

With the change to T.O.Y. there have been three songs that Taranczewski identifies as having Lovecraft leanings. Of those, "Beyond Sleep" surely ties into the Dream Cycle concept that was mentioned before—"blue sky night / your life fades out of sight / working in white rooms / dreams made in ancient looms."[4]

This concept seems to carry forward in "The Day rhe World Disappeared," "when you will fall asleep / and the stars wave me to follow them / take my hand / welcome to wonderland."[5] However, an earlier verse seems to also weave in other Lovecraft oriented themes. "As the world disappeared into that great fireball / no movement / no sound / and I saw them dancing on the ground."[6]

Although the closing line of "Inner Cinema" is the line, "This is my dream,"[7] thus tying it back into the Dream Cycle, the first verse seems to show a far darker and more direct link to Lovecraft's Old Ones. "Strange voices deep inside / A thousand eyes watching me / Down at the seaside / Waves on the sea."[8]

While Oliver Taranczewski's various groups are the first I have covered who are so Lovecraft dominated to earn their own chapter, there are several others still to be explored. They will be addressed in the upcoming chapters of this book.

Chapter 9

NOX ARCANA:
DELVING INTO THE NECRONOMICON

A recent entry into the world of Lovecraft-inspired musical excursions comes from goth outfit Nox Arcana. The group was formed in 2003 by Joseph Vargo, a fantasy artist whose work focuses on the gothic, who also happens to be an accomplished composer and musical performer. Vargo reveals that Nox Arcana's first album, *Darklore Manor*, "also utilized Lovecraftian elements to take listeners on a musical journey through an abandoned Victorian manor on the New England coast that harbors an ancient darkness." While this might be seen as just a warm up to Lovecraft, the band's second release, 2004's *Necromonicon*, made a full-on tribute to his work.

Working within a Lovecraft landscape was certainly nothing new to Vargo, and the artist relates, "Though I'm known mainly for my gothic artwork, I've also painted an assortment of dark, Lovecraftian images. These paintings are among my most surrealistic works. I've also had several short stories published, two of which, 'The Coroner' and 'Darkness Immortal' involve Lovecraftian themes."

When he describes the new album, it is very easy to hear both the admiration he has for Lovecraft and his writing, but also the reverence and attention to detail that has been paid to the source work.

Whereas many bands have written a song or two that were inspired by Lovecraft's writing, we wrote *Necromonicon* as a full concept album that pays tribute to the Cthulhu Mythos. All of the tracks and titles were based specifically on Lovecraft's work, and we used different musical styles to convey the various themes. For example, "Alhazred's Vision" has an Arabian feel to it, while "Temple of the Black Pharaoh" has an exotic Egyptian flavor. For "The Haunter of the Dark" we utilized eerie pipe organ music to convey the feeling of a dark, gothic cathedral. A thunder strike was added at the climax of this song because Lovecraft's story culminates with a lightning storm. We also used sound effects to simulate the sound of swarming insects, since, according to Lovecraft, the *Necronomicon*, or "Kitab Al Azif," as it was originally called, was named after the insect-like sounds of demons in the Arabian desert. Other howls and shrieks were used to convey the sounds of the monstrous Great Old Ones. The CD has several creepy narrations that tell of The Great Old Ones, describing them individually, and the CD booklet contains a story about the discovery of the *Necronomicon* and an overview of The Cthulhu Mythos.

The entire package is also full of sinister artwork depicting the ancient lords of darkness. We really wanted to create something that would do justice to Lovecraft's work and would also motivate people who were unfamiliar with his stories to seek them out and read them.

Vargo further related the following:

Although he intentionally left much to the readers' imagination, Lovecraft was a very descriptive writer and often made mention of certain sounds like mad, piping music and shrieks and wails. His stories also built an ominous sense of dread, and I think we were able to capture an overall feeling of creepiness and foreboding horror on *Necromonicon*. Lovecraft's tales of sorcery and ancient gods inspired us to utilize primal percussive sounds and compose melodies that were both hauntingly hypnotic and dramatically powerful.

The artist/writer/musician was drawn into Lovecraft in a rather unique manner. His story is as follows:

After viewing my dark fantasy artwork, several people had asked if I had ever read Lovecraft. After numerous recommendations, I picked up one of his collections of short stories. At first I didn't think that some of the individual stories were that special, but as I read more, I began to see how many of his works were linked together to form a larger mythology. He was a true innovator who took themes from folklore, ancient history and science fiction and bound them together in a way unlike anyone before. His stories interwove witchcraft, inter-dimensional travel, subterranean underworlds and monstrous alien entities in a way that no one had ever conceived. After I read more of his work, I started to recognize his true genius and fully realized why he is considered to be the father of the modern horror story. Some of his original concepts for stories like "From Beyond" and "Within the Walls of Eryx" were brilliant cutting-edge works of science fiction at a time when the genre was beginning, and many of his ideas are still used in books and movies.

When asked about his favorite Lovecraft stories, Vargo lists them as, "mainly his classic tales like 'The Case of Charles Dexter Ward,' 'The Haunter of the Dark,' 'Shadow Over Innsmouth' and 'The Dunwich Horror.' Of his lesser-known works, my favorites are 'The Hound' and 'The Horror at Red Hook.' It would be great to see someone do an accurate movie adaptation of one of these stories. And if anyone does, we'd love to provide the soundtrack for the film."

Vargo's experiences with releasing an album based on the writings of Lovecraft, despite his obvious enthusiasm for the source material, has not been all positive. He reveals the following in this regard:

When we released *Necromonicon* we began getting criticism from some narrow-minded people who were ignorant of the true facts about the book. They thought that the CD contained actual ancient, black magic spells that could be used to summon demons. We sent out press releases that stated that our CD was based on the fictional writings of H.P. Lovecraft, who had invented the concept of the book and its title, but it's incredible how many people think that the *Necronomicon* is real. It really is a true testament to Lovecraft's genius. Unfortunately, there are numerous misconceptions about the *Necronomicon* as well, and most of the people who think that the book actually exists believe it to be some sort of satanic bible. This can probably be attributed to the paperback version of the *Necronomicon* that was written and released 40 years after Lovecraft's death, which contains fictitious magical spells. Our CD was based solely on Lovecraft's concepts of the *Necronomicon* and his Cthulhu Mythos. We didn't want to utilize any of the embellishments of later writers, or the paperback version of the book that was written in an attempt to capitalize on Lovecraft's success.

The album itself truly is an inspired work, and may well be the best (at least most authentic) Lovecraftian music ever produced. I would consider it to be progressive rock, but it is certainly different from any other progressive rock CD. Indeed the band might not even consider it to be such, and I'm not completely sure it is, but it really feels like prog in many ways. Truly there is little "rock" involved in the disc, but the emphasis on electronic type symphonic arrangements seem to make it feel like prog to this writer. Their own description in the liner notes reveals refers to it as "this dark symphony, based on H.P. Lovecraft's legendary book of shadows contains pulse-pounding orchestrations, sinister melodies, gothic choirs and ominous chants."[1] That comes pretty close. I would say that this would be great film soundtrack music, but that really is putting limitations on it. Indeed, the whole disc seems to be one creation, building as it goes along. It has a lot of elements of classical music, but certainly would not fit there. It is dark, and obviously the subject matter could place it in the realm of gothic music, but again, that only fits so well. The lyrics for the most part are delivered as spoken words; the only song that has any kind of real singing does so in the form of a ritual.

Nox Arcana might not be a household name, and their music might be very hard to classify, but in *Necronomicon* they have produced what might be the most impressive and effective musical interpretation of the writings of H.P. Lovecraft ever. Vargo is joined on this release by William Piotrowski. The music though, might seem to be the sonic equivalent of Vargo's artwork. The musicians have paid very close attention to details from Lovecraft's work, a sure sign of their admiration and reverence for the source material. Many of these were mentioned by Vargo in his descriptions, but I feel it is important to reiterate them because he was right on the money. They use electronic insect sounds, since the language that words like "Cthulhu" were supposed to be derived from is one spoken by an insectoid race. A song like "Temple of the Black Pharaoh" has a decidedly Egyptian tone. "The Haunter of the Dark" ends with the sound of thunder, a nod to the story climaxing with a lightning strike. This is a first-class effort that should be a thrill for fans of the legendary horror writer. One thing is certain, flowing as one unit this disc starts off a bit slowly and continues to grow to a thrilling and satisfying conclusion. While there are both recurrent and newly emerging themes, each song seems to carry the whole album forward. This disc is definitely one of the most interesting of 2004, and one that both fans of creative dark music and fans of Lovecraft should really give a try. It also includes some dramatic examples of Vargo's graphic art, and a very informative booklet.

The song "Mythos" begins the disc. The buzzing of insects and evil choral vocals present the theme of this track. The vocals are a spoken powerful reading describing the background of Lovecraft's Mythos.

"The Nameless City" comes next. Furtive dark music with eastern tones begins this one. As the track carries forward it gains a dramatic movie soundtrack-type texture, gradually building in intensity and moving the tension forward. This cut, basically an instrumental, brings in choral vocals more as an instrument later. It is quite powerful and ominous.

On "Alhazred's Vision" Eastern tones in a symphonic gothic style start this, and it gradually builds in frightful tones. This instrumental does not wear out its welcome.

Another instrumental, the title track starts with a somber chorale texture. It is still symphonic in nature, but has a more electronic texture than the cut that preceded it.

A dramatic and mysterious faster paced electro-symphonic texture creates the main focus of "Ancient Shadows" with dark chorale vocals and eastern textures appearing over-top to flavor it. This is one of the more dynamic tracks, running through very progressive rock like movements as it carries forward. It ends abruptly.

"Azathoth" is a very brief (less than half a minute) spoken word narration over the top of keyboard elements.

Although it begins with more of the chorale vocals, as "The Black Throne" carries forward a slightly noisy keyboard sound gives it a very minor industrial tone.

"Nyarlothotep" has a mysterious Egyptian sound. It is another brief (under a minute) narrative.

Next up is "Temple of the Black Pharaoh." Appropriately dark Egyptian sounds create the texture of this haunting cut. It is one of the strongest compositions on the album. This one has actual singing in the form of understated dark chanting.

The most electronic sounds thus far start "Eldritch Rites," another spoken word piece. The narration here features an even more understated approach.

"The Haunter of the Dark," another, dark haunting atmospheric piece, has the some of the most neo-classical elements of the CD. It ends, as the story does, with the sound of thunder.

"Yog-Sothoth" is a one-minute cut that features a spoken narrative over a tolling gong and percussion.

A driving, but understated rhythmic texture starts "Guardian of the Gate," and they gradually build it in dark and ominous tones. This is another stand out cut.

Mystical pounding textures create the soundscape that is "Lords of Darkness."

"Dagon" is another brief narrative. The weird sounds that provide the backdrop here are among the strongest sounds of the disc.

More electronic driving tones create the main focus of the early segments of "The Stars Align." As this carries forward a vigorous percussion and dark keyboard elements create some of the most energized and powerful sounds of the album so far. This one comes the closest to rocking of anything so far.

"Ritual of Summoning," a less than half a minute piece starts appropriately with a whispered incantation. Weird swirling sounds begin to build as the intensity of the magickal invocation also increases in intensity. This ends in a powerful crescendo that leads into the heaviest cut thus far.

The music on "Cthulhu Rising," although sharing themes with some of the earlier tracks, is the most powerful and articulate to this point. It is very intense while still not moving into a full "rock" vein. This is certainly proof that the album just keeps getting stronger and stronger.

Next up is "The Great Old Ones." A hammering sound begins this, and a powerful melody with the most symphonic sounds of the CD overlaid takes over. It is the most dynamic and potent number on show, making it the perfect climax for this dark adventure. A noisy crescendo dissolves into brief chaos before silence takes it.

While that number is the last real song on the disc, the adventure does not end there. After a couple minutes of silence electronic sounds and processed vocals enter, comprising the first of two unlisted tracks. It dissolves into insectoid tones.

A short reprise of the processed words followed by a quick buzzing shows up to end the disc with this final hidden song. It is a fitting conclusion to what is arguably the finest H.P. Lovecraft inspired musical work of all time.

Chapter 10

THE DARKEST OF THE HILLSIDE THICKETS: LOVECRAFTIAN HUMOR SET TO MUSIC

It seems appropriate to devote an entire chapter to this Vancouver based outfit. The group has not had merely a passing acquaintance with the work of H.P. Lovecraft. Indeed, it is fair to say that the author's presence is the entire basis of their existence. As mentioned earlier in this book, the group's name even comes from a line in the Lovecraft story "The Tomb"—"I will tell only of the lone tomb in the darkest of the hillside thickets..."[1] Their website even includes what they call, "The Darkest of the Hillside Thickets Mega-Cthonic Guide to All Things Lovecraftian."

The band was formed in 1992, by a group of musicians quite involved in the works of Lovecraft. As described by band founder and spokesman Toren Atkinson (AKA Toren MacBin): "It was the call... the call of Cthulhu... which we heard collectively in 1992 and knew it was our duty to spread the will of Cthulhu throughout this world via sympathetic vibrations known only through our unclean instruments of rock. And the monster costumes helped too!" This sort of answer exemplifies the band's approach to the material. It is a stance of tongue-in-cheek homage that is shown in the lyrics and all other aspects of the band's work. Another example is contained in Atkinson's response to my question of what Lovecraft's writing has to offer music—his answer? "Subject matter that doesn't involve getting booty and/or adolescent whining."

In truth their first Lovecraft related piece was on their first demo. That tape was called *Gurgle Gurgle Gurgle* and, as Atkinson relates, features "three bad songs, but great graphics." The Lovecraftian number present on that offering was "Cthulhu Dreams." This was later re-recorded for their first full album, *Cthulhu Strikes Back*. The number is a mostly instrumental eleven-plus minute journey into weirdness. It serves as an effective sound-based illustration of what a Cthulhu-influenced dream might be like. To those unfamiliar with the story "The Call of Cthulhu," I can tell that the Old One gathers his followers by calling to them in their dreams. He is most effective with artistic souls. Listening to the track truly does seem to put one in the mind of what that experience might feel like were you to be one of those chosen.

The band's second demo tape was *Hurts Like Hell*, and featured nine songs. The majority of those were re-released later on the album *Great Old*

Ones. Therefore those pieces will be addressed in looking at that disc. There were three other pieces on the tape, though. One of those is "Worship Me Like a God." Because that track was re-recorded for *Cthulhu Strikes Back*, it will not be addressed here. Of the two remaining numbers only one is blatantly Lovecraft related. That cut is described by the group as "merely a mild Mellotron musical maelstrom"[2] entitled "Screams From R'lyeh." That title, of course, refers to the resting-place of Cthulhu. All of the songs from their next demo, *Cthulhuriffomania!* appear on *Great Old Ones* and will be addressed in the coverage of that album.

Although not all of the band's output center around material by Howard Phillips Lovecraft, certainly a large chunk of it does. The group even include "required reading" in many of their liner notes. An example of their recommendations taken from the notes for the song "Shoggoths Away" from the aforementioned first full CD *Cthulhu Strikes Back*, is "'At the Mountains of Madness,' by H.P. Lovecraft." That song (while certainly taking liberties with the material) is a wonderful mix of horror, humor and rock music. The lyrics include such memorable lines as "While on a flight one day I passed over the polar city / And curious sat down to see what I could glean / Behold a nightmare pit that splashed with piping shapeless monsters / I packed them in the bay of my B-17 / Shoggoths Away."[3]

According to the *Encyclopedia Cthulhiana*, Shoggoths are "entities created by the Elder Things as a servitor race billions of years ago."[4] As to the music of the piece, a driving bass line begins it, and the track is mostly metallic. It features sound clips from a famous film—think of the CD title and then put another word for imperialist kingdom in place of "Cthulhu" and you'll have the right series of movies.

Other examples of Lovecraftian lyrics abound in the work of this outfit. Looking just at that same disc one finds the obvious in the track "Goin' Down to Dunwich," a definite reference to "The Dunwich Horror." Indeed, that story is listed as the "required reading for the number." Still other pieces have the leanings without them being foretold by the titles. Bells and metallic tones begin the piece, after movie sound bites. The cut seems to combine metal and punkish formats with processed vocals. Sound effects add to the mayhem, and one break sets a very strong mood.

"Unstoppable" is one such piece. The notes for that one read, "Rumour has it that *The Necronomicon* can make you all powerful. Let us know if you find a copy."[5] The lyrics include the line "I've elbowed with the Old Ones."[6] The mode here is more on the punk end, less metal, but both are present. The track features some very quirky segments, and the break contains some quite spooky moments.

The notes for the track "Hook Worm" state that "I really don't know what this song is about. However, the wisenheimers among you will notice the references to the Fungi from Yoggoth. Never heard of them? Then H.P. Lovecraft's 'The Whisperer in the Darkness' is for you."[7] According to the *Encyclopedia Cthulhiana*, the Fungi from Yoggoth is another name for Mi-Go, which will be addressed just a bit later in this chapter. The very beginning of the track is a bit Rushish, and the track itself is in a nice metal mode. The bass line on the instrumental break has a very nice tone.

"Protein" is another example of less obvious Lovecraft leanings. They explain the song's theme as being "What if Nyarlathotep gave you the power to kill everyone in the world, including your loved ones. Maybe someday this will be more than a philosophical question."[8] More clues are found within the lyrics, "I had a dream the Crawling Chaos said / 'I need for you to fill everyone with lead' / He filled me up with protein, I gave the magic sign / He gave me X-ray vision and now the world is mine."[9] A smart metallic number, this piece is very well arranged.

Although a few songs on show with this album are not Lovecraftian in nature, the HPL connections don't end with the previously covered pieces. Indeed "Yig Snake Daddy" is based on the Lovecraftian "Curse of Yig" by Zealia Bishop. The piece is based on a rock and roll sort of structure with metal stylings. The conclusion to this cut is unusual. One could call it "the ending that just won't end."

While "Worship Me Like a God" has no blatant links to Lovecraft's work, the general tone certainly qualifies. Musically thrash and punk influences merge here, and this cut has some very quirky overtones.

Even the text on the centerpiece of the album packaging is Lovecraft-related. "There have been aeons when other things ruled on Earth. They had great stone cites and the remains are still to be found. They died vast epics before man came, but there are arts which can revive them…When the stars come round again in the cycle of eternity."[10]

With *Great Old Ones* the band reissued older songs that were by that point unavailable. In case you didn't catch it, that in itself is a clever double meaning since this material was all "great old ones" and much of it is about the Great Old Ones. Although there was no "required reading" listed on the release, the Lovecraftian tracks abound. "One Gilled Girl" includes the lyrics "Out beyond the Bay of Innsmouth / Caught in a fisherman's net / She came and rescued me / And set my heart free / Though she's a hybrid from above / We fell in love."[11] The reference to "The Shadow Over Innsmouth" is, of course, unmistakable, although presented in the Thickets' usual humorous way. For those who have not read the story, you'll have to take my word on it, as I don't intend to spoil the surprise. Musically the song could be described as "The Ramones take on H.P. Lovecraft."

The track that follows it, "Jimmy the Squid" could certainly be seen as continuing in the "Shadow Over Innsmouth" vein. A spoken lecture introduction starts it. As the song proper enters its meaty main riff is quite cool. As it drops to the verse only the rhythm section remains. This one is definitely a highlight of the album and includes both tasty guitar work and some killer vocal arrangements.

With "Chunk" the band seem to have tied together many elements of Lovecraft's Mythos, while not truly singling out any one. The opening verse goes, "In the city where the people dwell / Winds from out at sea sweep in a horrid smell / It's been a million years since they smelled it last / They cannot realize the danger sweeping fast."[12] With the second stanza the group work in themes from different Lovecraft works. "In asylums restless patients scream / Visions of Cthulhu every night they dream / They see the signs of chaos beyond the wall of sleep / Their minds retain a knowledge that ours refuse to keep."[13] The third verse refers fairly directly to "The Whisperer In the Darkness." "In the mountains where the Mi-Go mine / People disappear from time to time / If I told you why you might go insane / But it has something to do with canisters for your brain."[14] This excerpt from that story somewhat explains the usage of the term "Mi-Go.":

> It was of no use to demonstrate to such opponents that the Vermont myths differed but little in essence from those universal legends of natural personification which filled the ancient world with fauns and dryads and satyrs, suggested the kallikanzarai of modern Greece, and gave to wild Wales and Ireland their dark hints of strange, small, and terrible hidden races of troglodytes and burrowers. No use, either, to point out the even more startlingly similar belief of the Nepalese hill tribes in the dreaded Mi-Go or "Abominable Snow-Men" who lurk hideously amidst the ice and rock pinnacles of the Himalayan summits.[15]

To give more detail here, would again cut into the first time enjoyment of the story, so we'll leave it at that. The final verse, though, continues with more Lovecraftian references, "At the center of the universe / writhes a loathsome God thing that couldn't be much worse / Larvae pipe and dance about the bubbling froth / Orbiting the Outer God that is Azathoth."[16] Musically, this is a rocking cut that has an intriguing texture. The guitar solo is especially tasty.

"Flee!" is another with obvious Cthulhu references. "Flee mortal flee in fear / Cthulhu's coming the end is near."[17] As it carries on the band sing, "Flee mortal soon you'll know / Cthulhu deals the final blow / We are his voice and it's over due / To sing of what's in store for you / Pain, death, insanity, death."[18] This one has a more metallic texture at first. Then it drops to a drums and voice arrangement for the verse, but a metallic guitar riff makes up the main musical structure. It dissolves to chaos amidst chants of "insanity, death!"

The Lovecraft references in "Please God No," (while a little less obvious) remain, nonetheless. "Can you hear the thunder / Can you see it crack / Can you see it stretching / Stretching through the black / Stirring in the steeple / Up on Federal Hill."[19] Just the use of "Federal Hill" ties this one into Lovecraft's work quite well as it, along with many other sites in Providence, Rhode Island, show up frequently in his writings. It continues later with "See the Haunter / Watch it fly / Membranes pushing to the sky."[20] The reference to "haunter" seems to indicate Haunter of the Dark, both a story by Lovecraft and an entity within. That term is another name for the being known as "Nyarlathotep." This has a straightforward rock and roll texture. Its old school rock brought into a modern punk vein mode is quite cool. Atkinson stressed to me after seeing my draft that, "'Please God No' is definitely a musical adaptation of 'Haunter of the Dark.' The lyric 'take this red-veined oddly angled stone' refers to the Shining Trapezohedron in the tale."

With "Six Gun Gorgon Dynamo" we find the following lines presented, "She's the one of the million Favored Ones / She's the Black Goat with a Thousand Young."[21] Drums are the intro to this one, and with an echoed "whew", we're off on a frantic high-energy ride. It has some killer guitar textures and is oh-so fast. Atkinson said that, "'Sesqua Valley' is a reference to the setting that Lovecraftian pastiche artist Wilum Hopfrog Pugmire uses."

The CD includes on its back booklet cover a series of short letters that would seem quite at home in any Lovecraft tale. Examples of these include:

William,   June 26, 1991

You were right! They ARE in the hills. I went to the spot last night, taking the items you mentioned, and I watched them. They found me out quickly enough, but the precautions did indeed help. I explained my intentions, and they seemed willing enough to open a dialog. The things they knew!...[22]

In a later letter the writer explains that "The Old Ones have told me what the next best step is, and I have followed their instructions."[23] In another nod to "The Whisperer In The Dark," those instructions lead him to bring four jars with head that later are revealed to be those of the members of the band. You will know if you have read the story, or find out when you read it—and you should read it—that much of it centers around brains in cylinders.

The final letter states that "I have at last been called back to the hills, and given my final instructions by the Old Ones, for they have completed their work and are headed back into deep space. I have been recruited into this group of ageless men."[24] It continues revealing the duties of this band.

> We are to prepare for the Clearing Off in a very special and I must add, interesting fashion. We have assumed the roles of artists, musicians specifically, and will begin to use this pretense to seek out the young more receptive individuals in a way which will not compromise the whole. In this incarnation we can rest assured that the bulk of human fodder will not take us seriously, nor pay us undue heed. The idea seems fool proof, but it will take time. Already we are working on our "performances"...[25]

The tale is a fairly intricate and effective way of weaving the band into the Lovecraft Mythos and making them an integral part of it.

Although their next disc, *Spaceship Zero*, was the soundtrack album to a non-Lovecraftian science fiction film, three songs with links to the author show up nonetheless. Perhaps the most obvious of these is "The Innsmouth Look," the band once again turning to "The Shadow Over Innsmouth" for inspiration on this one. It also includes a reference to "Dagon" in the form of "E.O.D" (Esoteric Order of Dagon). "I met her at the E. O. D. / She sank dew claws into me / We stepped out to watch the tide come in / She said a little swim would do some wonders for your skin / I shed my old self, slipped into the sea / One glance was all it took / She gave me the Innsmouth Look."[26] Both of these terms are explained in the *Encyclopedia Cthulhiana*. The Esoteric Order of Dagon is described as a "cult devoted to the worship of Dagon, Hydra and Cthulhu."[27] And, as mentioned before, drawing from "The Shadow Over Innsmouth," the trusted Encyclopedia serves up this explanation for the term "The Innsmouth Look": "Hereditary condition which takes its name from town of Innsmouth, Massachusetts, in which the majority of the people possess this malady."[28] Musically, this one is hard-edged, fast-paced and driving. It rocks out quite well.

"The Sounds of Tindalos" is another definite Lovecraft mythos based track that shows up on the CD. The lyrics to this one have little explicit reference to the author, though, the main crux of the connection being related to the title. The story by the same name was actually written by Frank Belknap Long, but the Hounds became associated with Lovecraft's mythology when he mentioned them in "The Whisperer In the Darkness." Beginning with a bass line that feels a lot like early Alice Cooper, this one is quirky yet accessible. Not many bands can pull that combination off. It gets quite punky at times and features a very tasty guitar solo.

"The Chosen One," while less blatantly Lovecraftian in title has lyrics that call to mind many of the author's stories. "Like the girl that we met / At the serpent mound / Like the thing that we saw / In the ultrasound / Like the path in the woods / That the natives shun / Like the hair on the mole of the chosen one."[29] Starting with the sounds of a car running off and an ending of another song, this one is quite quirky and driving. It shifts gear later to a more raw and punky segment.

In 2002 Chaosium Games sponsored a release by the band to coincide with a new rule set for their "Call of Cthulhu" game. More precisely, Atkinson explains it this way:

> The d20 Call of Cthulhu game was licensed from Chaosium. Wizards of the Coast published the d20 version, and it was Mat Smith at Wizards of the Coast made the CD happen. The CD tied into game play if you played it on random. The liner notes contained special rules depending on what song was playing. For example, while "Colour Me Green" is playing, a "random character in combat is nauseated for 1d4 rounds."

The disc, entitled *Let Sleeping Gods Lie* covered no new ground musically. Instead it was a compilation of various Lovecraftian pieces from their older releases. The cover and concept, though, plus the strength of the material made it one of the best discs in the collection.

Atkinson (who lists his favorite H.P.L. stories as "The Rats in the Walls," "The Call of Cthulhu," "The Shadow Out of Time" and *The Case of Charles Dexter Ward*) describes the draw that he felt to Lovecraft (and the aspects that have kept him as a fan) in this way:

> Three separate aspects of HPL fascinated me when I first read him. Given that I was already into monsters, there was that aspect that drew me in. The florid use of antiquated words was another—it was like nothing I had read. Thirdly, the Lovecraftian philosophy that mankind is a speck in the cosmic scheme of things. Take out these elements and you've still got an author who is fantastic at establishing mood and great at crafting a many-layered yarn, and ultimately that is what has kept me a fan.

While that compilation has been the last we've heard from the Thickets in terms of musical releases, the band is still active, and getting ready to unleash a new batch of Lovecraftian music in the latter part of 2006. As Atkinson describes the disc, it is, "tentatively titled *Supercthonic*. A good portion of these will be Lovecraftian, but I don't want to say more since we're still working on them."

Chapter 11

HISTORICAL HUMOR:
THE H.P. LOVECRAFT HISTORICAL SOCIETY

Cthulhu Lives! This is the name of a live action Lovecraft based game that serves as the basis for the operations of The H.P. Lovecraft Historical Society. According to their official website their motto is "Ludo Fore Putavimus: a Latin phrase meaning 'We thought it would be fun.' And it is."[1] With that brave credo the group have not only created a society for the game, but also artistic endeavors based on the works of Lovecraft. Sean Branney is sort of the ring leader of the group and has lead them through (among other things) not only the creation of two albums of music, but also one of the most faithful adaptations of H.P. Lovecraft's work to cinema in the form of their film *The Call of Cthulhu*. While movies are not the focus of this book, suffice it to say that their period silent movie treatment of the story is very strong and comes highly recommended to fans of the author.

That brings us to the music the group has produced. Of the two CDs they have available, the first was released in 2002. Entitled *A Shoggoth on the Roof*, as one might guess this disc is a version of "Fiddler on the Roof" reworked with Lovecraftian themes. For fans of the author (particularly those with a good sense of humor), this is a pretty awesome album. I should admit here that since I generally am not a big fan of musicals, much of this music is new to me. Granted, I knew a handful of the originals. The point I'm making is that, even with that form of ignorance I still appreciate the disc. These guys do a very professional and creative presentation that will probably have you dying to see the full stage production. This is an unusual, but quite interesting album, and just plain lots of fun.

Act I starts off the disc and opens with "Tentacles." A classical organ processional starts this, then (after running through) ethnic music takes over for the opening spoken narrative. The whole cast joins in on the chorus of "tentacles." As the narrator begins his description of Cthulhu he joins in song and the full musical approach takes the track. This is bouncy and very fun. Various Lovecraft characters get their moments to speak including Herbert West (made famous in the story "Herbert West—Reanimator"), Randolph Carter (of "The Statement of Randolph Carter" fame) and more.

Next up is "Arkham Dunwich." This old world tinged balladic cut takes on very cool textures here and works exceptionally well with the lyrical switch. Originally "Sunrise, Sunset," "Arkham, Dunwich" seems an obvious one. Both names refer to places that are frequent locations of Lovecraft stories.

The theme on "Byakhee Byakhee" is more of the same with the group's spotless take on the music and the Lovecraft based lyrics. After a summoning some weird sounds emerge in the mix at times. Listening to the cheery vocal describing the taking by the Byakhee makes for a great and clever contradiction. For those who don't know, Byakhee is revealed by the *Encyclopedia Cthulhiana* to be "Creatures resembling bats, birds, moles and decomposed humans."[2]

A pounding starts "Shoggoth Prayer," then a pretty backdrop creates the motif for this prayer to call Cthulhu. The arrangement here is very cool.

The next track on the disc is "If I Were A Deep One." It is hilarious. "If I were a deep one—blub, blub, blub, blub, blub."[3] This reworking of "If I Were A Rich Man" is awesome. The arrangement gets quite powerful at times.

They follow that one with "To Life," the piece that ends Act I. This cheery number deals with "Herbert West—Reanimator." It works well, but isn't one of the strongest cuts here. The lyrics are quite funny, though. The "die, die, die" chorus is a definite winning touch.

Opening up the second act is "The Nightmare." This one feels like Monty Python does a full Broadway musical with Lovecraft at its heart. This number doesn't work as well as some the rest, though.

"Victim of Victims" comes next. This has a playful texture but is another that is only moderately strong.

In a bit of a step up they pull out a song called, "Very Far From the Home I Love." This one is musically stronger than the last couple. It is not as over the top as some of the rest are.

Continuing the upward momentum, they next bring out "Do You Fear Me?" Organ music begins it. The lyrics are hilarious and the arrangement is very strong.

The final track of the album is "Miskatonic." It is another cool one and a great conclusion to the whole story and musical.

The following year the group released *A Very Scary Solstice*. This was a newly expanded version of something they had had around since 1998. The disc is an album of humorous reworkings of well-known holiday songs. These are drastically reworked, but very well performed holiday songs.

Opening up the set is "Have Yourself a Scary Little Solstice." It comes in with jazzy guitar, making this feels a first like a jazz trio track, but then after an extended intro it turns to a more muzak/jazz arrangement. The cut that is the basis for this should be obvious. The lyrics are well done, possibly the bridge section being the most clever, "Stars return as in olden days, as foretold in crazy lore / Great Old Ones gather near to us, giving fear to us once more."[4]

Next in line is "Freddy the Red Brained Mi-Go." Feeling much like the well-known rendition, this is of course based on "Rudolph the Red Nosed Reindeer," and it is very funny. I think my favorite verse—but you have to understand the joke and follow the asterisk—is this, "Then one foggy Solstice even / [Hastur}* came to say / Freddy with your brain so bright, won't you scare some folks tonight?"[5] The biggest part of the humor to this one comes with the notation that corresponds to the asterisk—"* not to be sung aloud."[6] In Lovecraftian Mythos, Hastur is often referred to in the Mythos as "the nameless one" or "he who must not be named," because any time you say the name "Hastur" aloud there is a good chance that you will anger him to the point where he will materialize and kill you.

"Great Old Ones Are Coming to Town" is sort of a modern gospel rendition. It is high energy and fun. "You'd better watch out; you better go hide / An Elder Sign's needed for this Yuletide / Great Old Ones are coming to town."[7] An Elder sign, according to the *Encyclopedia Cthulhiana* is, "magikal symbol which the Elder God N'tse-Kaambl (or possibly the Elder Things) created."[8]

A multi layered beautiful traditional arrangement of "The Carol of The Bells," except for the lyrics, makes up the mode of "The Carol of the Olde Ones." This is one of my favorites. "Eons have passed; now then, at last, prison walls break / Old Ones awake! / Madness will reign, terror and pain, woes without end where they extend."[9]

Next up is "Silent Night, Blasphemous Night." Starting just on piano, this is a very traditional take on the cut, with the change of the lyrics really the only difference.

"Awake Ye Scary Great Olde Ones" is done with a great choral arrangement. This one is both pretty and powerful. Based on "God Rest Ye Merry Gentlemen" the theme here is far different from on that song. "Awake ye scary Great Olde Ones, let everything dismay / Remember Great Cthulhu shall rise up from R'lyeh / To kill us all with Tentacles if we should go his way."[10]

Based on "Angels We Have Heard On High", another traditional chorale approach makes up "Mi-Go We Have Heard On High."

"The Shoggoth Song" is a fun little dittie based on "The Dreidel Song."

"It's the most horrible time of the year / With the nights growing longer / The evil is stronger / And there's much to fear / It's the most horrible time of the year."[11] With an opening verse like that, I don't need to tell you that this is not the same song as "It's the Most Wonderful Time of the Year," even though it might sound like it. They use a keyboard dominated, nearly lounge lizard approach on "It's The Most Horrible Time of the Year."

Based on the Jose Feliciano number "Feliz Navidad," "Es Y'Golonac" is bouncy and fun. The *Encyclopedia Cthulhiana* describes the being in question in this way: "Great Old One who takes the form of a flabby headless human with mouths on the palms of his hands. Since Y'golonac takes possession of a human when he arrives, the exact details of the form may vary according to the person chosen.[12]

Next in line is "Away in a Madhouse." "Away in a madhouse, confined to my bed / From visions and nightmares that filled me with dread."[13] So begins this piece that is fairly traditional at least in terms of the music and voice. However, the insane laughter that serves as accompaniment is a bit different from any version I've heard before.

A very traditional playful treatment makes up the bouncy music of "It's Beginning To Look a Lot Like Fish-Men." The term fish-men is a reference to the Lovecraft story "The Shadow Over Innsmouth."

On "I Saw Mommy Kissing Yog-Sothoth" a distant scratched record type sound makes up the main texture. It's like your listening to it on an old cheap record player. The rendition itself is a cool bounce guitar based jazzy take.

Feeling like it was recorded by a church choir, pipe organ and all, "O Come All Ye Olde Ones" is the next song on the album.

"I'm Dreaming of A Dead City" is a rather stripped down arrangement. This song goes on a little too long and while a very faithful musical rendition doesn't do much for me. The lyrics, however, are great. "I'm dreaming of a dead city / Where Deep Ones swim in depths of night / Where Cthulhu's sleeping while stars go creeping / Until the time when they are right."[14]

"Dance the Cultists" is based on "Deck the Halls." They take a fairly traditional choir with organ approach to this arrangement, too.

The next track, "He'll Be Back For Solstice" is again played like one of the traditional age-old songs we all grew up listening to. "He'll be back for solstice / 'Cause R'lyeh will rise / When he's free then you will see / But won't believe your eyes."[15]

"Mythos of A King" is based on "The Birthday of a King," a song with which I'm not familiar. A church organ starts this. A choral vocal performance moves it forward. This is another that feels like it could have been done in a church service. The lyrics those, tell the story of Lovecraft himself. "In the little village of Providence / There wrote a gentle man / Filling countless reams from his ghastly dreams / And a mythos thus began."[16]

With another very traditional bouncy arrangement "Here Comes Yog-Sothoth" is short, but fun.

A variant on "Little Drummer Boy," "Little Rare Book Room" is based in a fairly traditional and definitely dramatic approach.

Based on "Good King Wenceslas," "Demon Sultan Azathoth" is another cut from the muzak/old time Christmas song tradition. This one is made more intriguing with tuned percussion. It's another very brief one.

I guess they had to have a song called "Tentacles" on both discs. This is a pretty arrangement of female voices, piano and strings that is created on the basis of "Silver Bells." "Tentacles, tentacles: it's Solstice Eve, and it's scary / In my dream hear my screams, soon we shall all see R'lyeh."[17]

Next in line is "Do You Fear What I Fear?" While I like all the verses, I think the last one is my favorite. "Said Cthulhu to the human beings / 'Do you know what I know? / The stars, the stars, soon will be in line / I shall reclaim that which was mine / I shall reclaim that which was mine!'"[18] This is a great rendition that again feels like it could have come from the golden era of Christmas songs.

Considering that "Cthulhu Lives!" is the name of the game and the reason for their being here, it seems obvious that they would have a song with that title. Starting with a little kid speaking, this rendition of "Jingle Bells" is a whole-family sing along type of number. "Oh! Cthulhu lives, Cthulhu lives, deep down in the sea / In the city of R'lyeh, waiting to be freed."[19]

Based on "The Hallelujah Chorus," "Oh Cthulhu" is another strong, and quite standard take, with some killer vocal layering. It serves as very satisfying conclusion to the album.

There is also a more recent CD from the group, this one featuring the soundtrack to the film *The Call of Cthulhu* mentioned earlier. I won't go into depth on descriptions of the instrumentals contained on the disc, but I'll say that the group did a great job of capturing the musical textures of an old silent movie, while still managing to bring it up to date.

Sean Branney had the following to say about the group's music:

Our music has come in two flavors: sincere and satiric. With the sincere music (the soundtrack to *The Call of Cthulhu*) our intent was to recapture the flavor of a pit orchestra from the 1920s and create a sound that would help tell the story dramatically. I think our composers were quite successful on both fronts. The music has a period feeling and it carries the momentum of the plot while reinforcing the emotional experience of the film.

In terms of our parodies (*A Shoggoth on the Roof* and *A Very Scary Solstice*) our intent has been to keep the music of the source material intact, and apply the Lovecraftian colors on top of the music. The humor comes from the horror and nihilism of the music when combine with lovely, familiar songs.

When asked what Lovecraft's work had to offer to music, Branney said, "First and foremost, I think that H.P.L.'s writing is inspirational. His worlds and world-view has inspired countless musicians, artists, writers and other artists. Many musicians have found their own muse in his writings and they have proved a catalyst to great new compositions inspired by Lovecraft."

Branney also spoke about what drew him to H.P.L. and what has kept him as a fan in the following way:

> The first story I read was "The Rats in the Walls," and it freaked me out. I had never read anything quite like it. His style evoked an atmosphere and world that was simply disturbing to visit. The story's not particularly frightening, but it's unsettling in a good way. I remain a fan of H.P.L. because I think he puts mankind in its place. We are very small specks on a speck of dust swirling about other specks of dust in a universe consisting of unimaginably huge amounts of dust. His mythos keep mankind in check by reminding us that we're not the first things in the universe, won't be the last, and we certainly aren't the most important or most powerful. Second, he uses language to evoke an atmosphere which unsettling and unnerving. A lot of people write him off for his sometimes-excessive use of vocabulary, but there's a lot more to his writing technique than a reliance on sesquipedalian verbiage.

When asked about his favorite Lovecraft stories, he had this to say, "I like 'The Call of Cthulhu.' It's a great story. I'm also fond of 'The Rats in the Walls,' 'The Shadow over Innsmouth,' *At the Mountains of Madness*, 'The Whisperer in the Darkness' and 'The Dunwich Horror.'"

It seems obvious that with the passion and energy The H.P. Lovecraft Historical Society have for Lovecraft's writing and for doing what they do that we have not heard the last of them. Since everything they've done thus far has been quality, I see no reason to believe future offerings will be anything less. They are certainly a group on which H.P.L. fans should keep their eyes (and ears) glued.

Chapter 12

STRANGE AEONS:
A MUSICAL TRIBUTE TO H.P. LOVECRAFT
AND THE CTHULHU MYTHOS

2001 saw the release of a collection of music by various artists entitled *Strange Aeons*. According to the liner notes, *Strange Aeons* is "a musical tribute to H.P. Lovecraft and the ever expanding 'Cthulhu Mythos.'"[1] Steve Lines "directed and produced" the disc, but there are a number of artists who contributed to it. Disc one is described in those same notes as "the album proper" and disc two is "a bonus collection of outtakes, demos and alternate mixes. It also includes several tracks which would have been included on disc 1 if there had been enough room so their inclusion here should not infer that they are in any way inferior to those recordings on disc 1."[2] Like any various artists compilation this one has both strong and weak material. Personally I am quite fond of the contributions from Childe Roland, and less taken by those by Stormclouds. Among other contributors to the disc are Brian Voth (otherwise known as Fireaxe—see Chapter 6) and science fiction/horror writer Brian Lumley.

The format of the CD is to alternate between a poetry/prose reading and an actual song. This, while intriguing, seems a bit strange after a while. Frankly, I would have to also say that the disc might have benefited from being cut down to one CD. However, there is plenty here to like, especially for fans of the writer whose work inspired it.

The idea for the album comes from Steve Lines. He also wrote most of the lyrics and provides much of the music. Add to that the fact that he organized the whole project and produced the recordings and it will be pretty obvious that Lines is committed to this collection. With that in mind, it should come as no surprise that he had quite a bit to say about the production. Here are his words in the aspect of bringing musical life to Lovecraft's work:

> When I began writing the songs for *Strange Aeons* I wanted to get away from what I saw as the usual style of Lovecraftian music, which seemed to be either ambient/heavy metal or gothic in tone. I have nothing against these styles of music and indeed have several Lovecraftian albums in these areas, but I felt that there was no reason why you couldn't have more melodic songs with folk or rock (or even pop) sensibilities. The Lovecraft inspired songs that I recorded

with my own band, Stormclouds, were melancholy folk in tone, except for the overtly psychedelic/eastern flavour of "What Do They Say?" However I also wrote the lyrics for all the other music on the album. The material by Childe Roland is very '70s rock in flavour and inspiration showing the influences of Bowie, Bolan and Mott the Hoople amongst others. There is a more sinister tone to the lyrics to suit the style of Childe Roland's material and he did a wonderful job of writing and arranging the music. I knew the Petals were very psychedelic and adept at writing strange music so I gave them the Clark Ashton Smith inspired lyrics "The Maze of Maal Dweb" and they turned them in a wonderfully bizarre song. I picked this version from three radically different demos that vocalist Cary Wolf sent me. Because I knew that Lodovico Ellena's band, Astral Weeks, were masters of eastern flavoured, West Coast style psychedelia, I gave them the lyrics to "The Black Pharaoh."

There is plenty of scope within Lovecraft's writings to adapt stories or sonnets to any style of music from classical to hardcore punk—you just have to be sympathetic to the subject matter. With *Strange Aeons* I tried to present a wide variety of musical styles based on the writings of HPL and other disciples of the Cthulhu Mythos. Lovecraft's writing is atmospheric and deals with (in the main) alien concepts and beings: a fertile breeding ground for great musical compositions. I can almost hear the brooding 20 minute instrumental titled "The Call of Cthulhu" or the 3 minute punk thrasher "The Black Hounds," or what about the Dreamlands concept album based on *The Dream-Quest of Unknown Kadath*?

Lines also had plenty to say about what drew him to Lovecraft and what has kept him as a fan:

I first came across the works of H.P. Lovecraft when I was a teenager back in the early '70s. At that time the shelves of W. H. Smiths and other stores were stacked with the writings of many of the great pulp writers such as Clark Ashton Smith, Robert E. Howard, Frank Belknap Long and Robert Bloch as well as their more recent "disciples," L. Sprague De Camp, Lin Carter, John Jakes, Fritz Leiber, Jack Vance and many others. I read all these avidly, drawn to several authors by the covers by such great artists as Frank Frazetta and Bruce Pennington. Amongst these of course was H.P. Lovecraft. I can't remember why I picked up a book by Lovecraft, though it was probably because he was quoted on the back of the Clark Ashton Smith paperbacks, which I'd read and absolutely loved. It wasn't too long before I had collected all the Panther editions of H.P.L.'s stuff. I was fascinated by his stories; the careful unfolding of facts and events inexorably leading to an awful conclusion; the narrator telling his tale while hovering on the brink of insanity or about to be consumed by some terrible doom or hideous monster; the creation of unspeakable tomes and blasphemous sects and the terrible, alien creatures constantly waiting behind sealed gateways for their chance to return to claim what was once theirs. The idea that Mankind was an insignificant aberration within the cold, uncaring Universe appealed to me (and still does).

Although it's been over thirty years since I discovered Lovecraft (and all the other authors mentioned above) I still read and re-read their stories, especially in these times of interminable "fantasy" trilogies. In fact I'm probably more influenced and inspired by their writings now than I was back in those dim heady days of the early '70s. I am in regular contact with many of today's Cthulhu Mythos writers and have illustrated several Mythos related books and magazines so I am still deeply immersed in the writings of Lovecraft and his disciples—and long may it remain so!

When asked about his favorite Lovecraft story, Lines said, "This probably changes day by day, but constant favourites are *At the Mountains of Madness*, *The Dream-Quest of Unknown Kadath*, 'The Shadow Over Innsmouth' and 'The Call of Cthulhu.'"

The first disc opens with "Strange Aeons," performed by Lines himself. Weird sounds create a creepy sci-fi texture over which a narration is delivered dramatically. This is a powerful start to the disc and ends in dark Hawkwindish noise. The song is not only performed solo by Lines (he does the vocals, keyboards and effects), but the lyrics were also written by him. Even with the opening sentence the links to Lovecraft are obvious. "From undimensioned spheres, the Old Ones swept down to primal Earth and beneath their mighty tread all creation bowed."[3] This essentially tells the story of how the Old Ones came to be imprisoned in an endless slumber. Later it speaks of Elder Gods intervention. "Across the ravaged Earth these ancient Gods waged war and The Old Ones were imprisoned or locked in deathless dream, not in the spaces known to man, but in the angles inbetween."[4]

The aforementioned Roland is up next with "The Necromonicon." If the last cut felt a bit like the weird Hawkwind, this one comes across as a solid rocking take on their more straightforward sound. This rocker is a bit more raw and stripped down than a lot of that band's output, but features a couple very tasty guitar solos. The lyrics again come from the mind of Lines, while Roland handles vocals and all instruments, and wrote the music as well. The words of the song are very much in keeping with Lovecraft's themes. The beginning sounds very much like the way that H.P.L. might have started one of his stories, "I know not who might find this note, as I write here in my room, gripped in a fevered madness and waiting for my doom."[5]

The situation that brought about this fate is apparently a reading of the dreaded book. Just the thoughts of what that book contains drive the narrator to suicide. The descriptions of the contents are also quite good.

Vast gulfs there are that yawn beyond the gates of which we dream, the Old Ones wait and watch the stars in spaces in-between. And Cthulhu dreams in R'lyeh, imprisoned in the deeps, but in death He does not die, Cthulhu only sleeps.

There are things that mortal man was not meant to know. The ravings of an Arab poet have blasted my soul...[6]

"The Telegram" by Ramsey Campbell is another spoken word piece with sound effects at the ending. On this one Lines provides the effects while Campbell recites his own words. Again the opening lines seem to me as if they could easily have been drawn from any number of H.P.L. stories. "Come at once to Kingsport. You are needed urgently by me here for protection from agencies which may kill me—or worse—if you do not come immediately."[7] It goes on later to speak of the terrors by which this narrator is threatened. It also ends with a chant/spell type recitation. Campbell himself disagrees with my assessment, saying, "To be honest, I don't think Lovecraft ever overwrote like that. I did when I was fifteen and should take all the responsibility—I mean, 'kill me or worse?'" Nonetheless will stand by my statement, as in my opinion it feels a lot like many similar statements uttered by characters in H.P.L.'s tales.

Campbell also shared some of his views on the marriage of H.P.L.'s work with music. He said that when it comes to that topic Lovecraft offers, "potentially a good deal, I'd say. It was Fritz Leiber who pointed out how similar to music Lovecraft's prose is, in the sense that the words are often orchestrated, with phrases developed and varied or expanded each time they're repeated." He also put forth the following in regards to what drew him to the author and has kept him as a fan:

> He remains one of the crucial writers in the field. He united the American tradition of weird fiction—Poe, Bierce, Chambers—with the British—Machen, Blackwood, M. R. James. He devoted his career to attempting to find the perfect form for the weird tale, and the sheer range of his work (from the documentary to the delirious) is often overlooked. Few writers in the field are more worth rereading; certainly I find different qualities on different occasions. I still try to capture the Lovecraftian sense of cosmic awe in some of my tales, and "The Darkest Part of the Woods" has a little of it, I think.
>
> I should point out that his mythos is only one of his devices for conveying something larger and more awesome than is shown. It's the easiest to imitate and has been added to far too much, not least by me. Ironically, Lovecraft invented it so as to get away from occultism that he regarded as over-explicit and over-conventionalized, but that's exactly what we imitators have made of it. Read the man and not pale copies of him. On the other hand, such different and excellent writers as T. E. D. Klein, Thomas Ligotti, Caitlín Kiernan and Poppy Z. Brite have developed his methods in their own highly individual ways.

When asked about his favorite Lovecraft tale, Campbell said this:

My absolute favourite (as it was his) is "The Colour out of Space," which finds the perfect symbol for his sense of the indifferent alienness of most of the cosmos. It's a tale that moves through gruesomeness and terror to awe. I'm very fond of *The Case of Charles Dexter Ward*—a great sustained performance—and "The Rats in the Walls" and the restored "Shadow out of Time." But I could list you a dozen more I wouldn't be without.

Stormclouds make their first contribution with "Midnight Sun." A slightly rough around the edges ballad, this one doesn't do a lot for me, feeling a bit amateurish. It features a noisy guitar solo that doesn't seem to fit the backdrop. The line-up of the band on this track are Lines (acoustic guitar—who also wrote the music and lyrics), Melanie Townsend (vocals) and Roland (lead guitar).

Brian Lumley's first poetry reading is "Tindalos." More atmospheric Hawkwindish waves of keys serve as the backdrop to the narrative of this one. It evolves up in intensity and weirdness as it carries on. Lines provides the keyboards over which Lumley recites his own words that tell a tale of the place called "Tindalos." An excellent explanation of this place can be found in the *Encyclopedia Cthulhiana*. Tindalos, according to that source, is a "city which may exist on Earth far in the past, on a faraway world near a black hole, or even floating throughout time, contemporaneous with all space yet unable to intrude upon it."[8]

Next on the agenda Roland returns, this time with what seems to be the companion piece to the last one, "The Hounds of Tindalos." This rocker again has a slight Hawkwind feel, but actually links more closely to a '50s sound mixed with elements that lean towards Jamaican grooves at times. This feels quite "cheery" and has some killer moments in its arrangement. Once again, Steve Lines wrote the words and Childe Roland adds his music, vocals and all instrumental performances to complete the picture. According to the *Encyclopedia Cthulhiana*, the hounds of Tindalos are, "creatures which come from the distant past, or possibly another dimension. The hounds appear much like green hairless dogs with blue tongues, or like black formless shadows; it is difficult to be sure of the hounds' true form."[9] A key point comes with the next sentence of that entry. "They dwell in Tindalos, a city of corkscrew towers, but have been known to travel to other places and times to attack their prey."[10] These words tie in quite well to the writings of Lines on this song. Lines' lyrics speak of a journey back in time, during which the narrator encounters the hounds. "I can hear them breathing / I can hear them howl / The Hounds of Tindalos are on the prowl / through outrageous angles / They scented me in Time."[11]

The next poetry reading is "The Shore of Madness" by Susan McAdam. Windy sounds create the backdrop for this poetry reading. The lyrics here are actually a sonnet written by Ann K Schwader. Schwader spoke of her particular interest in Lovecraft in this way:

> Lovecraft's work is closer to very dark science fiction than straight horror, which is probably what drew me to it. (I am an active member of both SFWA—Science Fiction Writers Association and HWA—Horror Writers Association) He was also able to actually chill the reader without resorting to "splatter" tactics or graphic sexuality, which I still appreciate. I'm not sure what keeps me a fan, but I suspect his very dark view of the universe—and the multitude of things which can be written/read about his original stories—has a lot to do with it. His work rewards rereading.

She also revealed that her favorite Lovecraft stories are "'The Thing on the Doorstep,' 'The Call of Cthulhu,' 'The Colour Out of Space' (first H.P.L. story I ever read, at about age 13), 'The Dunwich Horror,' 'The Whisperer In Darkness" and 'Imprisoned With the Pharaohs.'" The song itself ties lyrically to the previous two tracks with links to the Hounds of Tindalos.

Brian Voth (a.k.a. Fireaxe) is up next. Here he contributes "Dreamhound." Weird spoken words start this, and then a smoking metal texture takes the piece. This cut feels a bit like a rawer Iron Maiden meets Dio and Rush. Its high-energy approach is a great change of pace on this album. It is quite dynamic and ends with a bluesy nearly acapella verse. While the music, vocals and all the instrumentation is provided by Voth, Lines again contributes the lyrics. The words here seem to carry forward the themes of the last few tracks.

"Home" by Simon Clark is a processed narrative feels very science fiction oriented. Steve Lines provides the keyboards and effects as the only accompaniment to Clark reading the words that he penned.

Stormclouds returns with "Call of the Whippoorwills." An acoustic based ballad cut, this is also a bit rough and rather weak. It feels rather like a bad '60's folk group. The credits of the song remain the same as the last appearance by the group with the addition of Ken Flynn on acoustic guitar and bass.

Another reading by Ramsey Cambell, "Daoloth" is next in line. Again the words are by Campbell, who also provides the voice for the recitation. Lines, this time out, lays down nothing but creepy science fiction effects as the backdrop. This has processed vocals that have a very eerie texture. The entity whose name is the title does not actually come from H.P.L.'s work directly, but rather from Campbell's own story, "The Render of the Veils" which builds on Lovecraft's Mythos.

"The Maze of Maal Dweb," performed by The Petals is next. A competent psychedelic jam is the basis to this cut. This is not spectacular, but for fans of '60s psychedelia it should be a treat. The vocals are a little hard to take at times, though. A false ending gives way to a nearly acapella section. They do get bonus points for the sitar usage. This one definitely goes on a bit too long. Once again, Lines provides the lyrics to the song.

The Zoogs are up next and contribute "The Manuscript of Emily Zann." Violin starts this. This is quite appropriate as Lovecraft's tale "The Music of Erich Zann" focuses on a man (depending on interpretation) either calling or holding at bay unknown creatures with his violin. In the case of this piece, the violin carries through a pretty melody unaccompanied for a time, then weird keyboard atmosphere enters, and the melody twists into a creepy cacophonic minor key with a lot of dissonance. The sound effects eventually gain control with monstrous tones, infecting it. A frightening burst of sounds ends this. It seems likely that the artists credited with this track are pseudonyms, since their names are Steven Zann and Emily Zann.

The next instrumental cut feels a bit like a harder rocking version of early Pink Floyd. It is actually "Brown Jenkin" by Childe Roland. The piece resolves to an almost Bowieish segment before a nice break. The Bowie-like section comes back later, extended this time. In this instance while Lines gets co-credit for the lyrics, his name is accompanied by Roland's. The title refers to a character from the Lovecraft story "Dreams in the Witch-House." These words from the story give a good description of this being:

> But it was not in these vortices of complete alienage that he saw Brown Jenkin. That shocking little horror was reserved for certain lighter, sharper dreams which assailed him just before he dropped into the fullest depths of sleep. He would be lying in the dark fighting to keep awake when a faint lambent glow would seem to shimmer around the centuried room, showing in a violet mist the convergence of angled planes which had seized his brain so insidiously. The horror would appear to pop out of the rat-hole in the corner and patter toward him over the sagging, wide-planked floor with evil expectancy in its tiny, bearded human face; but mercifully, this dream always melted away before the object got close enough to nuzzle him. It had hellishly long, sharp, canine teeth; Gilman tried to stop up the rat-hole every day, but each night the real tenants of the partitions would gnaw away the obstruction, whatever it might be.[12]

Compare those words with these from the song, and the parallels are very obvious. "… Brown Jenkin with his terrible teeth is waiting there for me / It had what looked like human hands / And features old and wise / The face was after all human with shining evil eyes…"[13]

Next up is another poetry reading in the form of "Down to A Sunless

Sea" by Rod Goodway. This is one of the creepiest of the recitations here. At times it feels a little like Alice Cooper, while other segments bring just a small Hawkwindish texture. As it moves through its midsection those Hawk elements create a full early Hawkwind like section. Later a consistency like a cross between Hawk weirdness and dark psychedelia takes the track. Sounds of wind and sea end this.

The strongest showing by Stormclouds thus far, "The Midnight Sister" has a garage band, neo-psychedelic texture. An instrumental break is both progish and quite strong. The lyrics here are by John B. Ford.

The next poetry cut is "Pickman's Painting" by Kevin Broxton: This creepy reading has sound effects as its backing. An echo on the voice is a nice touch. The lyrics are again by Steve Lines, but this time out Broxton's recitation is accompanied by Matt Woodward and Danny Maisey both contributing guitar and effects. These lyrics link incredibly well to Lovecraft's story "Pickman's Model." In fact, we'll take a look at both the opening verse and a similar excerpt from within Lovecraft's story. First, these are the lines from the song:

> I gazed in stunned horror at the canvas on the wall and held out my brandy glass as my host began to pour me yet another drink my hand shaking and unsure. Never had I seen such work, which at once appalled and fascinated with an unholy nameless dread. It was Copp's Hill Burying Ground and from broken tombs canine creatures crawled from unknown catacombs. They were ghouls feeding he said.[14]

Now note the similarities in this excerpt, from the story on which Lines drew his conceptions:

> By this time Pickman had lighted a lamp in an adjoining room and was politely holding open the door for me; asking me if I would care to see his 'modern studies.' I hadn't been able to give him much of my opinions—I was too speechless with fright and loathing—but I think he fully understood and felt highly complimented. And now I want to assure you again, Eliot, that I'm no mollycoddle to scream at anything which shows a bit of departure from the usual. I'm middle-aged and decently sophisticated, and I guess you saw enough of me in France to know I'm not easily knocked out. Remember, too, that I'd just about recovered my wind and gotten used to those frightful pictures which turned colonial New England into a kind of annex of hell. Well, in spite of all this, that next room forced a real scream out of me, and I had to clutch at the doorway to keep from keeling over. The other chamber had shown a pack of ghouls and witches over-running the world of our forefathers, but this one brought the horror right into our own daily life!
> God, how that man could paint! There was a study called 'Subway

Accident,' in which a flock of the vile things were clambering up from some unknown catacomb through a crack in the floor of the Boston Street subway and attacking a crowd of people on the platform. Another showed a dance on Copp's Hill among the tombs with the background of today. Then there were any number of cellar views, with monsters creeping in through holes and rifts in the masonry and grinning as they squatted behind barrels or furnaces and waited for their first victim to descend the stairs.[15]

Astral Weeks contributes "The Black Pharaoh." A slightly metallic, almost progressive rock style works nicely here. A killer eastern tinged break is included later. On this one the lyrics again come from the fertile pen of Lines. The title character, is a name sometimes used for Nyarlathotep, but there are also other meanings for the term.

The sounds of tides and seagulls mixed with eerier tones make up the backdrop for the next reading, "Innsmouth Jewelry," by Loretta Mansell. The narrative includes severely twisted and altered sounds. Extremely weird tones end it. Lines contributes the lyrics along with the keyboards and effects that accompany Mansell's recitation.

Childe Roland makes another entry with "At the Mountains of Madness." Eastern sounds start this and run through in a short intro, then silence takes the cut for a time. A "Munsters" theme meets Hawkwind texture creates the main element for the song proper. This instrumental is quite cool and ends abruptly. This time around Roland is the one responsible for every aspect of the number.

"The Black Litany of Nug and Yeb," by Robert M. Price, starts normally, but a weird pairing on sections makes it strange. This is a bit too bizarre for me, and way too long and repetitive. It is sort of a piece of musical theater in that each voice used is essentially playing a role. The words here are written by Joseph S. Pulver, Sr. Robert M. Price takes on the role of "High Priest" while Loretta Mansell, Steve Lines, Jim Xavier and Bradley Dexter all take on the parts of acolytes.

Backwards tracking and a cool arrangement make "What Do They Say?" by far the best Stormclouds offering here. I'm a sucker for Eastern tinged music, and touches of those also add to the experience here. Exotic processed words overlaid serve another plus. The extended jam, while repetitive, is quite cool. The lyrics on this one includes Lovecraft's infamous couplet.

"The Stormclouds of Their Return" by Joseph S. Pulver Sr. is next. Appropriately the sounds of a storm serve as the only backdrop to this poetry reading. The words are delivered (by Pulver himself) in a very unemotional and matter of fact manner that adds a certain horror to their already frightening meaning. This serves as a strong conclusion to the first CD. "This is the season of Their Return, the flung-open days and months and strange aeons of the Old Ones lost in despairing deliriums have passed…"[16]

"Strange Aeons (Demo)" by Steve Lines opens the second disc. This is (as the title suggests) a demo of the album's opener and still very effective.

The next demo comes from Childe Roland. It is an acoustic based rendition of a song from the previous CD. While "The Necronomicon (Demo)" is this is rougher than the other version, it is still quite cool.

"Invocation to the Void," which was written (the lyrics) by Thomas Ligotti, is read here by John B. Ford. This is a great narration, at least as good as most on disc 1. It is one of the most dramatic. The atmospheric textures that provide accompaniment get quite weird, but are very entertaining.

With "Dunwich Town" Childe Roland provides another rocker that has some Hawkwind like textures. This also almost has a "Mersey-Beat" sound at times. The lyrics to this one are also from Roland.

Eerie horror movie tones with processed narration make Steve Lines' "The Whisperer In Darkness" a very strange piece. Here Lines' recitation of his own words is accompanied by the keyboards and effects of Jim Xavier.

Next up is "The Ghooric Zone (demo)" by The Gugs. Starting with peculiar textures, as the song proper comes in this feels like a Nik Turner (of Hawkwind) composition. This one is very solid and although a bit rough, one of my favorites on the set. The lyrics to this one are credited to Haydon Atwood Prescott.

Contributed by Simon Clark, "Home (Different Mix)" is another version, less understandable, of the track from the first CD.

Another by Stormclouds, "Beyond the Fields We Know (Demo)" takes up the next position on CD 2. This rough take has a fairly intriguing folk type arrangement. They should have fleshed this one out more as it is one of their stronger cuts. The lyrics here are written by Lines.

Another poetry reading, "The Ghosts of Cydonia" (written and read by John B. Ford), with its eerie arrangement is a strong one. Lines provides only effects to accompany the voice.

I would have liked to hear a finished version of "The House on the Borderland (Demo)" by Childe Roland, as even in this rough draft take it is a strong, albeit, under produced and raw number. Steve Lines wrote both the lyrics and the music to this one, but Roland handles all the instruments and vocals.

Sound effects serve as the backdrop to this narrative, "Eclipse" by Joel Lane. It is one of the stronger ones, and the lyrics to this one are awesome. While Lane gives voice to the words he wrote, he is accompanied by Chris Davis (guitar feedback), Steve Davis (bass feedback), Nick Borrie (guitar feedback) and Steve Lines (keyboards). The lyrics seem to speak at points directly to Lovecraft himself.

...Reporter of the endarkened age, your words have filled my head for twenty years, framing the night behind this smoke painted sky. We would not have been friends. Your letters scare me more than your stories: wave upon wave of cold bigotry and hatred, tipped with the broken ice of jargon. Objectively speaking, the Semitic race... You praised Hitler's vision, but died before he could show the world what prejudice means. We know objectivity is the mask of horror.

At the end of this century, your vision still speaks to us; and so does your blindness. I look up at the burning sky, and can see nothing but eclipse.[17]

Roland puts in another effort here with "Midnight Sun." This is a folky and quite entertaining track. The words and music come from Lines, but Roland provides all instruments and voices.

"Petition to Tsathoggua" by Robert M. Price is next. This one has Hawkwindish weirdness far in the back. The recitation is a bit weak, though. It is essentially a prayer to the dark one. The words to this one come from Richard L. Tierney.

Black Monolith puts in the next track in the form of "The Thousand Young (Demo)." The cut comes in with sounds like you might expect to hear in a pornographic movie. Eventually this begins to give way to odd sound effects and then weird textured demonic voices. It never moves far away from that, however, never moving to anything one could call "a song."

Spawn of Chaos is next on the bill with "E'Ch Pi El." This punky stomper feels just a little like Hawkwind at times. It is very short. It's also very fun. The lyrics (seeming at times to talk about H.P.L. and at other points about characters from his stories) were written (as was the music) by Steve Lines.

The narrative that is the next number ("Y'Golonac" by Ramsey Campbell) has some extreme weirdness for its backing. It has a texture much like Hawkwind during the Michael Moorcock era. The lyrics were also written by Campbell.

"Lizzy (Demo)" by Thunderhead is next. It is amateurish, but shows promise. The harmonica solo is a nice touch. The lyrics are quite strange. While I am including this song here, because of the Lovecraft nature of the whole collection, this one seems to be strictly written about Lizzy Borden and has nothing to do with H.P.L. Lines wrote the music and lyrics and also provides all the instrumentation. Holly Hudson sings this like a small child.

The next poetry reading is by Steve Lines. It is a Hawkwind-like treatment slightly based on the story "The Rats in the Walls," with which it shares a name. The track, though, shares much of its lyrical structure with "Brown Jenkin", and in fact has much to do with "Dreams In The Witch-House" as well.

The demo version of "Brown Jenkin" by Childe Roland comes next in line, and even in this rough form, it is still great.

Another cool reading, the next track is "Vacant Souls" by Tim Lebbon. The lyrics are written by Lebbon and are exceptionally strong. It begins with this line to set the scene, "I saw faces in the walls."[18] As it carries forward we get a more clear explanation of what those words mean. "They were familiar to me in some repulsive way, and yet I could not name any of them. If I had known these people, whose images were carved into rock a billion years old, they were different now, changed." [19] This theme seems to relate indirectly into several Lovecraft tales, and, although altered, fairly directly to "The Tomb." The final segment is the most jolting. "And then I saw a face I did recognize. It was twisted out of shape, and I realized suddenly that the distortion had not yet happened, but was soon to come."[20] The final line realizes the horror in style. "The face glaring back at me, moodily inert, was mine."[21]

Brian Voth contributes his demo of "Dreamhound" here, as before under the name Fireaxe. This comes across as quite rough, but it is also very robust.

Author Brian Lumley contributes another poetry reading in the form of "The City Out of Time." This one is another freaky and processed science fiction like recitation. His words and voice are accompanied by Steve Lines' keys and effects.

It might be a demo, but Childe Roland's take on "At the Mountains of Madness" on the second disc is potent. Frankly, I'd have to say that it is at least as good as the "finished" one.

"The Night Music of Oakdeene" by Michael Cisco is next in line. This weird one is an incantation ritual with peculiar voices and effects serving as the backdrop. The lyrics here are by Brian Lumley and consist of a non-human chant type recitation. The unspoken notation "(repeat 13 times—if you dare!!)"[22] at the end is a nice touch.

While CD 1 featured a version of "What Do They Say?" by Stormclouds, here Childe Roland does an acoustic version. This is another strong entry from an artist who doesn't seem to disappoint.

Another Hawkwind-like narrative is up next with "When They Return" by Steve Lines. This one is another that falls into the "tastefully weird" category. It also serves to end the set. It refers to the re-arrival of the Old Ones. The tasty lyrics include this opening, "They lie awake in the unending night whilst uncounted epochs slowly unfold and, talking in their tombs, they mould mankind's dreams. When stars come right, thresholds will crumble, torn asunder."[23] The piece ends with these lines, "A strange new aeon will have begun. I will laugh as mankind's cities burn and greet the Old Gods when they return!"[24]

This album, then, represents a fairly large chunk of Lovecraft based sounds. While not all of it is great, some of it is. It will certainly appeal to anyone who is a Lovecraft completist, as it will to those into role-playing in the Mythos. This chapter will also take us into the final coverage of the book, the one that addresses the various bands and sounds that don't fit into any of the other categories.

Chapter 13

MORE MYTHOS MAYHEM:
OTHER ASSORTED APPEARANCES

There are some other notable instances of Lovecraftian music that don't really fall under any of the musical styles addressed thus far. The bands in question don't have a strong enough element of Lovecraft (or in some cases enough material) to warrant their own chapter. Therefore, they will be covered in this chapter, in no particular order.

Coming out of Long Island, New York in the late 1960s, Blue Öyster Cult's brand of hard rock at times leans close to heavy metal and then at other times runs close to progressive rock. Their lyrics often flirt with the dark and touch on both science fiction and horror. With some songs co-written by science fiction authors and an obvious enthusiasm for science fiction and horror stories on the part of guitarists Buck Dharma and Eric Bloom, it should come as no surprise that the group is one of the more literary bunch of rockers around. It should also be a given that they have touched on the works of Lovecraft occasionally, and such is the case. While often times the reference is only a passing one amongst a seemingly unrelated set of lyrics, there are quite a few songs containing such gems.

The first such occurrence comes with the 1976 album *Agents of Fortune* and the track "E.T.I (Extraterrestrial Intelligence)." While the lyrics certainly speak of a UFO related theme, certainly the lines "All praise / He's found the awful truth"[1] set a tone that is consistent with that of a lot of Lovecraft's themes. In addition the cut includes a reference to "the king in yellow." This would seem to tie to a mythical play in the Lovecraftian Mythos that centers around a character by the same name who is an avatar of Hastur or Nyarlathotep. The song, essentially a "thinking man's metal" number is well written and arranged. It includes keyboards that at points sound like a flying saucer and at other times call to mind a 1950s science fiction film.

The 1988 album *Imaginos*, that actually began as a solo project, but was forced into becoming a B.O.C. album by the label, features no less than four songs that contain Lovecraft links. The first of these is the disc's opener, "I Am The One You Warned Me Of." The lyrics, "When destiny assigns wisdom / Known to me / The starry wisdom,"[2] are definitely in keeping with Lovecraft's mythos. Although nothing is specifically mentioned beyond that here, that same allusion returns later in the album. The term "the starry wisdom" frequently appears in Lovecraftian texts in reference to having an understanding of the meaning of the stars. The cut has a metallic texture, but doesn't quite fall into that genre. It is quite catchy and tasty and the chorus is especially effective. The later segments turn exceptionally meaty with a number of intriguing instrumental changes.

"Les Invisibles" again does not show explicit references, but there are several lines that seem to possibly be derived from H.P.L. The line "Beneath the Polar Mountain"[3] seems to point to Lovecraft's *At the Mountains of Madness*, while "Aerial races / In rotation over / The magical casement / Visions of a parallel world"[4] seems to indicate a non-specific, but fairly strong link to the author. While in some ways this doesn't alter drastically from the track that preceded it, this one has an almost funky texture at points and a very interesting vocal arrangement. This one is a slightly stronger track, while still maintaining a similar texture to the other song. There are some exceptionally meaty instrumental works here. The number also has a segment that comes across almost like modern progressive rock.

Certainly the most persistent references to Lovecraftian mythos to be found on *Imaginos* come with the song "In the Presence of Another World." Several lines seem to link fairly directly into the imagery and creation of H.P.L. "In the promise of another world / A dreadful knowledge comes / How even space can modulate / And earthly things be done"[5] certainly has much of the texture of Lovecraft's overall body of work, and space modulating fits in well with many of his themes of the stars and space and their impact on Earthly outcomes. The following lines found near the end of the song could be seen to refer to Cthulhu, "Your master is a monster / Your master / Born of a yolkless egg / Your master He has dominion over animals / Your master He walks the world Entrail diviner / Your master And when the stars are right / Your master He locks the door behind the door behind the door / Your master The milky way abyss inclines."[6]

The song itself comes in with a tentative, mellower, mysterious sounding texture. The first verse is sung in balladic fashion over a haunting and distant acoustic guitar dominated arrangement. The slowly bring more elements into this progression, then shift gears to burst out into metallic power—still tempered by progressive rock like keys. The vocal arrangement on the chorus to this one is especially effective and they throw some tasty guitar work into the mix. Later a prog rock oriented bridge moves the cut onward into a spacey sort of jam. This gives way to a false ending, then that spacey segment returns with some nice vocal lines (singing the "your master" part) come over the top. This is gradually reworked with more energy and power added to the mix as it carries forward. This segment is quite effective and after running through for quite some time, it serves to end the piece.

The final track to be featured on *Imaginos* that has links to H.P.L. is "The Siege and Investiture of Baron Von Frankenstein's Castle at Wisseria." Here the sole reference is another mention of "The starry wisdom." On this track the sound of thunder gives way to percussion. Then keys come over and lead the track until a meaty riff takes it from there. This one is quite metallic, and very tasty. This has an anthemic feel to it, and reminds me just a bit of Kiss at times. They drop back to a guitar jam segment later, and then launch into a fast paced soaring jam. From here the cut eventually moves back to the riff driven section that preceded it. It turns very metallic and dramatic later, running through some rather neo-classical segments. Then the music shifts towards more powerful progressive rock with a new energized vocal arrangement and guitar excursions taking it. As this carries through, the emphasis shifts to the keyboards, which begin creating neo-classically-tinged arrangements within. This takes the cut down to its eventually exceptionally gradual concluding segment.

2001's *Curse of the Hidden Mirror* disc includes the most blatant and direct link to the Lovecraftian mythos, though. It came in the form of the song "The Old Gods Return." If the title were not enough, the lyrics certainly cement the connection. "... Now is the time the old gods return / Now is the time the old gods return / Exactly when the world is not expecting it / Exactly when we're sure of ourselves / That's exactly when the old gods return / And sweep our cities back into hell..."[7] Musically the song was a fairly quirky hard rocking number, that was quite well written. With the literary bent of the band it seems likely that although these tracks are the only ones so far, they will move into Lovecraftian territory again some day—perhaps when the stars are right.

A very early entry into the Lovecraftian musical world came from a group called "The Liverpool Scene." This 1960s group were basically a bunch of beat poets with a more rock sound. Their 1969 release *Amazing Adventures of the Liverpool Scene* included the track "2 Poems for H.P. Lovecraft." With a title like that it would be hard to miss the links to the author, but the lyrics spell them out even more clearly.

> Miskatonic river / Flowing through a landscape that is always evening / Accusing eyes in the empty streets of Innsmouth / Strange movements out on the reef / Tumuli on hilltops / Trembling in the thunder / Behind the gambrel roofs of Arkham / 'In his house at R'lyeh / Great Cthulhu sleeps' / amid / alien geometries / perspectives / walls shifting as you watch them / slumbering / in the Cyclopean dripping gloom / waiting to wake like Leviathan /when his children shall call him.[8]

Australian rockers Jo Jo Zep and the Falcons, formed in 1976 released one Lovecraft inspired song, "Cthulhu."

Alternative rock/post punk band The Fall were formed in 1977 in England. They have released one Lovecraft oriented song during their long career, "Spector Vs. Rector" from the 1979 album *Dragnet*. The link here is quite minor, though, simply the usage of the name "Yog Sothoth" in the lyrics. The music on this one is really quite odd, coming across at first as a stripped down hard rock, garage band sound. As it carries forward there are moments that call to mind 1970s hard rock, but also elements of The Knack's "My Sharona." All of it, though is with a nearly spoken, shouted vocal. This track definitely isn't for everyone. It very much has a decidedly stream of consciousness approach to it.

Browne Jenkyn is a Celtic band that pays tribute to Lovecraft in many ways. First, of course, is the name of the band – albeit misspelled from the Lovecraftian character. Looking around at their website it also becomes obvious that they have Lovecraft ties due to all the graphics and other elements that come into connection with his work. And, according to band member Del Merritt, they are the only group to ever record the one song that H.P.L. himself wrote. He explains it in the following way:

> The only Lovecraftian song we have recorded is the one he wrote. It appears in the story "The Tomb." We call it "Fill up Your Glass" and wrote music for it to sound like an old drinking song. We couple it with a traditional Irish tune called "Morrison's Jig." I have written other mythos-connected songs, but we haven't recorded them yet.

In the story where it appears Lovecraft introduces the song with the following sentence. "One morning at breakfast I came close to disaster by declaiming in palpably liquorish accents an effusion of Eighteenth Century bacchanalian mirth, a bit of Georgian playfulness never recorded in a book, which ran something like this:"[9]

The lyrics to the song begin with the following verse:

> Come hither, my lads, with your tankards of ale / And drink to the present before it shall fail; / Pile each on your platter a mountain of beef / For 'tis eating and drinking that bring us relief: / So fill up your glass / For life will soon pass; / When you're dead ye'll ne'er drink to your king or your lass![10]

As might be expected (or perhaps not) this is a fairly standard Celtic drinking song based on acoustic modes. It's fun and very traditional. It sounds like it was recorded in a small pub in the days of old.

Merritt also revealed that, 'If you're interested, there is a sea chantey I wrote about "The Shadow Over Innsmouth.' My other band the Sea Dogs (which sings traditional chanties and sea songs—go figure) performs this song."

Speaking about writing music to suit Lovecraftian themes, Merritt had this to say:

> Working in a traditional music field (in this case Celtic/British) your options are kind of limited to the capabilities of acoustic instruments. I want my songs to sound as if they could have been written centuries ago, albeit by someone perhaps less than sane. Dark, rustic moods pervade much of our music to begin with, so Lovecraftian themes fit right in. Dissonant chords and slightly "improper" note patterns can add the feeling of insanity or otherworldly inspiration. However, for the songs which I have sent you ("Fill Up Your Glass" and "Innsmouth Town") the words are the connection rather than the music. On "Fill up your glass" Lovecraft created a very convincing 18th century-style drinking song, so I tried to write appropriate music for the period. He did an excellent job recreating the structure of songs from that era and I wasn't about to mess it up.

He said that he feels what Lovecraft has to offer music is, "imagination, one of the things lacking most in today's music." He further explains it in this way:

> Lovecraft's stories make you think, and not necessarily the way you've been told to. That's an excellent lesson for musicians and songwriters. Conceptually, of course, he gives lyricists a whole realm of material to write about that strays from typical themes of love or reminiscence found in most music. Cryptic lyrics and mysterious, ominous sounds are far more interesting.

He had even more to talk about when asked about what drew him to H.P.L., and what has kept him a fan.

> I have always been interested in folklore and mythology, especially the darker side (this will happen to any young imaginative person growing up in a state abounding in legends of its own "official demon"). Reading horror tales as a kid you inevitably come across H.P. Lovecraft, usually "The Dunwich horror" (which appears in so many horror compilations). Noticing his very effective use of folklore and myth, I felt like I had discovered a world where I belonged. Inside every dark crop of trees there were satyr-like beings, graveyards were passages to fantasylands and every abandoned house held a story of secret cults or unfathomable creatures waiting for me to peek through the window. Though I am much older, I am still drawn to those same things (only a person with a little kid trapped inside would name his band after a witch's familiar). Reading Lovecraft can still make me feel like a kid being dared to peek through the window of an ancient, decayed house. How cool is that! Very few authors can do that for me.

Merritt says that his favorite Lovecraft stories are "The Rats in the Walls," "Dreams in the Witch House," "The Cats of Ulthar," "The Unnamable," "In the Vault" and *At the Mountains of Madness*.

Famlende Forsøk is a Norwegian trio who have a sound that is nearly impossible to categorize. The group has many Lovecraft influenced works. In fact their disc *One Night I Had A Frightful Dream* contains only one track whose lyrics are not from written by the author. That track, though, is actually an original composition speaking of Lovecraft. *The Return of the Monster Attack* album also includes a track, namely an extended reworking of "Cthulhu Lives" that takes its inspiration from H.P.L.

Hans Christensen details the band's adaptations of Lovecraft creations by saying the following:

> Lovecraft writes very little about music. I do not think he cared much about it at all. "The Music of Eric Zann" describes discordant violins. When we started in '88 we used samples of sounds he describes—night ravens in "The Dunwich Horror," whales in "The Shadow Over Innsmouth" (sounds from the sea deep), dripping of water in "At the Mountains of Madness" (deep cave like), human voices in "The Festival" and so on. We did some concerts and demos, and people thought they sounded very much alike. So we decided to add arrangements of Arabic sounding chamber music, a bit like Univers Zero or Third Ear Band. Only two tracks succeeded in this, "The Festival" and "At the Mountains of Madness." The LP is mixed on computer-and we used a lot of electronic sound manipulations.

> We have used a lot from the mythology of *The Necronomicon*, his greatest invention to my mind, also a few more romantic shorter poems and a letter. The last track is my tribute to Lovecraft-written in Norwegian and translated into English. The vinyl version is issued on a German psychedelia label, probably the wrong market. It has sold poorly, 200 copies out of 500 pressed. Lovecraft was a dilettante and amateur, so are we.

He further describes his feelings about H.P.L. in the following way, "I like his ideas. I think he sometimes is a terrible writer technically, but he captures a mood, maybe because he lived in fear—close to madness. Others in the band think he is a very good writer."

The first of the discs we'll examine here is *One Night I Had A Frightful Dream*. The music is quite weird and spooky, but also very cool. They include both organic and electronic sources in producing their soundscape. Brian Voth (Fireaxe—see page six) guests on this disc.

This opens with "Supernatural Horror In Literature." Weird sounds begin the cut in ambient ways. This backdrop is ever so slowly built upon. A thesis that H.P. Lovecraft wrote by the same title is read over top of this background. This is quite interesting. The backdrop is a melancholy sedate creeping music. Bass guitar comes in to end it.

More weird keys start "The Dunwich Horror" and form both the background and insect like electronic chirps. Then a mellow soothing melody emerges over top. This has another spoken recitation taken from Lovecraft's writings. Cacophonic piano eventually takes it, feeling both playful and scary, while other musical elements foretell doom. This turns into a RIO (a free form jazz like style of progressive rock known as Rock In Opposition) like jam for a short time, and then ends.

Noisy weirdness makes up the backdrop to "The Shadow Over Innsmouth."

"The Gardens of Yin" is the next track, and water coming down starts it, then pretty keys enter. This backdrop serves to create the scenario over which the reading plays. This is one of the most effective cuts on the album.

Ambient keys and a mournful sax serve as the accompaniment for this reading, "Dream-Quest of Unknown Kadath."

"The Festival" follows that one in sequence. This one comes in with the weirdest elements of all, building a mellow melody that feels both pretty, but also otherworldly. It gradually builds into a dramatic and very well fleshed out song. This is another standout. Violin and flute play over the top of this melancholy cut. Eventually the pace ramps up to a nervous pattern, moving steadily faster and faster. It drops back to near atmosphere for the closing line.

Weird effects start "Al Azif," joined shortly by flute. The cut begins building, but only a little. This one is another that is very weird. It gets very noisy is it carries on.

A feeling of impending doom comes in with the ambient sounds of "The Ancient Track." This again builds only a little, but is an effectively creepy piece of atmosphere. This eventually gets louder, but the effect is of an ever-closing atmosphere of fear, but also wonder. Eventually it gives way to a new movie soundtrack type melody, but this only stays for a short time, instead dropping back to near silence to gradually end.

"At the Mountains of Madness" is up next. Sound effects start this and plaintive violin wails come in over top. Other instruments throw hints of a melancholy melody that never full comes in. Instead, it drops back to only sound effects for the backdrop of the first reading. Then some more melody emerges after the voice retreats, building gradually, but dramatically. When the speaking returns the melody lines remain seeming almost to seek to quiet the speaking. This is another standout track.

Sci-fi like sound effects conjuring up pictures of a flying saucer, begin

"A Gentleman From Providence," then eventually disappear. Ambient sounds take over and barely accompany the recitation at first. This eventually builds up as it carries on, becoming more and more threatening. Weird as it is, this one is very cool. The sounds eventually take over and begin to resemble those that started it. They crescendo and a guitar "laugh" enters and echoes to end the piece. This is the only lyric not written by Lovecraft, but rather written about him.

From *Return of the Monster Attack*, "Cthulhu Lives!" starts with weird horror movie type sounds. The voice comes across as the sounds become even more twisted. This thing wanders through eccentric sounds of odd spoken words and waves of nearly noise-oriented sound. The track carries on for over eight minutes and is one of the most unique listening experiences you are likely to have. The lyrics are credited to H.P.L. but from what I can tell they are just a serious of Lovecraftian names like "Nyarlathotep" and "Cthulhu.' This one isn't something you will listen to often, but it is worth checking out, even if just for its uniqueness.

An electronic artist, Matt Cece records under the name E.M. and has released two CD's thus far. Both are almost entirely influenced by Lovecraft. The first disc, *E.M. Volume I* (admittedly the titles aren't the most creative parts of these discs) was released in 2002 and features twenty one tracks—fifteen of which are inspired by H.P.L.

The second cut on the CD is the first with Lovecraft tendencies. It is "Oylath-Leen." Like all of the material here, this is instrumental. There isn't a lot of music present, instead the track focuses more on waves of what might be considered sound effects and noise.

The two pieces which come next are related. They are "Celephais I" and "Celephais II." The first one is essentially more of the same type of material that made up the first previous number, with perhaps a bit more drama in the mix. There are some sounds on this one that lead one to think of the theme song to the Dr. Who television series. Also, there are moments where you might imagine that you are hearing voices. This one gets pretty weird at times.

At right around five minutes in length, "Celephais II" is the longest track on the disc. It starts with some white noise, feedback type sounds that are a bit hard to take. These seemingly rise and fall with other elements emerging in the backdrop. It turns more towards pure noise later, but then shifts completely for a moment into some of the most musical sounds of the CD. This then gives way to a short respite of silence before more of the noisy elements return to repossess the track. It runs through like this for a time, and then drops to more sedate science fiction oriented sound effects.

"Kaman-Thah" is up next. In many ways it is the most musical piece thus far. There are still plenty of elements of science fiction noise like sounds, but there are also definite segments of melodic journeying. While this is still quite strange, I find it to be amongst the most listenable material on show here. At less than two minutes, it is also very short.

After a non-H.P.L.-related piece, Lovecraftian territory is returned to with "Night Takes Hold of the Moths." Although not as noisy in its beginnings as much of the other material here, this one is perhaps darker and more dramatic. It still has only ambient textures, but this one is almost catchy in a dark, disjointed, creepy way.

"Gnophkeh" is next and this one is even more musical, albeit in a noisy, bombastic way. In some ways it feels a lot like a jazz sort of texture, but perhaps jazz on some distant world. It does drop down mid-track to more white noise, but then the bubbling sort of swirling musical lines re-emerge to carry forward.

There is another track next that isn't related to H.P.L.'s work, but then the track is regained with "Ngranek." Some extremely dissonant, but still almost beautiful noise starts this, feeling a bit like feedback. As it carries upward this is both jarringly painfully and strangely pretty. This is a short and unusual track.

Next on the agenda is "Mutation and Madness." This comes in feeling a bit like a surf guitar maelstrom. It's sort of like the distant sounds of some kind of Hendrix guitar fest run through a buzz saw. At about halfway through its length it shifts into a less musical, more noise oriented zone. It kind of wanders a bit from there, moving along into what sounds like an explosion at one point. This one is definitely strange, but also rather intriguing. It is one of the more effective pieces on this CD. The track that follows it is not related to Lovecraft's works.

The next Lovecraftian number on this CD is "Hatheg-Kla." (Not to be confused by the track from Bal-Sagoth; they are just sharing the title.) This one seems rather tentative at first with fairly sedate waves of sound being woven around one another. Then pieces of noise emerge to shatter the relative calm. Eventually just odd sounds gives way to a chirping keyboard sound that ends it.

"Dry Cold Air" is next, and this one sounds rather like its title. It feels a bit like a still air that just sort of hovers about. You can almost see your breath hanging in the midst of this piece. Some of the keyboard textures make one think of the sounds of the wind circling about. Another non-Lovecraftian piece follows this one on the disc.

Sedate and rather pretty (yet mysterious) tones begin "Tanaria." It stays in this general format for quite some time, but eventually a glaring, screeching sound takes it. Then just textures that feel like the wind end the composition.

"Magah Birds Sing Blithely as They Flash Their Seven Colors to The Sun" is next and it is one of the most dramatic pieces on show here. While it still remains fairly rooted in atmospheric noise-like territory, there are some definite moments of melody and the general texture of the piece is quite interesting.

The next cut is "Cataclysm." This one is rather bothersome to me. While the general elements of the track are not that different from a lot of the material here, at times it feels like it is stuck in some endless loop. Still, a later segment feels a bit like the cackling of some mad type of bird. After this it moves out into some rather creepy, but more melodic textures. There is still enough noise and weirdness there to make it seem like some alien landscape, but there are elements of melody in the mix, too.

"Baharna" comes in with layers of feedback and echoey textures. It works along these lines, setting up layers of call and response type feedback loops. I don't know that anyone would accuse this sound experiment of being "music," but it is actually rather interesting.

The final Lovecraft excursion on this CD comes in the form of "Qoth Nargai." It seems to flow straight of the chaos of the previous cut and is essentially a one-minute onslaught of weird sound textures like we heard in that number.

E.M. Volume II was released in 2004. This time out of twenty-three songs only ten were infused with Lovecraft inspiration. The opening cut is the first of those, and is entitled "Partially Reconditioned." After the previous disc it should be no surprise that waves of odd keyboards make up the textures of this track. This doesn't really go far, instead just laying down lines of ambient sounds and tones. The next cut on the disc is not related to Lovecraft.

"Hunger of Insects in Dry Places" is the next cut on the disc that has ties to the author. It comes in rather tentatively. The sounds here feel a bit like tuned percussion at times. This one is an interesting paradox, feeling both organic and synthetic at once. It is also the most "musical" piece from E.M. to this point. Several non-Lovecraft related tracks follow this one.

"Kuranes" is the next piece on the disc with ties to H.P.L. It starts with a surging, swirling sort of science fiction sound, much like a force field or something in an old sci-fi movie. Eventually melody comes in, but very far back in the mix, almost inaudibly. This one ends quite abruptly.

Seeming to come straight from the sudden conclusion of the last number,

"Gnana" comes in with a very pretty, but hauntingly frightening sound. This is certainly the most effective musical piece from E.M. so far. This feels like it could be part of a soundtrack to some horror film. It's sedate, but dramatic. There are several more non-Lovecraft related tracks after this one.

The next composition on the album which has roots in the works of H.P.L. is "Sung In Clear Accents." A pretty flowing keyboard line begins this in dark, melancholy ways. It moves through in this way for a while then eventually becomes noisy and rather cacophonic for a time. Then it drops back to the layers of sound that started it.

While the next few cuts are not related to the author, once "Nature's Gift Valley" kicks in, we are in for several tracks that have their inspiration in H.P.L.'s work. The cut comes in with a noisy chiming, a bit like tolling bells. Other elements enter to accompany this sound, but generally this texture remains in control. It doesn't wander far, but instead lays down a solid layer of texture and doom. Later it transfers the control from the bell sounding keys to more atmospheric ones.

Spacey waves of tentative keyboard tones begin the next one. "Not An Exit" is about three-minutes of this sort of atmospheric sounds. It's actual more effective than that description might make you think it would be.

"The Shocking Truth" comes up from the last piece with even weirder tones and sound effects. This is strictly textural and ambient in its approach. It feels to me like something that might have been in the soundtrack to *2001 A Space Odyssey*.

The final Lovecraft related track in this series is "Picture-Perfect." More musical, yet still rather textural, sounds begin this one. They start to build in a dark and rather gothic approach. This one could have been in the soundtrack to a horror film. It is actually quite pretty and one of the standout numbers. While it ends this series of Lovecraft related pieces, there is still one more composition on the disc that ties into H.P.L.'s work.

After several non-Mythos associated pieces, "Tekeli-Li" enters to end the disc. This is the most intriguing piece from E.M. It has a lot of beauty, but also a sense of mystery and darkness. It is a backwards tracked piece of keyboard experimentation. Even so, it manages to bring in a good amount of melody and musicality.

Cece describes the process of creating these two CDs this way:

When I did *E.M. Volume I*, it was mostly experimental. I had just bought some new synths and wanted to play with them, get some new sounds. But the first few recordings turned out a lot better than expected. At the time I was on one of my yearly H.P.L. binges and had just finished reading Dream Quest [*The Dream-Quest of Unknown Kadath*] for the first time. That story and others were in my head, which created something that spilled out into those recordings. I went back and read Dream Quest again. It was easy for me to match emotions from the songs with sections of the story.

When I got around to putting *Volume II* together, I wanted to expand. I wanted to create something that was a little more accessible to the average listener—cleaner and not as raw as Volume I, but still having the general sense of dread and horror to shine through the sounds. So I picked up the books again.

Of the appeal that Lovecraft's work has towards the creation of music, Cece had these things to say:

H.P.L.'s stories are about the darker side of humanity, a side which not many like to think about or even acknowledge. But reading his works and confronting that dark side on paper has given us insight into ourselves. Influence and creativity work hand in hand, and his works have helped me to create something tangible that I enjoy listening to and that holds a lot of meaning for me. Maybe E.M., and other H.P.L.-inspired music can do the same thing—open people's minds and show them something about themselves that they wouldn't have seen otherwise.

Cece lists his favorite Lovecraft stories as *The Dream-Quest of Unknown Kadath*, "The Shadow Out of Time," "The Dunwich Horror," *At the Mountains of Madness*, "The Shadow Over Innsmouth," "The Temple," "Cool Air," "The Thing on the Doorstep," and "The Color Out of Space." He adds, though, "Those are the first that come to mind—so many good ones." When asked about his first introduction to H.P.L. he said, "Growing up, I was always a fan of fantasy/horror/sci-fi, and after I was introduced to the work of H.P.L. through a friend in high school, it quickly became an obsession." He continued by saying the following:

The man had such a command over the English language that you notably feel every single thing that goes on in his stories. The fear of the unknown, the sheer panic and terror... And not only this, but year after year I find myself picking up the books and re-reading them, still experiencing the same emotions, finding more and more metaphors that relate to our own fears even now, nearing a century after these stories were written.

A project with a similar musical style is AKLO. This one is another one man "band," that man being Eric Sandberg. The disc is officially described as "Eleven tracks of atmospheric music created to invoke the themes, characters and moods of H.P. Lovecraft..." Well, if an album that is billed that way doesn't belong in this book, I don't know what would. That disc, *Beyond Madness* was released in 2005, but Sandberg is working on the follow up

which should be out either by the time this book is published or shortly
thereafter. The name, AKLO, by the way, refers to the language which is
used by priests of the Great Old Ones in rituals.

When asked about creating music that had Lovecraftian textures,
Sandberg had this to say:

> Lovecraft wasn't a huge success during his lifetime, but many people clearly
> recognized his genius. Other writers were so impressed that they often wanted
> to use his creations in their own stories. Lovecraft not only permitted this, he
> encouraged it.
>
> Lovecraft still inspires countless writers to pick up where he left off and
> expand upon the themes he gave us. And that's exactly what I want to do--but
> with music instead of words. I want to explore the moods and emotional tones
> springing from the Lovecraftian mythos, and hopefully build on them as well. I
> want to create music that is dark, lush, atmospheric, claustrophobic, dreamlike,
> unnerving, mind-expanding—in short, music that fits the same description as
> Lovecraft's writing. I let these sensations be my guide. When I play the music
> back and feel something akin to what I feel while reading Lovecraft, I know I'm
> on the right track.

When confronted with the question of what he feels Lovecraft's work has to
offer the world of music Sandberg said this:

> Lovecraft's work practically screams to be interpreted musically. It invokes
> such powerful atmosphere, mood, and feeling--things music is ideally suited to
> convey. Lovecraft, even with his mastery of language, repeatedly plays with the
> idea that some things can't be expressed in words. It's only natural for
> musicians to want to try expressing them in their medium.
>
> On top of this, there are the things Lovecraft offers to all our art and
> culture: his compelling visions and ideas, such as the way he casts the universe
> as hostile and, by human standards, insane. Concepts like this lend themselves
> richly to music as well as every other medium, and it's easy to see why he has
> such a lasting influence on the world's creativity. Isn't it the psychically
> hypersensitive "artists and poets" who pick up on the brainwaves emanating
> from the sleeping Cthulhu?

Sandberg spoke about what drew him to H.P.L. and kept him as a fan in the
following way:

> The thing I associate with Lovecraft more than any other macabre writer is a
> sense of astonishment. His stories don't merely disturb, they amaze.
>
> When I first discovered Lovecraft, I had an immediate sense that this was
> something huge. At the time I had very limited access to his work or
> information about him, so it seemed like it was an immense dark mystery
> waiting to be delved into. But even now, with all his work on my bookshelf and

more online information than I can read, I still feel like I'm scratching the surface. Which is probably as Lovecraft would have it. He built mysteries into his work that just refuse to be solved.

Another reason Lovecraft stays fresh is that his stories are not just fiction. The specifics are fiction (Cthulhu, *Necronomicon*, Innsmouth, etc.), but the stories imply new ways of looking at our universe that are more like philosophy or psychology. For instance, a story like "The Call of Cthulhu" says that as humans we can no more understand our universe than a spider can understand the soda bottle it lives in. Not something we like to think about much, but it's undoubtedly true.

Sandberg lists his favorite Lovecraft tales as "The Shadow Over Innsmouth," "The Thing On The Doorstep," "From Beyond," "The Colour Out of Space," "The Festival," and, "of course, 'The Music of Erich Zann.'" Looking to the CD it does share some territory with E.M. Certainly the music is dark and textural and basically all instrumental. I would have to say that this rises more up towards the level of "real" music rather than atmosphere. It also probably can be seen to share some musical ground with Nox Arcana at times, and I would see this as a good companion to Nox Arcana's *Necronomicon* album in terms of playing one after the other. Although, I'd probably throw this one on first because it might pale a bit in comparison to that masterpiece.

It opens with a track called "Intro." I suppose that's rather appropriate. So is the music on this one, which essentially sets a tone for the rest of the disc. It is composed of waves of keyboards layered atop one another in a dramatic and mysterious montage of sound. There is really no one predominate musical motif here, but just a series of atmospheric elements to create a mood. This essentially leads directly into the next number.

"The Lurking Fear" comes next and starts with a short audio clip of a man talking about the emotion of fear. Then a persistent pounding begins along with waves of keyboards that are both pretty and disquieting. This is a very effective effect of being both beautiful and frightening. The spoken word sound bite shows up again later as this drops towards space music. Echoey waves of sound seem to compete with that pounding backdrop in a rather psychotic tapestry that also has more elements of spoken sound bites. This one doesn't go far, but the emotional effect it has on the listener is powerful. Sandberg says of this one, "The quotes in 'Lurking Fear' are the opening lines from Lovecraft's essay 'Supernatural Horror In Literature.' I processed it to sound like it might be a recording left over from Lovecraft's time, or even Lovecraft's own voice, but, sadly, it isn't."

"Rue D'Auseil" takes its name from the street on which the building where Erich Zann held his musical vigil was said to exist. The sounds of wind and keyboard elements begin this. Then, appropriately, a violin like sound (it might be processed violin, but I'd guess it's keyboards) starts to weave a melody. This fights for control with other sounds and a swirling wave of violin like texture add a psychotic, urgent, nervous texture to the track. This one is definite change of pace and one of my favorite numbers on the disc. It drops back later to just the wind then keyboards gradually begin a chiming sort of texture that rises up from this. Then after a time the original tones return to carry the piece forward and eventually end it.

Next up is "Brain Cylinder." This cut starts very gradually with just spacey keyboard tones making up the early segments pretty well unaccompanied. After a time, though hints of melody come across. These are delivered in the form of more keys that weave a dramatic and frightening, almost oppressive texture. About two minutes in a new noisy sound that feels a bit like an old sci-film representation of a computer shows up. This doesn't stay around for long, though, eventually leaving just the atmospheric type textures that started it. However, those "computer" sounds return at points, but not with the sort of prominence they had before. The title, of course, refers to the devices in the story "The Whisperer in the Darkness."

Referring to the cult discovered in "The Call of Cthulhu," "Swamp Cult" begins with sounds that one might hear in a swamp. Insects and other atmospheric tones seem to fight for control of the piece. Eventually, though, chanting in the form of processed loops emerge. Then the track begins to take on a techno sort of approach as noisy percussion and harder edged sounds begin to show themselves. This beats and pounds for a time before it returns to the modes that began it. There are more weirdly processed vocals later, and eventually the pounding returns, but not so cacophonic. A short percussive, rather chaotic segment ends it.

The sixth piece on the album is entitled "Exham Priory." It takes its title from the building in which "The Rats in The Walls" takes place. An electronic percussive sort of sound begins this one and starts a nervous sort of pounding building sound. Waves of techno like keyboards flirt over the top. This grows gradually on these elements, but then drops to just a percussive sound. Then more noisy keys in kind of a swirling pattern (probably to represent the sounds of rats scurrying about) enter, but eventually this moves back to the sounds that preceded it.

The oddest number on show here, "Tillinghast's Notebook" comes next. This one has an oddly processed spoken voice set over the top of weird and rather nervous sounding atmospheric keyboards. This one sets an intriguing mood, but is very strange. It does take on more musical elements at points, but is just plain weird. The title is derived from the story "From Beyond" where the main character is Crawford Tillinghast.

Next up is "Yuggoth." A dark, ambient, mysterious tone begins this and very gradually the piece starts building on that foundation. This is another very odd one with just varying elements of textural keys and sound effects in seemingly random patterns making it up. While odd, I would say that it doesn't rise quite to the level of strangeness that the previous one did.

Taking its name from a location of "The Horror at Red Hook," "Red Hook Alley" is the next song on the CD. The opening elements of this one, with its slow sludgy deep textures (along with dripping water) remind me a bit of a track that I doubt anyone reading this book has ever heard. I once did a series of three songs based on a bass guitar solo that I played. Loaded with echo and distortion and dropped to half speed the sound was very similar to the deep tones achieved on this. I'm not sure if that is how he obtained that texture, but I wouldn't be surprised if it was. In any event, Sandberg eventually pulls this sound far into the backdrop and then brings across what feels like a saxophone (but might be keys) to create a jazzy sort of tone, but still with a very dissonant, dark and creepy texture to it. This track, while definitely high in the weirdness quotient, is one of my favorites on the disc.

"Nyarlathotep" is the next one on the album. That title should be no stranger to anyone who has read along this far, since that it an entity that has been mentioned many times previously. White noise sort of sounds begin this and rise up (along with a rhythmic sound that really couldn't be called percussion) ever so slowly. After a time, though a new rhythm pattern that almost feels a bit funky comes in amidst the weird keyboard layers. As electronic fast paced lines of keys begin to dominate, this feels just a bit like a darker Kraftwerk. This piece never moves far from these roots, instead working within that motif to create varying textures as the track moves on.

The disc closer shares its name with Cthulhu's home, "R'lyeh." This is not a very dynamic piece, but is quite powerful nonetheless. It is pretty, but still dark and mysterious. It does manage to convey a sense of majesty that one would expect. This one is without question one of the strongest pieces on show here, and for that reason makes a great disc conclusion.

The Unnameable is an Australian group that is composed of two gentlemen, Clinton Green and Andrew McIntosh. Their music fits somewhat into the same field as the last couple acts, but they lean perhaps more heavily on sound effects and ambience. They also seem to have a healthy dosage of space rock—well at least the space part—in their arsenal. As those last couple entries all their music is strictly instrumental. I suppose strictly isn't exactly accurate as there are occasional voices, just nothing lyrical at all. In any event, both Green and McIntosh were kind enough to share their views about creating Lovecraft based music and about Lovecraft's work in general. In terms of what methods they use in creating Lovecraftian textures, McIntosh had the following to say:

> Lovecraft's stories all seem to be ultimately about despair. The only time I've read about a happy ending that I remember is *The Dream-Quest of Unknown Kadath*, which is more a fantasy than horror. For the most part, there are no happy endings unless you count mutating into a sea creature that never dies, worships Cthulhu and tries to breed shuggoths like at the end of "The Shadow Over Innsmouth" as good (it'd suit me). So I would say that "a Lovecraftian texture" is one of unrelieved misery. We've managed to do that by making our sound dark, sullen, and mainly unpleasant. In a lot of ways to really get the full feeling of one of Lovecraft's stories into sound you'd want to start with a pretty nasty, threatening sound and build it up into an orgasm of despair. We tend to be a bit more restrained with that, although there could be exceptions (like with the concept we're working on at the moment).

While Green has a similar take, he has his own way of describing it. "The whole concept of the band is to create music or soundtracks suitable for Lovecraft stories. We had heard other Lovecraft tributes, which usually consisted of cheesy heavy metal. We both came from drone/noise music backgrounds, and thought threatening dark ambient soundscapes would be more suitable." Green had this view of what Lovecraft's works can offer to the world of music, "What I personally like about Lovecraft is the atmosphere he creates—dark, brooding, hints of unseen threats. Lovecraft is all about atmosphere. We try to create that atmosphere with sound." McIntosh had more to offer on the subject too:

> … just the imagery and the creatures. The problems here are how seriously do you want to take it, and what kind of music you like to do. If you were into rock or pop you might have a bit of fun poking fun at it (there is in fact a fellow from Singapore who does folk music with some rather funny Lovecraft lyrics [note he is referring to a filker—see the next chapter] if you're dead into darkwave or extreme metal you could make the whole concept behind Lovecraft's writings your life's work. We tend to lean towards taking the idea seriously as far as creating our sound is concerned and somewhat less seriously as far as promotion is concerned. My favourite Lovecraft inspired music is Rudimentary Peni's *Cacophony*. [It's] one of my favourite albums of all time, actually.

McIntosh spoke about his introduction to Lovecraft and the lasting appeal of his work in the following way:

> The first I heard about Lovecraft was in the book *The Fantasy Book* by Franz Rottensteiner. Despite its name it tended to look more at horror writing. This

was when I was in high school and I was heavily into science fiction and Lovecraft's ideas of creatures trying to take over the world "from beyond" seemed to fit with that. These days I don't go much for it as science fiction, I prefer the horror element. I go through stages with Lovecraft. It's hard to say I'm a "fan" since I really don't care much for his writing style and his blatant racism. What I like are the ideas and the concepts and what can be done with them. I think that's why Lovecraft's work is popular with fans, as people can take it and make it their own. It's a great thing especially compared with today's "intellectual property" obsessed corporatized "culture."

In contrast, Green is taken with Lovecraft's style of writing. When asked about what drew him to Lovecraft's work, and has kept him as a fan, he said, "The horror of the unknown is of interest, and I love his arcane, eccentric prose style as well." When asked to list his favorite tales by H.P.L. he named off "Dreams in the Witch-House," *The Case of Charles Dexter Ward*, "The Colour Out of Space," *At the Mountains of Madness*, "Out of the Aeons," and "many others." His musical cohort listed his as "Probably the more well-known, longer ones like *At the Mountains of Madness*, 'The Shadow Out of Innsmouth,' and any of them connected with the Cthulhu mythos." He added, "'Dagon' is pretty good."

The first release from the group came in 2002 and had a title that certainly sounds like it could have been lifted from one of H.P.L.'s tales. That disc was *But of That, I Will Not Speak...* The first track from that release was "This, No Human Creature May Do." The opening segments of this are nothing but ambient sound effects, but after a time what sounds like a creepy Gregorian chant, but then an "oh" sound enters. This carries the track forward for a time with the elements gradually rising in volume. A couple of minutes in waves of processing begin to play on these sounds, swirling and modulating them around. It never really wanders far, but rather builds on the same patterns and themes throughout its length.

They follow that piece with "You Fool, Warren is DEAD!" You have to give these guys some kudos for that title. The title to this one is the last sentence of the story, "The Statement of Randolph Carter." The "song" itself is echoey, dark and very sparse. Truly, there is nothing here that really could be called "music." Instead they are content to create their atmosphere with varying elements of effects and the like.

Considering that the core of much of the Lovecraft Mythos is based on the idea that the underbelly of all existence is a dark and horrifying terror, I can certainly see the Lovecraftian element in a title like "Life is a Hideous Thing." It is of course also lifted directly from the opening line of Lovecraft's "Facts Concerning the Late Arthur Jeremy and His Family." This next piece on the disc is a bit more musical than the cut that preceded it, but is sort of a creepy, synthesized form of ambient weirdness. Like a lot of the other tracks by this group it never really moves far from where it began, but the number is only a little over three minutes in length, so it doesn't feel redundant or monotonous.

"Space Belongs To Me, Do You Hear?" is next in line. Odd synthesizer drops begin it, then waves of sound come over the top in a drone that feels a bit like a synthesized version of white noise. Chirping, echoey sounds eventually join in and bring Hawkwind-like textures with them, but still that rather annoying synth loop remains. This one has a rather high learning curve, and it's the one piece by a group that just doesn't really work at all for me. It's just a tough listening experience. Yet, when that synth sound goes away, it feels like someone was hitting you with a hammer and quit—there is a sense of relief. It allows you to more fully appreciate the accompanying effects sounds that remain to close out the composition.

More noisy keys start "The Orbit of Yuggoth" off, and a supersonic sort of spacecraft zooming around a science fiction film texture enters. While this one is more odd noises and sound effects, it's not abrasive like the last one was. After a minute and a half or so, some hints of more melodic sounds show up. This still builds incredibly gradually. I hear some Hawkwind leanings on this one, too. My only complaint here is that for a track that's over thirteen minutes long it tends to stagnate a bit. They could have stood to work some more variety into the cut.

With what has to be one of the longer titles I've seen in a while, "Only The Most Accursed Rites of Human Blasphemy Could Ever Have Called Him" ends the disc. This one feels a bit like the Black Sabbath feedback fest "FX" to me. While it doesn't differ much in its approach from a lot of the other material from The Unnameable, I find it to be their strongest piece. Part of that comes from the fact that there is actually music in the form of some rather plinky guitar soloing going on here, but also because the sound effects elements and other textures just seem to get better here. Don't get me wrong; this is still very odd, but it just seems to work the most effectively.

The duo released a follow up (in the form of an EP) in 2005. Entitled *Graves Are Not Harde [sic] To Digg [sic] – Nor Acids Loth [sic] to Burn*, the disc featured three new tracks. The first of these is also the most massive. It is called "The Black Gulfs of Space." Odd textures begin it in sedate, yet unsettling ways. Eventually noisier waves of textural sounds enter and this becomes a scifi backdrop sort of piece. A couple minutes in this washes away then far quieter, but still very odd, elements take its place. The tones are somewhat rambling, spacey, yet rather seductive. They start to grow very gradually. There are times when this will definitely cause one to think of the more ambient, spacey modes of Hawkwind. A bass guitar manages to bring in some serious drama in a slow echoey sort of way later. This cut is nearly twelve and a half minutes of sparse, strange, experimental exploration. While it is not extremely energized or heavy, one can certainly not consider it easy listening. Even so, I must say that it does do a good job of conveying the feeling of the title, and it would be great music to inspire nightmares if you tried to fall asleep to it. This is dark and very creepy.

"Teeth and Claws Sharpened on Centuries of Corpses" comes next. Clocking in at less than half the length of the track that preceded it, this one is a bit less disquieting in some ways. Still, it has a way of giving you the feeling of the stale air of a sealed crypt that's a bit too active. Throughout most of its length the term ambient suits it quite well. However, about five minutes in it ramps up into noisy chaos that eventually drops away to a short, quieter outro.

"If I Am Mad, It Is Mercy..." starts with actual music, feeling a bit like a combination of chamber group motifs and folk rock. While the melody that is played has a pretty texture, the performance is anything but cute. The tune remains unchanged, but the pounding performance of it, along with the weird elements that accompany it, give a definite unsettling air to the piece. After a minute and a half or so (at less than two minutes, this track is the shortest of the three) the melody line drops away and leaves just the effects type sounds to carry it to the conclusion.

Formed in Houston, TX in 1988, Pain Teens was a husband and wife duo of Bliss Blood and Scott Ayers. The two created one of the earlier blendings of goth rock and experimental sounds, making them a pioneering group in the industrial genre. They recorded several songs whose basis was rooted in the works of H.P. Lovecraft.

Blood says the following regarding the creation of these songs:

Back when the Pain Teens began, it was Scott Ayers and myself. We were pretty heavily into psycho-actives, and we were creating music that was performed during, and attempting to musically approximate, those mental states. Often it was very trance inducing because of the recurring base rhythm loop, and filled with weird noises. I turned Scott onto Lovecraft's writing, which he devoured voraciously, and we both had a weird reference point for otherworldly sounds that we were creating, such as "This sounds like The Devil's Hop Yard" or "Those sound like the mindless piping demons surrounding Cthulhu," etc. We used titles like "Brown Jenkin," "The Unnamable" (that one is especially funny, because our music was often so devoid of any type of description), "Mindless Piping," and "Innsmouth."

Actually, "Innsmouth" was a long improvisation (20 minutes or so) that we recorded one night right after Scott had read the story. When we went back later and listened to it, we realized that it was the perfect soundtrack for the events in the story, right down to the creatures chasing the narrator out of town, rising up out of the sea in unending droves...

We were sort of using his writing as descriptions of the weird, nightmarish music that seemed to be sort of a parallel to the strange places he was describing in his stories. We used lots of disembodied voices from radio and TV that, taken out of context, seemed to be descending from somewhere in the ether or collective unconscious, like the auditory hallucinations experienced by schizophrenics (Scott had two friends from down the street, sisters who he had had relationships with, who both became schizophrenic), and we had some twisted '50s psychiatry book about hereditary insanity that we were obsessed with (which parallels Lovecraft's own family and beliefs that insanity was hereditary). Scott created dozens of musical pieces every week, and Lovecraft's stories were a rich source of song titles (he wasn't particularly good at naming his creations early on). We also got inspired by M.R. James, and there's a song on our first album called "Count Magnus" which has some heavy guitar riffs.

When asked what she thought Lovecraft's writing had to offer music, Blood said this:

Well, for people like us, who were interested in similar ideas—insanity, horror, transmigration of souls, out-of-body experiences, mutations, human culture wrecked by industrialism and pollution, (we lived in Houston, of course he lived in Providence, RI, an early industrial manufacturing center and desolated by pollution many decades before other parts of the US)—he is an articulate, imaginative, bizarre genius. We found a wise storyteller who reflected our current preoccupations with a dark wit and a peculiar prescience. He knew what was happening in our present, because it had happened in his present decades before. Anyone who has a way with words like he had, even his so-called "purple prose," is so interesting to read in this day of dumbed-down language and newspeak bullshit. It's funny, reading his stories is just like stumbling into some antiquated mansion and being accosted by a weird old man with some unnerving tale to tell about murder, mayhem, forces from beyond our cosmic realm. Most older folks nowadays can only tell you about what Tom Brokaw said on "Prime Time" last night.

When asked what lead her to Lovecraft and kept her as a fan, Blood said:

I experienced death at age 6, when my little brother died (much like Lovecraft and parents' deaths during his youth). I spent time every Sunday at the graveyard with my parents, and came to feel very comfortable there, I guess because I was too little to be afraid. Then at about age 8 I saw "The Innocents," one of the best ghost story films ever made, which absolutely terrified me. I was hooked on horror stories. I also saw an episode of "Night Gallery" with the story "Pickman's Model" which I didn't connect with Lovecraft until much later—but it scared me so much I turned the TV off before the end of the story! Somewhere several years later I got a horror anthology, and the only story that really stood out for me was "Pickman's Model," at which time I ordered copies of all his books from the local bookstore. I became a lyricist and poet, and Lovecraft's language and command of imagery has kept him consistently in the category of my favorite writers.

Even Joe Satriani, one of the rock world's most highly respected and influential guitarists, has put out a nod to Lovecraft. His *Time Machine* album, released in 1993 included a song entitled, "Dweller on the Threshold." As with all Satriani's composition, the number is an instrumental. It is a frantic, slightly mysterious piece that has both decisive progressive rock and fusion elements. It features a tasty bass guitar segment that leads into a spacey break that truly feels Lovecraft oriented. Eastern tones enter after a bit, and it turns appropriately weird for a time before returning to its roots. It ends in chaos.

A band with both a convoluted history (technically we are talking about two different bands) and a hard sound to pin down is Call of Cthulhu. As you can certainly gather from their most recent name, they are fans of H.P.L. The first real incarnation of the group (there was an earlier version just called "H.P.L.") was under the name "Agony Café." It was with this moniker that they recorded their first Lovecraftian music. In the late 1980s they released one album which included such songs as "Haunted House In Arkham," "The Haunter On the Dreamside" and "In the Light of Al Hazred's Lamp." Eventually (in the 1990s) the band was stripped down to a trio format and became Call of Cthulhu.

Carl Brandt, who is one third of the outfit, shared his ideas about how he creates a musical texture worthy of H.P.L.'s legacy.

> I try to create a feeling of insecurity and paranoia. I love the idea that either you die or just go insane. Horror is much more than blood and gore, the real horror is within—in your brain. It shivers your soul and destroys you without any physical traces.

When asked about what he feels Lovecraft's work has to offer music, Brandt says, "His short stories and novels are a piece of music itself, and his poetry is suitable to put music on, I've done it several times, so I ought to know... He created an ice cold music by playing at your veins."

Brandt describes the process of becoming a Lovecraft fan in this way:

I have always been reading a lot, I learned to read when I was about 5 years old, and early I began to read, and write poetry. I just loved the French decadents like Charles Baudelaire, Arthur Rimbaud and their companions and through Baudelaire I stumbled over Edgar Allan Poe and later on H P Lovecraft. I love to take down the old books now and then and enjoy them together with a good glass of Calvados in the light of burning candles—once a romantic fellow always a romantic fellow, I guess.

In regards to choosing a favorite Lovecraft story, Brandt said, "It's hard to pick just a few. It depends on moods, but a couple of stories I do enjoy almost anytime are *The Case of Charles Dexter Ward*, *At the Mountains of Madness* and of course 'The Call of Cthulhu.'"

The song, "Haunted House In Arkham," recorded under the Agony Café banner, is a melding of punk rock and grinding heavy metal. The only real connection I can make from the lyrics is the title, which makes up the bulk of the chorus. This one is a fine example of some of the rawer hard rock that was coming out in the 1970s and 1980s. It is tasty and just rough enough to maintain a certain charm.

With the song "Call of Cthulhu," this time by the grouping that goes by the same name, the Lovecraft influence is far more explicit. In fact, as this excerpt from the lyrics shows, Brandt both captures the general concepts and moods of Lovecraft's work, but also includes a fairly accurate quotation:

My eyes glows but my sermon is cold / I do prepare for his return / The dark clergyman of the old / invocation makes the air burn / So shudder in the dawn, of the Great Old One...

That is not dead which can eternal lie / within strange eons even death may die...

Dreaming in its house in R'lyeh / great Cthulhu waits to rise once more [11]...

Musically this one probably falls closer to the punk end of the spectrum. That's strictly due to the arrangement, though because the main riff has a crunchy killer metal styling to it. The percussion here feels a bit too artificial. The vocals (spoken) are also a bit on the harsh side and a bit too far up in the mix. Still, the cut does have its own particular charm and definitely works well, given the strength of the subject matter.

Another song by this incarnation of the outfit that draws heavily from the source Lovecraft is "He Who Whispers In The Dark." From the opening line, "Nyarlathotep; I'm the last in this crawling chaos,"[12] it's obvious from whence the lyrics come. It certainly doesn't end there, either. As it carries on, it seems as though each verse has its own particular Lovecraft reference. As an example here is the next one that doubles somewhat as a repeated (but altered) chorus. "You can hide try to run / Step inside try to shun / From the shadow out of time, out of time."[13] A later verse includes these words, "Shub Niggurath, the black goat from the woods with a thousand young."[14]

Of these songs, I think I like this one the best. Some of the vocals are in the spoken style of "Call of Cthulhu," but most of them are closer to what you might come to expect from The Sex Pistols, but cleaner in terms of production. It doesn't suffer from the percussion issues that "Call of Cthulhu" did, and at times the spoken word segments remind me a bit of Alice Cooper. It is a rather odd, but also quite fun rocker that even shows off some Hawkwind-like tendencies at times.

Unquiet Void is the working name of the musical artist Jason Wallach. He has been operating under that moniker creating dark, ambient instrumental sounds. With his 2004 disc *Poisoned Dreams*, he has turned his attention to Lovecraftian themes. The entire disc is composed of music meant to create a soundtrack to the author's work.

Wallach spoke of his interest in Lovecraft in the following way:

> In the 1980's my stepmother rented *Re-Animator* shortly after it came out on DVD. The movie really blew my mind at that time, it was so strange, disturbing, and funny. Then my brother and I saw *From Beyond* and I had to know who the hell was writing this stuff, it had such an intelligent foundation. Well come to find out that the stories were far more interesting and far more inspiring. I also like the fact that Lovecraft points out, through his work, a lot of logic and didn't waste time with romance in horror and all that jazz... the brother kept it real. I like the fact that he points out that no one is ever safe because anything can happen to anyone, anywhere at any time. Look at 9/11 for example, those people could never have predicted that was going to happen but it did and nothing could stop it. His ambiguity and descriptiveness, simultaneously, really disturbs you and keeps you on your toes. I like that a lot about his work.

He also says this about Lovecraft's draw to musicians:

> I think that Lovecraft's writing has such a wealth of inspiration to offer musicians and artists. There are and always will be purists that, no matter what you do, will dislike what you do and see it as blasphemy. With Poisoned Dreams I got lucky because the album is about a year old and it still gets reviewed and the reviews have been so positive. When you're dealing with something like Lovecraft, Tolkein, or even Machen, you risk pissing people off. However, sometimes it becomes an addition to that universe and becomes an inspiration in itself. People can tell when you are being sincere and when you're posturing... with The Unquiet Void I have to be sincere about what I'm feeling or it all goes south. I think that people who are truly and deeply fans of Lovecraft's work are deeply feeling and thinking individuals, some aren't, but

that really doesn't matter if the inspiration was there to help create. I think it offers a vast and rich vein of ideas that not only do you really need to understand on a deeper level than, "oh yeah, I get that," but that you almost need to believe in.

Wallach further describes the process of creating Lovecraft based music with these words:

With the creation of The Unquiet Void, in 1989 when I was 15, I intended to both use the project as a means of catharsis as well as explore my inner self and understand more about myself. I wouldn't say that I'm going for a Lovecraftian texture per se, but what happens is that the music I make, textures and all, are dependant upon what state I am in as far as my life is concerned. That's really the honest albeit simple answer to the question.

For instance, in the summer of 2000, I had what I believe to have been a nervous breakdown. To make a long story short I will say that it was the most unpleasant and ugly experience I have ever had. It was a time where I truly feared for my life and, even worse, my soul. I know that sounds corny but it's true, things got that desperate. One day I was alright and then the next I could tell something wasn't quite right though I didn't know what the hell was going on. It kind of crept up from inside and overwhelmed me—slowly at first and then suddenly. My behavior changed rapidly throughout the course of seconds and there were times I didn't know where I was or recognize my loved ones around me.

Now with that being said, once the smoke cleared enough for me to see straight I took up a job in retail. The three-year "recovery" afterwards was an uphill struggle let alone dealing with retail managers. I happened to have one who just loved power and loved to use it to make himself feel much more important than he really was. This guy made my life a living hell, not to mention that I was harassed by the assistant manager and it was made out to seem like I was some screwed up liar who loved to create drama which was not at all the case. I began to loathe humanity and I stayed with this company for self-discipline as I was rebuilding myself in lieu of my breakdown.

Where I am going with this is that it made me want to make all of humanity go away. About this time I became reacquainted with the writing of H.P. Lovecraft and realized that since (this was in 2002) I hadn't had an album out since 2000 that I might have a go at a Lovecraft-based album. *Poisoned Dreams* was that album and its structure was inspired by the book ending of the stories "Dagon" and "The Shadow Over Innsmouth" in Stuart Gordon's film *Dagon*. The film has some great moments in it but I was expecting something with fewer liberties taken in its adaptation, which solidified my interest in the project. However, at that time, I was unable to record on my own... so I decided to read instead. At some point during this process I decided to turn an album into a trilogy based on Lovecraft's theme of humanity being insignificant in the grand scheme of the universe.

I read and re-read those two stories (I had read "...Innsmouth" many years prior) and soaked up the details. I was all over the net searching for images and information, anything that would tell me what the hell it was all about. The beautiful thing about it all was that with all of my searching and with all of the information I read, it still didn't tell me much. I think that unsettled me quite a bit and I loved the fact of that. I began reading Lovecraft like crazy and I realized ambiguity was his style of writing making the fiction far more disturbing than anything I have ever read. I loved his ideas and his themes... speaking of which, I realized I had to find out who Lovecraft really was as a person. That search led me to a book by S.T. Joshi which was a biography on Lovecraft, and it blew my mind. I couldn't believe that someone's disturbing fiction was so inspired by his own life—that shocked me. So I spent the greater part of two years reading about his life and re-reading his stories to soak up detail. Looking back I guess you can say that's what inspired the textures of the music. Wanting to alleviate my own despair and explore Lovecraft's mythology at the same time, his life and stories just provided the structure to work within which was both liberating and stressful.

When asked about his favorite Lovecraft stories, Wallach says that they are, "'Dagon,' 'The Call of Cthulhu,' 'The Shadow Over Innsmouth,' 'The Dunwich Horror,' 'The Whisperer In Darkness,' 'Nyarlathotep,' 'The Festival,' 'The Hound,' 'From Beyond'... and the list goes on and on."

As Wallach stated, *Poisoned Dreams* is in fact the first in a trilogy of albums. *Poisoned Dreams* is the only one that has been released to date, though. It is eight instrumental tracks that represent an uneasy (appropriate to the name that they are recorded under) disquieting ambience. The first piece on the album is entitled "A Troubled, Dream-Infested Slumber." The cut begins with sounds that feel a lot like wind in a storm, but they grow into a full tempest. Then elements resembling monstrous roaring and a tinking a bit like Pink Floyd's "Echoes" emerges. The track begins growing upward ever slowly from there, and then a crescendo of noise enters to transform it. This really feels like some sort of powerful horrifying otherworldly storm for a time. Then a growing wave of keyboard textures come over the top of this backdrop to bring in new elements. While never becoming anything really musical, this one segues directly into the next number.

"Cyclopean Monolith" comes next and starts with a lot of noisy rumblings and crashing resembling an extended lightning strike. Then it drops back to more textural atmospheric tones—not yet musical, really, but more a controlled noise pattern. Eventually hints of other worldly, rather creepy music begin to emerge over this backdrop and rise ever steadily upward. Still rather cacophonic, this has a certain emotional appeal that really needs to be heard to be fully appreciated. While it is not overly "music" oriented, it really gets under your skin. Nothing happens very fast, but it does begin to take on more musical textures later. It just sort of starts to wrap around you with a dark nature that is both beautiful and unsettling. This is no relaxing "new age" music, but still it maintains the same sort of nature as much of that genre. I would hate to fall asleep to it, though, as the dreams you would experience would certainly be (as the album title suggests) poisoned. The press material for the disc says that, "Wallach provides an instrumental accompaniment to the other-worldly aspect of Lovecraft's disturbing prose." Listening to this track, it's easy to see the truth in that statement. Much of Lovecraft's work grows in increments becoming ever more frightening with the additional layers of imagery and horrors. That is a pretty apt description of this piece of sonic story telling, too. After building for the first ten or so minutes, it seems to drop back in intensity (this one is over thirteen minutes long), but the horrors just get more pronounced as odd sounds resembling monstrous voices are brought into the picture. This is one of the strongest cuts on the disc.

The most musical tones thus far, in the form of dramatic keys that feel like the soundtrack to a horror film start the next cut, "*Necronomicon.*" They move along ever so slowly and methodically, carrying the track by themselves with waves of sound for quite some time. Hints of a percussive track emerge beneath this eventually, and then begin to become more and more pronounced. Then an echoey, distorted sound, not unlike an alien monster's growling is heard several times. Then a new rhythmic structure emerges and begins growing. This feels at once more rock music like and a bit like the ticking of a clock. This rises in an almost Kraftwerk meets punk rock texture, with even hints of mid-era Hawkwind. The keys from the opening are still present even here. This rhythm basis, it must be noted, is the most rock oriented sound we've heard thus far and it begins taking more and more control of the composition as the other elements previously introduced seem to work their way in almost a fight for dominance over the music. As the arrangement becomes more lush, it begins to feel a lot like one of the keyboard based interludes Hawkwind frequently produces. Eventually it dissolves downward to more sedate patterns as it feels like the cut is winding down to nothingness. A scurrying, scratching sort of noise remains in the background to take the number after a time to its conclusion.

"Return to Innsmouth" starts by rising up from the ambient sounds of the prior piece. It has a rainy day sound, but also waves of dark and dramatic keyboards hint at some sort of powerful horror that is about to begin. This moves slowly upward as it carries forward and the sounds of the sea join the ever more intense modes of the storm. After a couple minutes an electronic rhythm emerges to accompany what has dropped back to nearly just the storm and wave sounds. This rhythm takes control for a while with more of the keyboard textures occasionally wafting over the top of this. The main emphasis by this point is the drumming sounds and the nature noises merged together to create a unique soundscape. Later it becomes more musical, again in a pounding rhythmic jam that seems to call to mind some of Hawkwind's work to a degree. This is another track on the album that is more easily accessible and a bit more "rocking."

Wallach continues on next with "The Esoteric Order," which comes out of a lightning strike or explosion that ended the last one. A very creepy sort of breathing or snoring texture is in the background along with what sound like footsteps and more echoey sound effects. Then a spoken recitation of "In his house at R'lyeh dead Cthulhu waits dreaming"[15] comes in repeated over and over to create a chant like effect that is both creepy and extremely effective. More chant like spoken distorted vocals enter later, when the cut begins to take on a more rock oriented rhythmic texture. As this carries on with the recitations fighting with weird keyboards and sound effects for control, it turns quite rock oriented and actually almost catchy in a weird way. At about five or so minutes in, it drops back to just noisy atmosphere to carry forward. This section does get a bit tedious, but eventually other nearly musical elements begin to take it from there. For a short while this gets extremely chaotic, but then it moves back into a new take on the chanting type of themes. Percussion with only more of the odd sounds to accompany it then takes the track for a while before there are more groaning, growling sounding keys occasional showing up. Then a recitation of Lovecraft's most famous couplet is repeated over and over in this mix. Eventually rhythmic sounds with just noise type sounds take it for a while, then more chanting enters. This combination eventually ends the track and segues it into the next one.

"The Shadow Over Innsmouth" opens with the sounds of storming. Then textural sounds that are somewhat keyboard-like in texture (in fact they may be keys, but aren't easily identified as such) come over top in the form of textures. Once again, this grows gradually upward. This one doesn't move quickly at all, instead moving along with only very minimal changes. Even so, it doesn't get boring, since the sounds of the storm and other unknown horrors work to keep an uneasy and rather frightening texture to the track. Late in the track choral vocal like sounds (in fact they might be processed or sample choir voices) come in to add a drama and power to the track. It is a well-needed boost to a number that was beginning to drag a bit too much. This section serves as the outro.

Weird undersea type effects start the next number, "We Shall Dive Down Through Black Abysses." Keys come over in definite unsettling waves of sound. Then a hammering, rhythmic structure comes in, followed by more dramatic keyboards as the cut builds upward. This one becomes quite lush and is another that is almost pretty, since it is more melodic than a lot of the material on the disc. This one has a sort of majestic texture to it, but also maintains a mythical horror quality and a sense of mystery. This is probably my personal favorite on the CD. It eventually drops back to atmospheric sounds and something that feels a bit like whale song to end.

"R'lyeh Rerisen" is the final cut on the disc. It comes in with sound effects left over from the number that preceded it. Then dark, but very beautiful waves of keys come in to join this element. The sounds merge and rise in a somewhat noisy, but still quite dramatic mode until it changes gear to resemble a noisy sort of horror film soundtrack with pounding percussion serving as the timekeeper in a nervous pattern. This is a track that becomes extremely creepy in its mood. It is also one of the louder numbers on show here. It drops back to mostly just the keys late in the piece and the arrangement is both powerful and lush. This mode ends it after a while.

Forma Tadre is the name of a solo project by German keyboardist Andreas Meyer. Under this moniker Meyer has produced several pieces, which are linked to Lovecraft's work. The first of these is "Date Unknown" which comes from the *Navigator* album from 1996. It is a creepy, ambient piece. It sets an intriguing and dark tone as it begins; more energy and Eastern tones enter later, but do nothing to alter the general mood of the piece. This one gets quite powerful and feels a bit like a cross between old Gary Numan and Nine Inch Nails. This dissolves into weirdness to end.

Coming from the same disc, "Mesozoic Tree Ferns" also takes much of its inspiration from Lovecraft, albeit less directly.

"Gates" is another song from *Navigator* that has Lovecraft influences. 1998's *Automate* included the track "Dagon."

Children of the Monkey Machine was created in 1999 in Sumter, SC by Matthew Newman. After releasing several remixes of Prodigy songs to the internet, Newman followed up that same year with a four part series inspired by "The Call of Cthulhu" and other Mythos stories.

Newman lists his favorite Lovecraft story as *At the Mountains of Madness* but adds that, "I enjoyed just about everything he wrote. I've always enjoyed his poem 'Nathicana' as well." He also explained a lot about the effect Lovecraft has had on his music.

> The biggest influence his work has had on my music production has been to focus on atmosphere and the emotions portrayed in that atmosphere more so than the specific composition of melody. I think a lot of my work is most noted for the textures that compose the body of the work. At Overclocked Remix, descriptions of my arrangements often reference a "wall of sound" or "interesting static textures" (static as in white noise, not non-dynamic). The

"wall of sound" concept is really a goal I try to achieve. Many layers upon layers that build a solid sound made up of individually interesting parts, but not so chaotic that it's incomprehensible. I think trying to strike a balance between chaos and order is a Lovecraftian balance that makes things frightening. Sort of the idea of trying to wrap your head around something that's too big to understand. Once you start to understand something, you realize there is much more than you can comprehend, and that's frightening. A professor I once had said that the most intelligent thing a person can do is realizing the things that they don't know. I think that fear and horror comes from that realization. It's really humbling to begin to tear apart a concept or a perception only to realize that for all your efforts, you're only scratching the surface. That futility of understanding seems to be the heart of "Cosmic Horror," to me. Dig as deep as you want, the "cosmic universe" still won't even notice.

I might not be able to craft atmosphere so rich that it evades comprehension, but if you set lofty goals, then when you fall short you're likely to still be ahead of where you might have been if you set a goal that you knew to be attainable. I had one of those moments with a track I arranged for the "Relics of the Chozo" project—an arranged album covering the entire OST of "Super Metroid." In the original "Norfair 1" track, it's very quiet. I listened to the original, emulated, track over and over searching it for my interpretation. I was positive I was hearing fragments of melody... but when I started describing it to some other people involved in the project, no one else seemed to be hearing what I was hearing. In the very absence of sound, the atmosphere created by the game and memories of it was churning away in my brain to produce something with a life of its own. My resultant original arrangement, which was not used in the final version of RotC but can be found on OCRemix, attempted to hold on to a sliver of that atmosphere. The image I constructed for myself was little Newt, from the film Aliens, sitting in her makeshift duct-work home, waiting to die with no knowledge of Ripley coming to save her. It seemed to fit the Lovecraftian model of the absolute horror of knowing that you have been made aware of unspeakable horror, can do nothing about it, and will meet that horror yourself.

A lofty goal. Maybe I succeeded, maybe I didn't. In the end, I think it helped me produce an interesting piece. Very quiet, very brooding.

The song "R'yleh: The Dreamer Awakens" begins with very ambient sounds. Then as this movies forward, elements of a fun, bouncy electronic pattern come and go. Eventually, though, this gives way to sounds of noisy chaos, but still not extremely loud. I'm not sure I'd really call it "a song," but more of a weird tone poem.

The second section of the "R'yleh" suite is "Rebirth." This one comes in with sounds that started in that first number. As it moves on weird monster like textures come over the top. This one is another odd piece of sound textures that doesn't exactly qualify as music. It certainly is unsettling, though. While the first cut was less than two minutes, this one comes in at over four.

Next up is "Mindflare." Sound effects begin this one, and it sounds almost like waves of static and white noise, in fact at points you can hear pieces of radio broadcasts coming into the mix. Tones like tolling bells also show up on this one at points. The main theme though is in the form of odd sound effects leaning towards noise. While some points have more sedate keyboard dominated elements, there really is no main song structure and the piece just sort of feels like random strange sounds.

"Desolate" closes out the four song thematic suite. While in some ways this doesn't differ much from the others, sound effects carrying most of the piece, there are moments of definite melody that show up. This one is probably the best of the four, but still not really something you'd sit down for a relaxing listening experience. There are sound bites of recitation on this one that speak of the city of R'lyeh and the return of the Old Ones. A spoken spell is also thrown in later on the track.

A later song, "Aphexian Nyarlethotep Dreams," while having the Lovecraft tie to the title really has nothing else in common with the author. Newman, in fact, thought that the track should not be mentioned here because, "it's primarily cut-up and repasted segments from the *Quake 1* album, by Nine Inch Nails (very Lovecraft inspired on its own) and tracks by Aphex Twin's *Ambient Selected Tracks Vol 2*. I really can't claim it as an original work, and as you've said yourself, it really doesn't have much to do with Lovecraft." Since I have seen the track listed in various sources as being related to the Mythos, it seems more accurate to leave it in and let his words speak for themselves in regards to the piece.

Formed in the year 2000, the Creepniks have released one song that is based on Lovecraft. It comes from their 2005 release *Graveyard Shindig*. One needs look no further than the first verse of that song, "The Shadow Over Elkhart," to spot the links. It should be pointed out that the band hails from Elkhart, Texas.

> Well I got me a girl, a little soft in the head / Whispers "The Old Ones are a-coming!" when we're lying in my bed / Unseen forces push from unplumbed space / They get your mother and your brother and the whole damned race / Spat up on a speck in the great stellar swirl / From the womb to the tomb, I tell ya man, we're doomed[16]

Each verse is packed with ties to Lovecraft's Mythos. In fact, looking to the rest of the lyrics (as relevant as they are it seems appropriate to include all of them) it seems like nearly every line is tied into Lovecraft's works.

> She screams out "IA!," every time I go and see her / "The Black Goat of the Woods," she says, is gonna come and eat her / Well I told her that she'd yanked my crank one too many times / Then the Colour came from Outer Space and

took her little mind / I say we're little bittie bugs in a great big world / I'm gonna beat those cosmic thugs 'cause I just gotta get my girl

Cruising 'round the other night, past my neighbor Obed's marsh / I glimpsed the Crawling Chaos before it sent me through the wash / Woke up a week later in an interstellar jail / My battrachian neighbor blinked at me, said "Welcome to Hell"[17]

This starts with a tentative, twangy guitar sound that has some signs of dissonance. Slowly it is built up into a rockabilly jam with a definite dosage of retro science fiction sounds. The vocals are a screamed sort of rockabilly rant that reminds me a bit of Screaming Jay Hawkins. In fact, there's a Hawkins vibe on this one in many ways. But interestingly enough I can also hear hints of modern King Crimson. This is a very listenable piece of musical pleasure. It's creepy, but still quite fun. At close to six minutes it's also the longest piece of music on the disc.

Johnny Lockjaw, one of the members of the group, talks about the process of creating Lovecraftian sounds in general (and specifically that track) in this way:

One thing that most of Lovecraft's characters seem to share is that their sanity is torn to shreds by the incomprehensible malignance that's thrust upon them. We try to capture this ruptured psyche in musical form. A tale of madness is more tangible when told by a madman. We start with a thematic idea. Our song "Shadow Over Elkhart" is a ridiculously dumbed down romp through the Mythos as told by a man who's thrown into this situation without any knowledge of what's happening on a larger scheme. He's a pawn and he can't see outside his little box of reality. And of course he goes stark raving mad toward the end. We tried to capture the essence of such an event in the music. The cacophony of the music is meant to mirror the psychological distress the poor bastard is going through. The vocal style is a further extension of this. It's not a pretty thing, nor should it be.

When asked what he believes Lovecraft's writing has to offer musicians and songwriters, Lockjaw said the following:

Lovecraft often writes in a very lyrical style. His word usage and overall style can definitely be exploited by songwriters. Aside from the mechanics of his writing, he created immeasurable worlds for thematic and conceptual development. There really seems to be no limit to how his work can be interpreted in any medium. Music in particular is a particularly open avenue of creation, and the spectre of Lovecraft's creation leaves a pallid shadow over those foreboding lanes.

Lockjaw describes his first exposure to H.P.L.'s work and its lasting impact on him in this way:

I first got into Lovecraft after reading his name in connection with Poe when I was 10 or so. I was an avid Poe reader and naturally drawn to the strange and moribund, so when I got my hands on Lovecraft, I was naturally hooked. No writer that I've ever read has a greater ability to write of outsideness than HPL.

It's easy to pick up on Lockjaw's enthusiasm and passion for Lovecraft's work. So strong is this draw that a question like which stories are his favorites gets a longer than usual response.

I've honestly got several. "The Dunwich Horror" strikes a real nerve with me every time I read it, largely due to the remarkable similarities between the Whateley clan and a certain decadent bloodline that runs through Elkhart. It's unsettling. And that introduction really knocks me on my ass. I'm also a huge fan of "The Shadow Over Innsmouth." One of my favorite Lovecraftian themes is genealogical decay. His writings on inherited spiritual sickness and human degeneration really creep the Hell out of me.

Hip hop is probably one of the last musical realms one would expect to find Lovecraft influences, but there are at least two hip hop acts who draw at least some inspiration from H.P.L. The second of these will be mentioned in the next chapter, but here we will be examining Humanoids. They are a three-man, Australian hip hop group whose lyrics are definitely drawn from H.P.L. All three members are also fans of the writer's work. The men who compose this outfit are MC 13th Son, MC Yvern and Ray Diode. While they are currently working on their second release, this is how MC 13th Son speaks about the influences of their 2004 debut, The EP *The Adyar Sessions Vol. 1*:

[The EP] was the result of two days sifting through texts at the Adyar Library of the Sydney, Australia chapter of the Theosophical society. Combining this with an obvious appreciation for the works of the Old Gent from Rhode Island, the have created an EP of downtempo, atmospheric and concept driven hip hop.

All four tracks on the EP are said to have Lovecraftian leanings, so we'll look at each of them (which, by the way, you can hear online at the Humanoid's myspace presence). The first one is "Human Eyes That Shine in The Night." It comes in feeling a bit like an acoustic blues jam. The flow of the cut seems to keep getting cut off at a point, though, with a weird sort of start and stop texture. Eventually, though, this resolves out into something that resembles a bluesy groove. It's almost a minute before the rapping enters. This one is quite an intriguing piece, and definitely very different than American hip hop. It almost feels a bit like beat poetry at times. It drops to an ambient weirdness to end. The line from this one that would probably be of most interest to H.P.L. fans is "Roadside assistance for Innsmouth collisions."[18]

The next number from them is "Ko Coralle." The cut starts with a jazzy sort of build up that feels like it could have come from some old movie. Then it shifts gear to more traditional sounding hip hop, but still built on that old school jazz sound in the form of samples and loops. It's definitely a much more traditional hip hop sort of sound, but also very tasty. At about 3:45, though, it drops back to just ambient spacey sounds to carry forward and finally end. One pair of lines early on calls in some of the Lovecraft leanings, "'So where you boys from?' – I'm not quick with the answers. / Yvern replies coolly, 'Arkham, Sir...'"[19] I think the most telling part is a section later which seems to call in "The Quest of Iranon" (addressed in an earlier chapter).

> Hey, you boys been 'round here before"?
> Asks a toothless old man, tapping the floor.
> "Yes, a long time ago, boy this place has changed".
> "But you boys sure haven't—you still look the same!!"
> he's getting kinda worked up and people are listening.
> I play dumb; act like there's something I'm missing.
> But he says he remembers us— "explorers from Arkham."
> Wonders how we still look young; he was just a boy then.
> I take a deep breath; I'm getting twitchy too
> I look at Yvern and he's turning blue.
> This guys asks too many questions, I thought noone knew.
> Thought we left it long enough—guess we missed a few.[20]

"Rock Steady Seti" is next in line and it definitely is different than the previous two cuts. This one starts with very weird musical textures, backwards spoken words and the like. This sort of odd backdrop becomes the playground for the rap. Eventually it shifts into a little more mainstream sound, but the odd elements remain. It shifts back down later to even more strange textures. This one is definitely a science fiction feeling track. It includes the line, "it's the call of Cthulhu."[21] I never thought I'd hear that phrase from a rapper, but I like it. A wailing horn that sounds a lot like a saxophone (but I've been assured is not) comes over this later in a mournful lonely sort of soloing. This takes the cut into something that feels like a twisted jazz jam for the early section of the outro. It eventually gives way to the twisted speaking and weird sound effects that started it to actually take it out. There are a couple more lines in this one that are obviously connected to H.P.L.'s work. "I'm the lurker on the threshold, holding the key."[22] "Or is it Arkham Asylum where your dreams are born?"[23]

The closer is a bit more obviously Lovecraftian from the title alone. It is called, "Arkham, Sir." The sound of a car driving and a small boy talking about the big bang theory begins this one. Sounds like mission control on a space shot come in at some points. Then it drops off to a very artificial sounding rhythmic groove for the rap. More organic sounds are also included here for a rather retro sounding texture. Then it drops to some weirdness with backwards quick clips of spoken sound bites and other sound effects. It moves back to the earlier section, but with more an energetic and potent approach to it. Of the four cuts, I'd have to say that this one is my favorite. It has a killer texture to it. The child returns later along with what seems like the sound of the sea for a tasty nearly instrumental outro. Other than the references to Arkham, and there are a few of those, this one also includes several other lyrical nods to H.P.L. R'lyeh gets mentioned in this line, "You'll never find R'lyeh unless your feet get wet."[24] Yet, this one, "Nowadays the Miskatonic library opens up late," shows a different Mythos entry. In a line very similar to one from one of the Blue Öyster Cult songs mentioned earlier, the King in Yellow gets a mention. Perhaps this duo of lines is the most telling of the whole song, though, "Release me, this haunter of the dark / Show me your starry wisdom, your divine spark."[25]

The group have some interesting things to say about what is involved in creating Lovecraftian textures in their musical landscape. Diode said that he feels that it involves, "dusty-textured rhythms, sitting on a bed of beats like cracked-leather (I hope it's leather), each track having it's own character and hidden secrets of narrative. Glacial reverbs caress each sound, replicating eerie breathing through blocked gills, as bass lines profess an undying love for those past the grave." I don't know how it could be worded more eloquently—or at least more lyrically. According to 13th Son, "We've attempted to evoke some sort of emotional response, but this wasn't limited to creating a 'Lovecraftian' feel specifically." MC Yvern had even more to add to this concept, encompassing the concept in general and specifically as it relates to their first album and the new one that is in progress. Here are his thoughts:

> There are certain techniques acoustically of course, none of which are essential to creating a "lovecraftian texture." Most essential is awareness of a current of cosmic cycles occuring outside the music.
>
> Lyrically, in our first EP, we explored the way knowledge opened up awareness of these currents, and some ways experience questions and impelled that search for knowledge. Resonance with known explorations through history, philosophy and science; such as the burning of the library at Alexandria, anomolous cases and debates of human eyes which have a kind of

phosphorescent glow, the fibonacci sequence and spiralling forms which occur throughout various scales in nature were sourced, partly from sessions in the Adyar library. Weaving through this, tales of exploration in pursuit of knowledge; the bitter experience of "hotel innsmouth" which suggests the downward pull of evolutionary regression which dogs any being attempting to spiral outside the concerns of the ego through creation and understanding... troubled occult explorers who never age and therefore have to retire to the desert for decades and return as weary strangers to their homeland—the Lovecraftian mark of alienation of those transformed by their journey outside the concerns of human culture...

The 2nd EP, at least in this stage of its development, suggests a more chanelling approach—deliberate attunement to elemental and cosmic cycles in such a way that through resonance these cycles can be expressed. Recorded on a water access only property near a national park on the Hawkesbury River (where I'm living at the moment), musically we tried to incorporate rocks, water, soil, bone and trees from this place into the music and give it something of a ceremonial 'backwoods' aesthetic.

13th Son said that from his point of view what Lovecraft's writing brings to the table when coupled with music is, "A rich mythology to explore. There's so many different ways to interpret his themes and ideas." From Diode's point of view it is, "A way to convey a metaphysical insanity in a pop song format." Yvern put it thusly:

Lovecraft offered the possibility of awareness of vast cosmic events and interests opening out from within the slightly loosened sections of usually tightly woven cultural fabric. The usefuless of this is, as I understand it, that Lovecraftian music doesn't demand a specific texture or genre, doesn't for instance need to be "epic" or "spooky" or "violent" or "ethereal" (although it can contain all these things), but the world hinted at through Lovecraft's writings can intrude into and transform the experience of any genre. This moment of transmundane transformation of cultural reality is a challenge to produce, and a rewarding project for the alchemy of composition.

Diode shared his own history with H.P.L. in terms of what drew him to the author and what has kept him as a fan in this way, "I'm a sucker for mythos." 13th Son's explanation was a bit more extensive:

I stumbled on him by accident when I was about 14 and have been hooked ever since. I think it's the grand scale on which his tales play out that I find so appealing. It's not just about here and now, it's about histories and tales that have back stories that reach across millions of years.

As one might have guessed from their previous replies, the most extensive of all three came from Yvern. He related the following:

Initially, it was the spark of Dario's [13th Son] love for Lovecraft's world that made me want to visit. Musically and conceptually we have continued to influence each other for the 15+ years we've been writing music. Reading Lovecraft I was drawn to the antiquarian style, the humility and groundedness of containing (for the most part) a deep and complex stream of existance within the forays of individual explorations, and therefore within the realm of the everyday, opening it out for transformation.

The opening of space for imagination continues to be one of the most important and subversive activities in a material culture, and Lovecraft's gift of a world which can be explored beyond the text is a testament to the integrity of his writing and devotion to a creative exploration of being human.

Finally, when asked about their favorite Lovecraft stories, Diode listed off *At the Mountains of Madness*, "Dreams in the Witch House" and "Herbert West—Reanimator." 13th Son said, "Definitely 'The Shadow out of Time' (the first tale I read). Also, *At the Mountains of Madness*, 'The Whisperer in The Dark' and 'The Call of Cthulhu.'" Once more Yvern's answer was the most thorough of the group:

I mostly try to avoid favourites, and each journey into the mythos produces different resonances depending where I'm at at the time.

The last thing I reread was *At the Mountains of Madness* and I was impressed by way that for the human narrator fear of the Old Ones was transformed to some extent into compassion: their disatisfaction with the alienating effects of mechnical technology and their trouble with the shoggoths, who morphed according to their desires but eventually turned against them, seems to reflect a profoundly human struggle with desire and creation.

Of course, special shout outs to "The Shadow out of Time," though, for revealing sunken cities in the deserts of Australia and bringing eons old horror closer to home...

A newer entry into the Mythos music realm (in fact, by the time this book sees print, it has not yet been released) comes from the upcoming album by Asmodeus X. This group, actually just three guys, has Paul Fredric (that name might be familiar—as the band name probably is—because he was mentioned earlier with another band, Morphine Angel, in the section on Gothic music) as one third of its lineup. In that outing Fredric spoke about the creation of the song "Breakfast With Cthulhu." That, however, was just one part of what he had to say about creating a Lovecraftian texture in music. Here are the rest of his very thoughtful concepts, along with his comments about the song that will be addressed here.

Creating a "Lovecraftian sound" is no easy task, precisely because Lovecraft aspired through so much of his work to create an "other-worldly" feel. He was often most successful in this regard not so much by what he said, but by what he hinted at, and the sorts of questions he inspired in the reader. In regards to music, I think this "unspeakable" aspect is most aptly illustrated in his short story, "The Music of Eric Zann," in which the main character describes the mute violinist's playing thusly, "...the shrieking viol swell into a chaotic barbell of sound" and later, "...it was not a horrible sound, but rather an exquisitely low and infinitely distant musical note."

And then of course there is Azathoth, who is surrounded by the sounds of 'idiot pipers.' Well, just what does an idiot piper sound like?

So here is the problem—how does one create an otherworldly quality that is genuinely unsettling, using totally familiar instruments like guitars, basses, and drums? The danger in applying modern day guitar rock sounds to Cthulhu-esque themes is that the result might be more comical than frightening. At the strumming of the first distorted guitar chord, the image likely to pop into ones head is that of a sweaty longhaired guy in spandex—probably not what Howard Philips had in mind.

So there are, I believe, two directions one can go with creating Lovecraftian music: the humorous path, or the serious path. The serious path is probably more in alignment with what H.P.L. was trying to accomplish with his writing, but the humorous path can be rewarding as well. The humorous possibilities in Lovecraft are in fact well established via role-playing games and movies like *Dagon*.

This brings us to Fredric's first attempt to take on Lovecraftian themes. That was the aforementioned song by Morphine Angel, and his ideas about that were addressed in the chapter that included the coverage of that act. He continued on his quest for Lovecraftian music, though, and describes it in the following way:

As I continued to work in the music medium, I was increasingly drawn to the use of electronic instruments—in particular the synthesizer and the theremin—in my effort to express this. When we started working on Asmodeus X we finally had the opportunity to really make some progress in this regard.

And so utilizing electronics, the Asmodeus X song "Darker Shores" came much closer to creating what I would consider a serious and somber Lovecraftian texture. This song was inspired more by Robert W. Chambers and his book *The King in Yellow*, which Lovecraft acknowledged as being his main inspiration for the *Necronomicon*. While drawing on the same non-natural essence as H.P.L., Chambers' world had a poetic and dreamy quality. As terrifying as Dim Carcosa and Hastur the Unspeakable might be, there is something about Chambers' writing that is also hauntingly beautiful.

So for this track we utilized digital instruments and sequencers to try and create a non-natural core to the song, and then analog synthesizers to wrap that non-natural core in a blanket of eastern mysticism and poetic bliss. The lyrics were intentionally kept vague so as not to over-define things for the listener—rather than tell people what was going on, the aim was to inspire the listener to begin considering these notions and impressions for himself.

Looking to the track itself, the most explicit Lovecraftian lyrical links in the cut come from the first verse. "The idiot pipers' song / Sing of a forgotten race / Sleep now in the angle of six / Dreaming of a familiar face."[26] The band produces an electronic, nearly techno sort of sound. The sound is really pretty hard to pin down, though, containing elements from many varied schools of music.

With this particular track, they start off with a keyboard sound somewhere in between piano and harpsichord. This moves in a rather dissonant, but mellow melody for a time before it is joined with other instrumentation. With the dissonance and the way the layers of sound are interposed there is a really unusual swirling pattern. It's not really part of the music, but an incredibly intriguing way that the waves of sound push each other around and away. The overall effect is something I've never really encountered before. It's also a great way of creating an otherworldly texture. The vocals are a mostly spoken sort of processed format that almost feel like they are done by a computer. The whole picture of this piece is something that has similarities to other forms of music, but in many ways is a completely new beast. I truly like it a lot. It has both an entertaining quality, but also seems to open your mind to another reality. I hear waves of space rock (á la Hawkwind and others) here on the verse chorus section, which has lost most of the dissonance, but the instrumental sections bring in all kinds of other sounds. I even hear a little Gary Numan in the mix. This one is one of the more exciting and unusual, yet at the same time maintaining a listenable quality, sounds I've heard in a long time.

As one might guess given his previous response, Fredric had quite a bit to say about what he feels Lovecraft's work has to offer to music. He puts it this way:

... a healthy dose of inspiration to be sure. Lovecraft's writings tend to leave one with far more questions than answers, and that perhaps is what is so disturbing about it. It instills one with a sense of wonder, and in becoming aware that the notion of a "safety-net" in the universe is but an illusion, we begin to experience dis-ease or even fear. The world will always have a plentiful supply of music that serves to help us forget about these things—in fact most people would probably rather just forget about the challenging questions of existence and enjoy the illusion of a "safe" universe controlled by a stern father-figure. There will always be a ready supply "safe" music in this regard. Consider the opening paragraph from the story "The Call of Cthulhu" about the merciful inability of the mind to correlate all its contents—like religion and philosophy, most music helps keep us "sane" by distracting us from the questions of existence.

But just as there is always a safe majority, there will always be an unsafe minority to balance things out. This is where the unnatural and alien influences like Lovecraft come into play. In a sense, all Lovecraft's stories are really just about trying to see the truth. One could argue in fact that perception of the truth is the highest virtue of Lovecraftian ethos. The problem is, truth is not always what we want to see or are even able to see.

Although most people are unconscious of it, much of music reaches at a sub-conscious level. Music can be like a key, in that it can "unlock" things within us. For instance, as most producers are aware bass sub-frequencies are more felt by the body as vibrations than they are heard by the ears or interpreted by the mind. This is a physiological fact, and yet most people would be at a loss to describe the "sensation of music," in terms of vibrations. What this means is that if one can capture the right tones and frequencies and put them together in the right combination, one can unlock certain hidden or lost potentials within one's self, and perhaps even in others. Like the man said, "That is not dead which can eternal lie, and with strange Aeons even death may die." Of course, it is really only the believers in the safety net that would need to worry about any deleterious effects from beholding "strange aeons." Those who wish to see themselves and the universe in its entirety without prejudice, should have nothing to fear.

So perhaps it is the sensation of an underlying non-natural current at the basis of all existence that is Lovecraft's greatest gift to us. In music, I find myself forever trying to re-create that sensation so that I might—even if for only a moment—see things as they truly are.

When asked what drew him to Lovecraft and has kept him engaged as a fan, once again, Fredric was not found at a loss for words.

I read my first Lovecraft around the age of 13. I believe it was *At the Mountains of Madness*. I didn't know anything about Lovecraft or his mythos at the time—it just looked like a cool book so I'd bought it. I didn't really understand a lot of what was happening in the stories, but again something about the mood drew me into it.

I wasn't aware of it at the time, but my own childhood presented many parallels to H.P.L.'s. For instance, I was born an only child on August 24 (H.P.L. was born August 20) and my father died while I was young. I was withdrawn, quiet, introverted, and would always choose sitting inside and reading a book to playing football or some such nonsense. Maybe this had something to do with why I found the Lovecraftian universe so palatable.

Lovecraft's universe is a thoroughly material one. Despite the fact it is often considered supernatural horror, there are actually no gods or similarly metaphysical entities in his universe. It is often mistakenly assumed that H.P.L.'s creations are merely a pantheon of 'evil gods', but in actuality it was his young friend August Derlethwho later attempted to add this sort of Greco-roman spin to the mythos. Rather, the bizarre inhabitants of Lovecraft's world are essentially material creatures and races of beings, either hidden under the sea (like Dagon), living in other mathematically postulated dimensions (like

Yog-Sothoth), or simply from another planet altogether (as in "The Whisperer in Darkness").

This material aspect is something very appealing to me as I've always been a materialist at heart. Despite the best arguments of Plato or Aquinas, I have never been able to see that the belief in non-material entities serves any higher function than manipulation of the ignorant masses by so called experts (often referred to as "priests").

Fredric said that his favorite Lovecraft stories are "The Call of Cthulhu," "The Shadow Over Innsmouth," and "The Whisperer in Darkness." And that brings us to the conclusion of our discussion of his bands and their contribution to Mythos music. It also brings us near the end of this exploration of Lovecraft based music.

Chapter 14

MISKATONIC MISCELLANY:
THE FINAL WORD

As one might imagine, a book of this nature is somewhat of a massive undertaking. Just in terms of making efforts to track down as much of the music as I could, and reach out and speak to as many of the artists as possible it has taken well over a year. That said, there are certainly things I have missed. In no way can this text be considered exhaustive. I have in the course of my research found other items likely to be Lovecraft related, but since I have been unable to get enough information on them, regarding either the artists or the recordings, I haven't allowed them to be included here.

I am also equally sure that there are things that I simply did not discover. I do know that several Internet based lists of Lovecraftian music have things listed on them that are not truly so. There are even a few instances of items I've included that I wasn't completely sure about. Without being able to reach the artist, though, the few times I have continued to feel that the case was strong enough to include some pieces, I have done so.

There are a couple of notable instances that I do know are said to be Lovecraft influenced, but in truth are not. For one thing, the group Le Orme has a song called "Beyond Leng." Several sources have attributed this cut as being related to Lovecraft. However, I got to communicate with the band, and they told me that they had not heard of H.P.L. and that the title was "just a name."

John Zorn has been credited with the Lovecraftian composition of "Necronomicon" and also the album *At the Mountains of Madness* with the band Electric Masada. However, Zorn told me that, while he is in fact a big Lovecraft fan, neither of these really are influenced by H.P.L. In the situation of "Necronomicon," Zorn said that it is "more inspired by Crowlean magick and hermetic philosophies." The other one shares a title with H.P.L., but Zorn stated that, "there is no direct inspiration from Lovecraft" on that one either.

Initially I didn't want to include "filk." As will be evident the next couple of pages I changed my mind. While there is really no one clear definition of this term, I'll try to explain my views of what this form of music is, and why I didn't want to cover it here. Filk is essentially a fan based (usually, but not always, focused on science fiction and fantasy themes) expression of lyrical themes with music. The style of music generally used for creating filk is folk or popular music. That brings up one of the key points. Most, but not all, filk is created by "borrowing" the music of other songs and creating lyrics to fit the singer's particular circle of fandom. You could almost think of it, at least in these terms, as being similar to the type of parody songs that Weird Al Yankovic is famous for performing. Another key point is that, even though some of these songs are recorded and even available for purchase, in general this is a hobby type of avocation. Furthermore, in most cases, the people creating the music would not consider themselves "professional musicians" by any sense of the word. Filk is typically done at science fiction and gaming conventions, and often not recorded. Because of all these factors, it is exceptionally difficult to track down all Lovecraftian filk and much of it really can be taken only so seriously. Those looking for more information on filk than I provide in this book would probably be well advised to turn first to Tom Smith, the self proclaimed "world's fastest filker."

Since my original dismissal of "filk" for the present project, I have been in contact with Mr. Smith and he caused me to rethink my position, at least in theory. Unfortunately, with the deadline looming, there is no way I can get into this exceptionally diverse and heavily populated art form. Perhaps if I revisit this book concept at a later date (in the form of a revised and expanded edition) I will devote a chapter or two to filk. Right now, I'll simply let him present his view on the concept to give another angle of the style.

A note on filk from the inside: there are several dialects of it —satirical, editorial, confessional, and the like... but I find the best way to look at it is as the musical variety of fan-fiction or fan art.

Filkers are, for the most part, amateur musicians expressing themselves in their chosen medium, exactly as fan writers or fan artists do. The difference is that these brave souls have to add an extra dimension to their work: performance. So, effectively, they have two not-necessarily-parallel skill sets to build, and many of them don't think of the second because it took enough courage just to get to the first.

Small wonder the filk community is so inviting, so forgiving. We're our own support system. Performance is looked upon as tertiary. First and foremost is being a part of things (a common enough circumstance in fandom, which is largely composed of people who will never hang with The Cool Kids, and are often amazed when they realize that there are other people like themselves out there). Sharing what's inside you is also up there at the top. The performance aspect, the skill with which you present yourself and your dreams, will ideally come later.

When they appear in filk, the Cthulhu Mythos are used more as a reference point rather than as a foundation. There are works adapting some Mythos stories or paraphrasing some concepts (insert shameless plug for a couple of my own songs, "Cthulhu Lite FM" and "House At Cthulhu Corner"), but simply mentioning Cthulhu out of context, e.g., in a hardware store or malt shop, is often enough to make the point or get the laughs. It's not that so many people are huge Mythos fans, so much as they know what it is and can use it as a touchstone... and, as with the Mythos creatures and situations themselves, the references are so contrary and discordant that they can be used to make an otherwise ordinary song extraordinary.

I've discovered that a few items *are* worthy of inclusion, although technically the music is not inspired by Lovecraft—but there is some other connection. The first of these involves guitarist extraordinaire Yngwie Malmsteen. The thanks segment of several of his albums includes a reference to Lovecraft. So, while there is no explicit musical reference, it is obvious that the author has touched Malmsteen's life.

There is also a rapper from Spain who goes by the name of "El Gran Cthulhu," which translates to The Great Cthulhu. While his music contains no references to Lovecraft's work, it is clear that he is a huge fan. In fact, El Gran Cthulhu (his real name is Eduardo Lozano Jiménez) says, "Lovecraft inspired me when I decided to choose for me the name of 'The Great Cthulhu' (the most horrible monster in his stories). This name goes with me, and tells people many things about my hip-hop. My flow is dark and dangerous too, because you can understand many things about these days." He also says that (not surprisingly) "The Call of Cthulhu" is his favorite Lovecraft story. He became a fan when his cousin, "spoke to me about the stories. He gave me a book: *The Tales of Cthulhu* or something like that. I liked it. So, I began to get more books. As a fan, one time I bought a shirt of Cthulhu in Madrid, and well, I have been using the name of Cthulhu during 7 or 8 years in the world of Spanish hip-hop."

There are also instances where I was unable after many attempts to either reach the artist for comments or get my hands on the music to describe it. Whenever possible, though, I have included lyrics, musician comments as well as my commentary about the music itself. If you notice any of them without one or more of these things, that is usually the reason for the omission.

In the course of my research I have also found a few songs that I've really drawn a blank on trying to verify. In other words, I have the songs, but either have not been able to reach the artists, or they neither confirmed nor denied that the songs had Lovecraftian inspiration. The first of these comes from an outfit called Smoke Blow and is entitled "Beyond the Wall of Sleep." They responded to me at one point, but never got back to me on the inspiration of the track. So, your guess is as good as mine. The gent who wrote to me said that he would check with the person who wrote the lyrics, but I never heard any more and further attempts at contact were never returned.

I had even less luck with the next one. I discovered a song called "Dagon" by someone going by the name of Mork Gryning, but my attempts to make contact there were never returned. Similarly I was unable to track down the group called Grotesque, but I did find a song by them called "Spawn of Azathoth." The band And Oceans... (or their management) also never returned my inquiries when I asked about the song "Cthonian Earth." The same was true of an outfit called Triptych and their piece "Arkham Verse."

That brings up another point. Any quotes not given an endnote and bibliography entry were from interviews that I actually conducted (usually by email). The one exception to this comes with Mike Korn's interview of Yyrkoon (still to come in this chapter). In reaching these various artists I found something very interesting out about them. It seems that no matter the artist's chosen musical style or particular niche, all involved seemed to be very helpful and interested in the project. It seems that the common interest in H.P. Lovecraft is a spark that resonates quite strongly in those who have "heard the call."

In general I posed the same questions to all of the artists in the book. I feel that there are two of those which I probably should address here from my own perspective. First, I asked them what drew them to Lovecraft and what has kept them as a fan. For myself, I came into his work through films like *Reanimator*, *From Beyond*, and *The Un-Nameable*. While those movies may not be tied with more than a tiny thread to Lovecraft's source material, I liked them enough to get me to seek out the books. Admittedly, H.P.L.'s archaic writing style took some acclimation. Frankly, I had never been able to enjoy Edgar Allen Poe because of this old world style of writing, and Lovecraft's tone is quite similar. The thing is, however, that the stories were strong enough to keep me coming back, and eventually I came to enjoy his style of prose.

From that point forward it was a foregone conclusion. He quickly became my favorite author and I began to devour all his works. Then I moved to biographies, the books about his letters, and anything else I could find with the Lovecraft connection. I think what I like the best about his work is that the feeling of dread is often so pervasive. It seems to me that many times the conclusion is known from the beginning—or at least guessed at—but something within keeps saying, "no, it can't be that—it's too horrifying." I guess in a way I find myself reading to discover that the truth is not what it seems at first to be. Then, as you work your way through the tale, it turns out that it is at least as bad, and sometimes even worse. There is a certain attraction to that sort of a piece.

That brings us to the other question I asked the artists—"what is your favorite Lovecraft story?" For me, I have to say that the top of the list is occupied by "Pickman's Model," "The Rats in the Walls" and "The Statement of Randolph Carter." That said, I'd be hard pressed to pick a Lovecraft tale that I don't enjoy. Those are just the ones that seem to resonate best for me.

It is also important to address one earlier article that has been published with a similar theme. I didn't actually know about the article until well into the research for this book, but S. T. Joshi provided me with a copy to have a look at. Allen Mackey wrote the article. It was entitled "Disciples of Zann or The Condensed History of H.P. Lovecraft's Influence on Heavy Metal." The article appeared in *Crypt of Cthulhu*, the "Eastertide" issue of 1995. I've tried unsuccesfully to reach Mr. Mackey, but I would like to address a few things he brought up in that article.

First there are a few groups Mackey mentions about whom I've been able to find nothing. The first of these is Mythos. According to Mackey, "There was also a group called Mythos, but I don't know if that name was a reference to Lovecraft or not."[1] Another of these outfits is Yog-Sothoth. To quote from Mackey's article, "I've heard of another group, this one from Canada, who were obviously influenced by the Old Gent—Yog-Sothoth. That's all I know about them."[2] In terms of naming, Mackey points out a couple more homages from the world of punk rock. He points to the singer for the Dead Milkmen, who apparently went by the name of H.P. Lovecraft for a while and also the guitarist of The Dwarves who played under the name "He Who Cannot Be Named."

Another act that I seem to have come up empty-handed on is the French band Catacomb (not to be confused with Catacombs covered earlier in this book). According to Mackey at the time he published his article the band had formed in 1990 and produced two cassettes. He pointed to their biography, which he says states that, "The lyrics are inspired by the myth of Cthulhu of H.P. Lovecraft...."[3]

While I was able to track down a Russian act called "Flegethon," they do not seem to be the band that Mackey mentions. He says that the group he's referring to is from Athens, Greece. He calls their album, *Repugnant Blasphemy*, "an awful offering,"[4] and it appears that it is their only offering. He points up to one verse from their song "Ancient Disgust," which begins with the line "When the stars and moon are in the right position."[5]

Mackey mentions the band Ripping Corpse, and admittedly they do have a few tracks that have Lovecraftian titles. I chose to omit them here as the lyrics (and liner notes) seem to make it quite clear that the source of inspiration is actually the Stuart Gordon films. Since those movies are based extremely loosely—in fact almost enough to say "not at all" on Lovecraft's stories, it simply didn't seem worthy of inclusion. Although, the liner notes do thank, among many others, Lovecraft himself. It should also be noted that the band Non Serviam, mentioned earlier in the book, was a spin off of Ripping Corpse.

Another case where I was unable to track down the group is Dunwich. Mackey says that the group hailed from St. Louis, MO, and apparently had released one demo. When Mackey contacted them via mail, he received a letter back from one of the members which expressed, among other things, "Lovecraft rules!"[6]

In another instance where it seems a newer group has overshadowed the original one, and looks to be the only incarnation I am able to track down, Mackey mentions an outfit called, "Paralysis." While I was able to locate a group by that name, the one he refers to is from New Orleans, but this one was from Greece. He states that at least their cover art is inspired directly from H.P.L.

Mackey also makes reference to the band Timeghoul, but (although he does list a few "choice" cuts) doesn't cite anything specific that is related to Lovecraft. According to the band's drummer, they never did any music that was related to the author. Another where Mackey suggests a mythos connection might be—but there isn't—is the case of Dream Theater. He points to their song "Ytse Jam" as possibly being derived from the fiction tome *Song of Ytse*. Actually the truth to the title of the instrumental is that the original name of the band was Majesty. Spell it backwards and you get "Ytse Jam."

Keep in mind that I point these things out not to ridicule or devalue Mackey's article, but rather to clarify for the reader discrepancies between his concepts and mine. He acknowledged not having full information, and I'm sure dug as deeply as he could to find the truth. I can attest to just how difficult some of this is to research.

Mackey quotes from a song by Milwaukee, WI based band Dr. Shrinker as being what he describes as one of the silliest references to the *Necronomicon*. While the fact that they mention H.P.L.'s creation does indicate that they are, albeit indirectly, involved with the Mythos it seems pretty obvious from the lyrics that the true inspiration is the Stuart Gordon film. That analysis was confirmed for me by Matthew Grassberger from the band who said the following:

Nope, none of our songs were directly based on Lovecraft's writings. I know he was inspiring to me with the descriptive writing style. I still am drawn to the northeast US only because of his stories. Incidentally, the only sticker on my bass is a Cthulhu "fish"! It has been on for years and is not coming off anytime soon.

Another one that Mackey mentions, which I am unable to confirm, is a band called "R'lyeh." He says just that, "I have evidence that there is a band called R'lyeh."[7] There are other bands that show up in his article that either have such a slim connection—mentioning Lovecraft in an interview or that had songs with titles like "From Beyond"—that I simply found to be too loosely connected or not definite enough to reference here.

Sources around the Internet say that the band Equomanthorn's 1994 disc *Nindinugga Nimshimshargal Enllilara* has lyrics that are drawn from the Simon Edition of the *Necronomicon*. While I am guessing that this is probably true, once again, I was unable to make contact with anyone involved, or even track down the music. Although, if the inspiration was strictly that source, then it doesn't really fit into the parameters of this book, anyway.

Two bands were brought to my attention by Craig Mullins from Unfilmable.com, but I had no luck reaching either of them. They are The Old Ones and The New Minority (which Mullins says includes a "Lovecraftian testimonial"). He also told me about a Weird Fiction collection on Valiant Death Records that included The Darkest of the Hillside Thickets, among others. That label never responded to my requests for information either. Another that was mentioned to me by several people is Moonspell, but again I've come up empty handed.

A gent going by the name of J. B. Lee is another act who seems difficult to track down. There are indications from looking around the Internet that this man has serious Lovecraft ties, but I have not been able to dig up the music or any other information on him beyond the fact the he released one set of four tracks entitled "Necronomicon," which proposedly were designed as "'imaginary soundtracks' for Lovecraft stories."

Nameless City seems equally difficult to dig up. All I can say is that the name of the band seems to indicate a Lovecraft connection, just like the title of their album, *Whisperer in Darkness*.

While there apparently at one point or another was an official site for The Talisdream Mission, it is no longer in existence. I was unable to track down the project any other way. All I know is that there was one release from the group out there entitled, *Mythos: H.P. Lovecraft's Cthulhu Nightmares*.

Another outfit that seems to have faded into the ether is La Voce de

Cthulhu, which translates to The Voice of Cthulhu. Beyond the name, I can tell you that the group did have several releases with Lovecraftian titles. These include "A Vision of Kadath," "Dagon," "The Shadow out of Time" and "The Sign of Shub-Niggurath." Beyond that, my searches turned up no information.

Another group which has pretty well eluded my research is Endura. I can tell you that they have released quite a few Lovecraftian titles, but I can't get my hands on any of the music or lyrics to verify the links. I also couldn't find any biographical or contact information for them. What I do know is that the suspected H.P.L. connections started with their 1994 release *Dreams of Dark Waters*, which included the songs "R'lyeh Awakens" and "Black Eidolon." In 1996 they put out *The Dark Is Light Enough* and it had the songs "The Stars Are Right," "Ubbo-Sathla" and "He Knows The Gate." "Dagon Is My Weapon" and "Cthulhu Fhtagn" both came from *Liber Leviathan* which was released that same year. Also in 1999 they released an album entitled *Elder Signs*.

I had a similar lack of luck digging up the band Mercyless. This French outfit released the album *Abject Offering* in 1992, and it included a track entitled "Nyarlathotep (Intro)." Once again, beyond that, I've come up with no information on this one.

In a related situation there is the group Necrosanct. I can't say much about the band, but they have one song entitled "Necronomicon" and another called, "Beneath Eternal Oceans of Sand" with lyrics borrowed mostly from Lovecraft's "The Outsider." I wasn't able to track down much else, except that the tracks come from two releases: 1991's *Equal In Death* and 1992's *Incarnate*.

Yog-Sothoth is another band that, at least from the name, is influenced by Lovecraft. This French outfit released one album, 1984's eponymously titled disc. While I haven't been able to listen to the music (there are apparently only three songs on the album) or reach the band, the music is described as free form jazz with progressive rock leanings. Interestingly enough, some of their countrymen later formed a band by the same name. I find nearly no reference to that group, though, but supposedly their music was rather Arabic.

Perry Grayson of Destiny's End mentioned the band Red Temple Spirits to me. Unfortunately, I haven't been able to find biographical information, lyrics or music by the band. So I'll take his word for it when he explains it like this, "can't recall the name of the song, but singer/lyricist William Faircloth was obviously influenced by HPL. The chorus goes something like "what lies beyond the wall of sleep...".."

Although the French band Yyrkoon returned my pleas for contact once (to either get some questions answered or their music or both), it came too late and without enough return information to fully include them in the book. Fortunately, my friend Mike Korn interviewed them recently for his publication *Wormwood Chronicles*. While it is good that I at least got this, it really points up how much this band belonged in the book. It's a shame I didn't have more luck with them.

Korn touched on their Lovecraftian elements in that interview. When Korn asked about the decision to base their latest release *Unhealthy Opera* around Lovecraft's work, Stephane Souteyrand replied in the following way:

> I'm really fascinated by H.P. Lovecraft's writings and his novels. I have been since I was a little boy. I decided to speak about Lovecraft's works in our previous album *Occult Medicine. Occult Medicine* was based on the story "[Herbert West:] Re-animator," which was the basis of the movie. With *Unhealthy Opera*, I tried to explore another phase of the writings of Lovecraft. This album is about Cthulhu, the Great Old One that sleeps in the deep blue abyss of the ocean and is waiting to rule the world again.

Korn mentioned "the horror from the sea," to which Souteyrand replied, "Yeah, that's the title of one of the songs on *Unhealthy Opera*. I treat this album like a concept album, where each song deals with another aspect of the Lovecraft concept." As they discussed several of the individual tracks it was revealed that the song, "The Book" is about *The Necronomicon*. Korn brought up the fact that many of the songs on the disc are centered around water and Souteyrand stated that, "In the main writing of Lovecraft, everything takes place near the sea, the ocean and their infinite depths."

Those who know a lot about H.P.L.'s life will know that he had an almost irrational fear of the ocean (and seafood—basically anything that came from the water). This, Souteyrand revealed, is something that he shares with Lovecraft. "I've been scared of the ocean since I'm a little boy because it's huge with no limits and you can't really know what's underneath the surface. This is a strong link I made with the writings of H.P. Lovecraft. That's what makes this such a personal album."

If you look for Lovecraftian music on the Internet you will also turn up a couple more compilations. The first of these is *At the Mountains of Madness—International Doom Collection*. Richard Walker of Solstice (a band featured on the compilation) told me that the only real Lovecraft related music on show here is the contribution from his outfit and one from Warning. The disc is also out of print, and I couldn't secure a copy of it. The other compilation that I found listed was *The Challenge from Beyond: A*

Tribute to H.P. Lovecraft. This one was released in 1999, and also seems to be out of print, but I was truly unable to find anything about it or the artists who were involved in the project (with the exception of Forma Tardre) who are addressed elsewhere in the book.

Looking to the future, there is a band called Arkham Hollow that have assembled in Vermont. They aren't included in any depth here because they have yet to record anything for public consumption. But they do say this about the effect Lovecraft's work has had on them:

> The Lovecraftian influence is displayed more often in mood and attitude than blatant recitations of stories. Songs like "Small Town Charm" and "Gravedigger" touch on themes commonly used in his stories, cursed little New England towns and the digging/robbing of final resting places. "'Til We Meet Again" is a spin on "The Thing on the Doorstep" dealing with issues of loosing ones free will to a supernatural fiend. "Blasted Heath" touches upon "The Color Out of Space" quite deliberately. "Pine Devils" echoes "Io Cthulhu" in the chorus with Crowley-esque rants in the verses, promising damnation upon the eventual return of both the singer and his demon of choice. That macabre melancholy and yearning for a lost past that Lovecraft displayed eloquently through out his works and life is echoed in "Passed Away." The band has also considered pulling out several other Lovecraft songs penned by others to add to their live sets, attempting in many cases to turn the heavy metal thunder into backwoods thrash.

They describe themselves as "possibly the only country/Americana band that counts HP Lovecraft as a primary influence." It seems obvious that music and lyrics deserve to be included here, but with nothing to be released until after publication, they just didn't make it. They will have an EP out later this year, though.

Before anyone contacts me saying that I botched the grammar when I use a plural verb with a noun that is a band name—I know the American grammar rule. However, I find that the English one makes more sense. They use a plural verb with a noun when that noun represents a group of more than one. I see it this way, if you use a pronoun to represent the group—let's say Metallica, for instance—it would be "they." That would call for a plural verb. Since the name of the band essentially performs the same function as the pronoun would, I believe that using the plural verb tense is correct. Besides, Lovecraft himself had some anachronistic writing idiosyncracies, so I can allow myself one.

I also would like to mention that I originally intended to include both a discography of the artists represented here and a listing of all H.P.L.'s literary works. On further consideration I decided that I would leave them out. This is solely for purposes of reducing the number of pages and thereby holding the cost down a bit for the buyers. In any event, the bibliography of Lovecraft is readily available from many sources. As to the discography, it is pretty well listed within each of the segments on the artists, therefore it would have been a bit redundant.

Finally, due to numerous PC crashes in the course of creating this book, I've lost a lot of names of people who I really should thank for their help. For that reason, and because the list would probably be a whole chapter in length, I'm going to pass on giving thanks to anyone here. It's not because I haven't been assisted in this process. Rather, instead of skipping someone who should have been mentioned, I'd prefer to not mention anyone. So, if you know that you were one of the people who pointed me in the right direction or gave me some much needed information, it is appreciated. Thank you very much. Feel free to drop me an email and let me know what you think of the finished product.

That pretty well sums up what that I feel needed to be made clear. I hope that for those of you who have yet to read Lovecraft, this book might serve as a trigger to get you there. Those amongst you who already enjoy H.P.L.'s work might well make an effort to find some of this music discussed. There is certainly a wealth of material out there, and it is always nice to see (or in this case, *hear*) interpretations of works that you enjoy. At least, that's what I feel.

BIBLIOGRAPHY

Chapter 1
1 Joshi, S.T. *H.P. Lovecraft Centennial Guidebook*. Cooke, Jon B. (ed.). USA: Montilla Publications, 1990
2. Lovecraft, Howard P. *Selected Letters II*. Sauk City, WI: Arkham House. 1968. 109
3 Joshi, S.T. *H.P. Lovecraft Centennial Guidebook*. Cooke, Jon B. (ed.). USA: Montilla Publications, 1990
4 Lovecraft, Howard P. "What Amateurdom and I Have Done for Each Other" (1921); rpt. *Miscellaneous Writings*. Sauk City, WI: Arkham House, 1995, 452.
5 Lovecraft, Howard P. *Selected Letters III*. Sauk City, WI: Arkham House, 1998. 166
6 Lovecraft, Howard P. *Selected Letters V*. Sauk City, WI: Arkham House, 1976. 16
7 Lovecraft, Howard P. *Selected Letters IV*. Sauk City, WI: Arkham House, 1976. 346; (ellipses as in original)
8 Lovecraft, Howard P. "The Music of Erich Zann." *H.P. Lovecraft: Tales*. New York, NY: The Library of America, 2005
9 Lovecraft, Howard P. "The Quest of Iranon." *The Doom That Came to Sarnath*. New York, NY: Ballantine Books, 1971
10 Lovecraft, Howard P. November 21, 1930 in a letter to August Derleth
11 Ibid.
12 Derleth, August. "Lovecraft and Music." *The Romantist* 4-5 (1980-1981)
13 Ibid.
14 Joshi, S. T. "Further Notes on Lovecraft and Music." *The Romantist* 4-5 (1980-1981)
15 Ibid.

Chapter 2
1 H.P. Lovecraft. "The White Ship." *H.P. Lovecraft*. Philips, 1967.
2 Lovecraft, Howard P. "The White Ship." *The Lurking Fear and Other Stories*. New York: Ballantine Books, 1971
3 Ibid.
4 Ibid.
5 Ibid.
6 H.P. Lovecraft. "At The Mountains of Madness." *H.P. Lovecraft II*. Philips, 1968.
7 Ibid.

Chapter 3
1 Harms, Daniel. *Encyclopedia Cthulhiana*. Hayward, CA: Chaosium, 1998 page 65
2 Univers Zero. *Ceux Du Dehors*. Cuneiform. 2001
3 Halloween. "Outsider." *Part One*. Musea. 2001
4 Lovecraft, Howard P. "The Outsider." *H.P. Lovecraft: Tales*. New York, NY: The Library of America, 2005
5 Halloween. "Outsider." *Part One*. Musea. 2001
6 Ibid.
7 Lovecraft, Howard P. "The Outsider." *H.P. Lovecraft: Tales*. New York, NY: The Library of America, 2005
8 Ibid.
9 Halloween. "Outsider." *Part One*. Musea. 2001

10 Lovecraft, Howard P. "The Wood." *The Ancient Track: The Complete Poetical Works of H.P. Lovecraft*. Edited by S.T. Joshi. San Francisco, CA: Night Shade Books; 2001

11 Lovecraft, Howard P. "Festival." *The Ancient Track: The Complete Poetical Works of H.P. Lovecraft*. Edited by S.T. Joshi. San Francisco, CA: Night Shade Books; 2001

12 Lovecraft, Howard P. "The Dream-Quest of Unknown Kadath." *The Dream Cycle of H.P. Lovecraft: Dreams of Terror and Death*. New York: Ballantine Books, 1995

13 Payne's Gray. "Sunset City." *Kadath Decoded*. 1995

14 Lovecraft, Howard P. "The Dream-Quest of Unknown Kadath." *The Dream Cycle of H.P. Lovecraft: Dreams of Terror and Death*. New York: Ballantine Books, 1995

15 Payne's Gray. "The Caverns of Flame." *Kadath Decoded*. 1995

16 Payne's Gray. "Moonlight Waters." *Kadath Decoded*. 1995

17 Ibid.

18 Lovecraft, Howard P. "The Dream-Quest of Unknown Kadath." *The Dream Cycle of H.P. Lovecraft: Dreams of Terror and Death*. New York: Ballantine Books, 1995

19 Ibid.

20 Ibid.

21 Ibid.

22 Ibid.

23 Ibid.

24 Payne's Gray. "The Way To Ngranek."*Kadath Decoded*. 1995

25 Ibid.

Chapter 4

1 Black Sabbath. "Behind the Wall of Sleep." *Black Sabbath*. Warner Brothers. 1969

2 Metallica. "The Thing Should Not Be." *Master of Puppets*. Elektra. 1986

3 Ibid.

4 Ibid.

5 Ibid.

6 Lovecraft, Howard P. "The Nameless City." *The Doom That Came to Sarnath*. New York: Ballantine Books, 1971

7 Rage. "Beyond the Wall of Sleep." *Trapped!* Noise. 1992

8 Rage. "The Crawling Chaos." *Black In Mind*. Gun. 1995

9 Harms, Daniel. *Encyclopedia Cthulhiana*. Hayward, CA: Chaosium, 1998 p 219

10 Ibid.

11 Rage. "Shadow Out of Time." *Black In Mind*. Gun. 1995

12 Lovecraft, Howard P. "The Shadow out of Time." *H.P. Lovecraft: Tales*. New York, NY: The Library of America, 2005

13 Rage. "In A Nameless Time". *Black In Mind*. Gun. 1995

14 Ibid.

15 Ibid.

16 Ibid.

17 Ibid.

18 Ibid.

19 Rage, *Soundchaser*. SPV. 2003

20 Ibid.

21 Manilla Road. "Children of the Night." *Mystification*. Black Dragon. 1987

22 Manilla Road. "Mystification." *Mystification*. Black Dragon. 1987

23 Manilla Road. *Out of the Abyss*. Leviathan. 1988

24 Manilla Road. "Out of the Abyss." *Out of the Abyss*. Leviathan. 1988

25 Manilla Road. "Return of the Old Ones." *Out of the Abyss*. Leviathan. 1988
26 Ibid.
27 Manilla Road. "Black Cauldron." *Out of the Abyss*. Leviathan. 1988
28 Ibid.
29 Ibid.
30 Ibid.
31 Manilla Road. "War In Heaven." *Out of the Abyss*. Leviathan. 1988
32 Ibid.
33 Manilla Road. "From Beyond." *The Courts of Chaos*. Leviathan. 1990
34 Manilla Road. "Megaladon." *Atlantis Rising*. Iron Glory. 2001
35 Manilla Road. "Lemuria." *Atlantis Rising*. Iron Glory. 2001
36 Manilla Road. "Sea Witch." *Atlantis Rising*. Iron Glory. 2001
37 Ibid.
38 Manilla Road. "Resurrection." *Atlantis Rising*. Iron Glory. 2001
39 Manilla Road. "Decimation." *Atlantis Rising*. Iron Glory. 2001
40 Ibid.
41 Ibid.
42 Ibid.
43 Manilla Road. "Siege of Atlantis." *Atlantis Rising*. Iron Glory. 2001
44 Manilla Road. "War of the Gods." *Atlantis Rising*. Iron Glory. 2001
45 The Official Bal-Sagoth Website. <http://www.bal-sagoth.co.uk/>
46 Bal-Sagoth. "The Sixth Adulation of His Chthonic Majesty." *The Cthonic Chronicles*. Candlelight. 2006
47 Mekong Delta. "Age of Agony." *The Music of Erich Zann*. Enigma. 1988
48 Mekong Delta. "Prophecy." *The Music of Erich Zann*. Enigma. 1988
49 Mekong Delta. "Epilogue." *The Music of Erich Zann*. Enigma. 1988
50 Lovecraft, Howard P., "The Music of Erich Zann." *H.P. Lovecraft: Tales*. New York, NY: The Library of America, 2005
51 Necrophagia. *Season of the Dead*. New Renaissance. 1992
52 Necrophagia. "Ancient Slumber." *Season of the Dead*. New Renaissance. 1992
53 Rigor Mortis. "Re-Animator." *Rigor Mortis*. Capitol.1990
54 Celtic Frost. "Morbid Tales." *Morbid Tales*. Metal Blade. 1984
55 Celtic Frost. "Nocturnal Fear." *Morbid Tales*. Metal Blade. 1984
56 Ibid.
57 Ibid.
58 Ibid.
59 Sacrifice. *"Necronomicon."* *Torment In Fire*. Restless 1986
60 Ibid.
61 Sacrifice. "Re-Animation." *Forward to Termination*. Restless 1987
62 Solitude Aeturnus. "White Ship". *Into the Depths of Sorrow*. Roadrunner. 1991
63 Lovecraft, Howard P., "The White Ship." *The Lurking Fear and Other Stories*. New York: Ballantine Books, 1971
64 Lovecraft, Howard P., "The Nameless City," *The Doom That Came to Sarnath*. New York: Ballantine Books, 1971
65 Entombed. "Stranger Aeons." *Clandestine*. Earache. 1991
66 GWAR. "Horror of Yig." *Scumdogs of the Universe*. Metal Blade. 1990
67 Ibid.
68 Morbid Angel. "Lord of All Fevers and Plagues." *Altars of Madness*. Earache. 1989
69 Morbid Angel. "Unholy Blasphemies." *Blessed Are the Sick*. Combat. 1991

70 Morbid Angel. "The Ancient Ones." *Blessed Are the Sick*. Combat. 1991
71 Ibid.
72 Morbid Angel. "Angel of Disease." *Covenant*. Giant. 1993
73 Ibid.
74 Morbid Angel. "Sworn to the Black." *Covenant*. Giant. 1993
75 Morbid Angel. "Prayer of Hatred." *Formulas Fatal to the Flesh*. Earache. 1998
76 Morbid Angel. "Hellspawn – The Rebirth." *Formulas Fatal to the Flesh*. Earache. 1998
77 Ibid.
78 Morbid Angel. "Covenant of Death." *Formulas Fatal to* the *Flesh*. Earache. 1998
79 Morbid Angel. *Formulas Fatal to* the *Flesh*. Earache. 1998
80 Morbid Angel. "Umulamahri." *Formulas Fatal to* the *Flesh*. Earache. 1998
81 Ibid.

Chapter 5

1 Lovecraft, Howard P., January 16, 1932 in a letter to Robert E. Howard
2 Thergothon. "Evoken." *Fhtagn-nagh Yog-sothoth*. Avant Garde 1991
3 Ibid.
4 Thergothon. "Yet The Watchers Guard." *Stream from the Heavens*. Avant Garde. 1994
5 Ibid.
6 Thergothon. "The Twilight Fade." *Fhtagn-nagh Yog-sothoth*. Avant Garde 1991
7 Tiamat. "Evilized." *Sumerian Cry*. Powerage. 1999
8 Tiamat. "A Winter Shadow." *The Astral Sleep*. Century Media. 2001
9 Tiamat. "Sumerian Cry Pt. 3." *The Astral Sleep*. Century Media. 2001
10 Ibid.
11 Vader. "Dark Age." *The Ultimate Incantation*. Combat. 1991
12 Ibid.
13 Vader. "Testimony." *The Ultimate Incantation*. Combat. 1991
14 Ibid.
15 Vader. "Breath of Centuries." *The Ultimate Incantation*. Combat. 1991
16 Ibid.
17 Ibid.
18 Therion. "Call of Dagon." *Lemuria/Sirius B*. Nuclear Blast. 2004
19 Harms, Daniel. *Encyclopedia Cthulhiana*. Hayward, CA: Chaosium, 1998, 73
20 Harms, Daniel. *Encyclopedia Cthulhiana*. Hayward, CA: Chaosium, 1998, 81
21 Deicide. "Dead By Dawn." *Deicide*. Roadrunner. 1990
22 Deicide. "Dead But Dreaming." *Legion*. Roadrunner. 1990
23 Hypocrisy. "*Necronomicon*." *Obsculum Oscenum*. Nuclear Blast. 1993
24 Electric Wizard. "Supercoven." *Supercoven*. Mia. 1998
25 Electric Wizard. "Vinum Sabbathi." *Dopethrone*. Music Cartel. 2000
26 Ibid.
27 Electric Wizard. "Weird Tales." *Dopethrone*. Music Cartel. 2000
28 Ibid.
29 Lovecraft, Howard P. "The Dream-Quest of Unknown Kadath." *The Dream Cycle of H.P. Lovecraft: Dreams of Terror and Death*. New York: Ballantine Books, 1995
30 Electric Wizard. "Eko Eko Azarak." *We Live*. Music Cartel. 2004
31 Electric Wizard. "The Sun Has Turned To Black." *We Live*. Music Cartel. 2004
32 Bethzaida. "The Outsider." *Nine Worlds*. Season of Mist. 1996
33 Ibid.
34 Pestilence. *Testimony of* the *Ancients*. Roadrunner. 1989

35 Massacre. "Dawn of Eternity." *From Beyond*. Relativity. 1991
36 Massacre, "From Beyond." *From Beyond*. Relativity. 1991
37 Massacre "Symbolic Immortality." *From Beyond*. Relativity. 1991
38 Ibid.
39 Sentenced. "Beyond the Wall of Sleep." *North From Here*. Spinefarm. 1993
40 Ibid.
41 Mercyful Fate. "The Mad Arab (Part One: The Vision)." *Time*. Metal Blade. 1994
42 Mercyful Fate. "Kutulu (The Mad Arab Part Two)." *Into The Unknown*. Metal Blade. 1996
43 Ibid.
44 Ibid.
45 Orphanage. "The Case of Charles Dexter Ward." *Oblivion*. DSFA. 1995
46 Orphanage. "At the Mountains of Madness." *By Time Alone*. DSFA. 1996
47 Lovecraft, Howard P. *At the Mountains of Madness*. *H.P. Lovecraft: Tales*. New York, NY: The Library of America, 2005
48 Darklands. "Dead But Not Dreaming." *Diablerie*. 1995
49 Disincarnate. "Entranced." *Dreams of a Carrion Kind*. Roadrunner. 1993
50 Lovecraft, Howard P. "The Tomb." *The Doom That Came to Sarnath*. New York: Ballantine Books, 1971
51 Disincarnate. "Entranced." *Dreams of a Carrion Kind*. Roadrunner. 1993
52 Solstice. "New Dark Age II.". *New Dark Age*. Candlelight. 1998
53 BloodHag "H.P. Lovecraft." *Dewey Decibel System*. Spork.
54 Ibid.
55 Ibid.
56 Non Serviam. "Which Eternal Lie." *Necrotical*. 1999
57 Ibid.
58 Ibid.
59 Ibid.
60 Nile. "Beneath Eternal Oceans of Sand." *Amongst the Catacombs of Nephren-Ka*. Relapse. 1998
61 Destiny's End. "Breathe Deep the Dark." *Breathe Deep the Dark*. Metal Blade. 1998
62 Destiny's End. "Vanished." *Transition*. Metal Blade. 2001
63 Chton. "Enemie." *Chtonian Lifecode*. Retribute. 2004
64 Chton. "Book of Black Earth." *Chtonian Lifecode*. Retribute. 2004
65 Ibid.
66 Aarni. "The Black Keyes (of R'lyeh)." *Demo*. 2001
67 Ibid.
68 Aarni. "Reaching Azathoth." *Duumipeikon paluu*. 2002
69 Aarni. "Lovecraft Knew." Currently Unreleased
70 Catacombs. "In The Depths of R'lyeh." *In the Depths of R'lyeh*. Napalm. 2006
71 Philosopher. "Within Aeons." *What Dwells Beyond*. 2003
72 Philosopher. "700 Steps of Deeper Slumber." *Thoughts*. Ruptured Silence. 2004
73 Philosopher. "Beyond Darkness." *Thoughts*. Ruptured Silence. 2004
74 Philosopher. *Thoughts*. Ruptured Silence. 2004
75 Philosopher. "What Dwells Beyond." *Thoughts*. Ruptured Silence. 2004
76 Philosopher. "World In Rapture." *Thoughts*. Ruptured Silence. 2004
77 Philosopher. *Thoughts*. Ruptured Silence. 2004

Chapter 6

1 Rudimentary Peni. "Architectonic And Dominant." *Cacophony*. Outer Himalayan. 1988
2 Rudimentary Peni. "Crazed Couplet." *Cacophony*. Outer Himalayan. 1988

3 Rudimentary Peni. "Sarcophogus." *Cacophony*. Outer Himalayan. 1988
4 Rudimentary Peni. "The Loved Dead." *Cacophony*. Outer Himalayan. 1988
5 Rudimentary Peni. "Kappa Alpha Tau." *Cacophony*. Outer Himalayan. 1988
6 Ibid.
7 Rudimentary Peni. "Memento Mori." *Cacophony*. Outer Himalayan. 1988
8 Rudimentary Peni. "The Old Man Is Not So Terribly Misanthropic." *Cacophony*. Outer
    Himalayan. 1988
9 Rudimentary Peni. "Sonia." *Cacophony*. Outer Himalayan. 1988
10 Rudimentary Peni. "Shard." *Cacophony*. Outer Himalayan. 1988
11 White Flag. "Cthulu Calling." *Step Back 10*. Just for Fun. 199912 Ibid.
13 White Flag. "Wake Up Screaming." *Step Back 10*. Just for Fun. 1999
14 Ibid
15 Lurking Fear. "Innsmouth Bay / Edge of Identity."
16 Ibid.
17 Harms, Daniel. *Encyclopedia Cthulhiana*. Hayward, CA: Chaosium, 1998, 347
18 Dayglo Abortions. "Spawn of Yog-Sothoth." *Here Today Guano Tomorrow*. Fringe. 1988
19 Ghost Run Wild Myspace Profile. <http://www.myspace.com/ghostsrunwild>
20 Ghosts Run Wild. "The Stars are Right." *From Beyond*. Valiant Death
21 Ghosts Run Wild. "Coffin Rock." *From Beyond*. Valiant Death
22 Ghosts Run Wild. "The Shadow out of Time." *From Beyond*. Valiant Death
23 Ghosts Run Wild. "Crawling Chaos." *Demos From The Dead*. Valiant Death.
24 Ibid.
25 Ghosts Run Wild. "Miskatonic Massacre." *Demos From the Dead*. Valiant Death.

Chapter 7

1 Fields of the Nephilim. "Reanimator." *Dawnrazor*. Beggars Banquet. 1987
2 Fields of the Nephilim. "The Watchman." *The Nephilim*. Beggars Banquet. 1990
3 Fields of the Nephilim. "Last Exit For the Lost." *The Nephilim*. Beggars Banquet. 1990
4 Morphine Angel. "Breakfast With Cthulu." *Project ISA*. Black Pepper Records. 1995

Chapter 8

1 Evil's Toy. "From Above Comes Sleep." *Illusion*. Metropolis. 1998
2 Evil's Toy. "Colours out of Space." *Angels Only*. Metropolis. 1998
3 Evil's Toy. "Timeless." Metropolis. 1998
4 T.O.Y. "Beyond Sleep." *White Lights*. A Different Drum. 2003
5 T.O.Y. "The Day the World Disappeared." *Space Radio*. BMG International. 2001
6 Ibid.
7 T.O.Y. "Inner Cinema." *White Lights*. A Different Drum. 2003
8 Ibid.

Chapter 9

1 Nox Arcana. *Necronomicon*. Monolith Graphics. 2004

Chapter 10

1 Lovecraft, Howard P. "The Tomb." *The Doom That Came to Sarnath*. New York:
    Ballantine Books, 1971
2 The Darkest of the Hillside Thickets. <http://thickets.net>
3 The Darkest of the Hillside Thickets. "Shoggoths Away." *Cthulhu Strikes Back*.

4 Harms, Daniel. *Encyclopedia Cthulhiana*. Hayward, CA: Chaosium, 1998, 274
5 The Darkest of the Hillside Thickets. *Cthulhu Strikes Back*
6 The Darkest of the Hillside Thickets. "Unstoppable." *Cthulhu Strikes Back*.
7 The Darkest of the Hillside Thickets. *Cthulhu Strikes Back*.
8 Ibid.
9 The Darkest of the Hillside Thickets. "Protein." *Cthulhu Strikes Back*.
10 The Darkest of the Hillside Thickets. *Cthulhu Strikes Back*.
11 The Darkest of the Hillside Thickets. "One Gilled Girl." *Great Old Ones*.
12 The Darkest of the Hillside Thickets. Chunk. *Great Old Ones*.
13 Ibid.
14 Ibid.
15 Lovecraft, Howard P. "The Whisperer in Darkness." *H.P. Lovecraft: Tales*. New York, NY: The Library of America, 2005,
16 The Darkest of the Hillside Thickets. "Chunk." *Great Old Ones*.
17 The Darkest of the Hillside Thickets. "Flee." *Great Old Ones*.
18 Ibid.
19 The Darkest of the Hillside Thickets. "Please God No." *Great Old Ones*.
20 Ibid.
21 The Darkest of the Hillside Thickets. "Six Gun Gorgon Dynamo." *Great Old Ones*.
22 The Darkest of the Hillside Thickets. *Great Old Ones*.
23 Ibid.
24 Ibid.
25 Ibid.
26 The Darkest of the Hillside Thickets. "The Innsmouth Look." *Spaceship Zero*. Divine Industries. 2000
27 Harms, Daniel. *Encyclopedia Cthulhiana*. Hayward, CA: Chaosium, 1998, 104
28 Harms, Daniel. *Encyclopedia Cthulhiana*. Hayward, CA: Chaosium, 1998, 152
29 The Darkest of the Hillside Thickets. "The Chosen One." *Spaceship Zero*. Divine Industries. 2000

Chapter 11

1 The H.P. Lovecraft Historical Society. http://www.cthulhulives.org
2 Harms, Daniel. *Encyclopedia Cthulhiana*. Hayward, CA: Chaosium, 1998, 42
3 The H.P. Lovecraft Historical Society. "If I Were A Deep One." *A Shoggoth on the Roof*. HPLHS. 2002
4 The H.P. Lovecraft Historical Society. "Have Yourself a Scary Little Solstice." *A Very Scary Solstice*. HPLHS. 2003
5 The H.P. Lovecraft Historical Society. "Freddy the Red Brained Mi-Go." *A Very Scary Solstice*. HPLHS. 2003
6 The H.P. Lovecraft Historical Society. *A Very Scary Solstice*. HPLHS. 2003
7 The H.P. Lovecraft Historical Society. "Great Old Ones Are Coming To Town." *A Very Scary Solstice*. HPLHS. 2003
8 Harms, Daniel. *Encyclopedia Cthulhiana*. Hayward, CA: Chaosium, 1998, 99
9 The H.P. Lovecraft Historical Society. "The Carol of the Olde Ones." *A Very Scary Solstice*. HPLHS. 2003
10 The H.P. Lovecraft Historical Society. "Awake Ye Scary Great Olde Ones." *A Very Scary Solstice*. HPLHS. 2003
11 The H.P. Lovecraft Historical Society. "It's The Most Horrible Time of the Year." *A Very Scary Solstice*. HPLHS. 2003

12 Harms, Daniel. *Encyclopedia Cthulhiana*. Hayward, CA: Chaosium, 1998, 340
13 The H.P. Lovecraft Historical Society. "Away In A Madhouse." *A Very Scary Solstice*. HPLHS. 2003
14 The H.P. Lovecraft Historical Society. "I'm Dreaming of A Dead City." *A Very Scary Solstice*. HPLHS. 2003
15 The H.P. Lovecraft Historical Society. "He'll Be Back For Solstice." *A Very Scary Solstice*. HPLHS. 2003
16 The H.P. Lovecraft Historical Society. "Mythos of A King." *A Very Scary Solstice*. HPLHS. 2003
17 The H.P. Lovecraft Historical Society. "Tentacles." *A Very Scary Solstice*. HPLHS. 2003
18 The H.P. Lovecraft Historical Society. "Do You Fear What I Fear." *A Very Scary Solstice*. HPLHS. 2003
19 The H.P. Lovecraft Historical Society. "Cthulhu Lives!" *A Very Scary Solstice*. HPLHS. 2003

Chapter 12
1 Various Artists. *Strange Aeons*. Rainfall Records. 2001
2 Ibid.
3 Lines, Steve. "Strange Aeons." *Strange Aeons*. Rainfall Records. 2001
4 Ibid.
5 Lines, Steve. "The Necronomicon." *Strange Aeons*. Rainfall Records. 2001
6 Ibid.
7 Campbell, Ramsey. "The Telegram." *Strange Aeons*. Rainfall Records. 2001
8 Harms, Daniel. *Encyclopedia Cthulhiana*. Hayward, CA: Chaosium, 1998, 300
9 Harms, Daniel. *Encyclopedia Cthulhiana*. Hayward, CA: Chaosium, 1998, 141
10 Ibid.
11 Lines, Steve. "The Hounds of Tindalos." *Strange Aeons*. Rainfall Records. 2001
12 Lovecraft, Howard P. "Dreams in the Witch-House." *H.P. Lovecraft: Tales*. New York, NY: The Library of America, 2005
13 Lines, Steve. Roland, Childe. "Brown Jenkins." *Strange Aeons*. Rainfall Records. 2001
14 Lines, Steve. "Pickman's Painting." *Strange Aeons*. Rainfall Records. 2001
15 Lovecraft, Howard P. "Pickman's Model." *H.P. Lovecraft: Tales*. New York, NY: The Library of America, 2005
16 Pulver, Joseph S. Sr "The Stormclouds of Their Return." *Strange Aeons*. Rainfall Records. 2001
17 Lane, Joel. "Eclipse." *Strange Aeons*. Rainfall Records. 2001
18 Lebbon, Tim. "Vacant Souls." *Strange Aeons*. Rainfall Records. 2001
19 Ibid.
20 Ibid.
21 Ibid.
22 Lumley, Brian. "The Night Music of Oakdeene." *Strange Aeons*. Rainfall Records. 2001
23 Lines, Steve. "When they Return." *Strange Aeons*. Rainfall Records. 2001
24 Ibid.

Chapter 13
1 Blue Öyster Cult. "E.T.I (Extraterrestrial Intelligence)." *Agents of Fortune*. Columbia. 1976
2 Blue Öyster Cult. "I Am The One You Warned Me Of." *Imaginos*. Columbia. 1988
3 Blue Öyster Cult. "Les Invisibles." *Imaginos*. Columbia. 1988

4 Ibid.

5 Blue Öyster Cult. "In The Presence of Another World." *Imaginos*. Columbia. 1988

6 Ibid.

7 Blue Öyster Cult. "The Old Gods Return." *The Curse of* the *Hidden Mirror*. CMC International. 2001

8 The Liverpool Scene. "2 Poems for H.P. Lovecraft." *Amazing Adventures Of*. RCA. 1968

9 Lovecraft, Howard P. "The Tomb." *The Doom That Came to Sarnath*. New York: Ballantine Books, 1971

10 Ibid.

11 Call of Cthulhu. "Call of Cthulhu." Timeless Arkham.

12 Call of Cthulhu. "He Who Whispers In the Dark." Timeless Arkham.

13 Ibid.

14 Ibid.

15 The Unquiet Void. "Esoteric Order." *Poisoned Dreams*. Middle Pillar. 2004

16 The Creepniks. "Shadow Over Elkhart." *Graveyard Shindig*. GraveWax. 2005

17 Ibid.

18 Humanoids. "Human Eyes That Shine In the Night." *The Adyar Sessions Vol. 1*. 2004

19 Humanoids. "KO Coralle." *The Adyar Sessions Vol. 1*. 2004

20 Ibid.

21 Humanoids. "Rock Steady Seti." *The Adyar Sessions Vol. 1*. 2004

22 Ibid.

23 Ibid.

24 Humanoids. "Arkham, Sir." *The Adyar Sessions Vol. 1*. 2004

25 Ibid.

26 Asmodeus X. "Darker Shores." As yet unreleased

Chapter 14

1 Mackey, Allen. "Disciples of Zann or The Condensed History of H.P. Lovecraft's Influence in Heavy Metal." *Crypt of Cthulhu* #89 1995

2 Ibid.

3 Ibid.

4 Ibid.

5 Ibid.

6 Ibid.

7 Ibid.

Internet Resources

Sites Featuring the Work of Gary Hill

Beet Café
http://www.beetcafe.com

Music Street Journal
http://www.musicstreetjournal.com

Wormwood Chronicles (under the name "Dark Starr")
http://www.wormwoodchronicles.com

Bands and Solo Artists

Aarni
http://www.aarni.info
http://www.myspace.com/aarni

AKLO
http://www.aklo.net
http://www.nightmaresforsale.com/aklo

Arkham Hollow
http://www.myspace.com/arkhamhollow

Asmodeus X
http://www.asmodeusx.com
http://www.myspace.com/asmodeusx

Babyland
http://www.babyland.info
http://www.myspace.com/babylandmusic

Bal-Sagoth
http://www.bal-sagoth.co.uk

Black Sabbath
http://www.black-sabbath.com

BloodHag
http://bloodhag.com
http://www.myspace.com/bloodhag

Blue Öyster Cult
http://www.blueoystercult.com

Browne Jenkyn
http://www.brownejenkyn.com

The Call of Cthulhu
http://www.myspace.com/lovecraftian

Caravan
http://www.caravan-info.co.uk

Celtic Frost
http://www.celticfrost.com

Chton
http://www.chton.com
http://www.myspace.com/chton

Cradle of Filth
http://www.cradleoffilth.com

The Creepniks
http://www.myspace.com/creepniks

The Darkest of the Hillside Thickets
http://www.thickets.net
http://www.myspace.com/darkestofthehillsidethickets

Deicide
http://www.deicide.com

Disincarnate
http://www.disincarnate.msanthrope.com

Djam Karet
http://www.djamkaret.com
http://www.myspace.com/djamkaret

Electric Wizard
http://www.myspace.com/electricwizard13monkey

Entombed
http://www.entombed.org
http://www.myspace.com/serpentsaints

Evil's Toy
http://www.toy-music.com

The Fall
http://www.thefall.info

Fields of the Nephilim
http://www.fields-of-the-nephilim.com

Fireaxe
http://www.neptune.net/~bev/Fireaxe.html
http://www.myspace.com/theburningblade

Ghosts Run Wild
http://www.myspace.com/ghostsrunwild

GWAR
http://gwar.net

The H.P. Lovecraft Historical Society
http://www.cthulhulives.org

Humanoids
http://www.myspace.com/humanoids

Hypocrisy
http://www.hypocrisy.tv

Steve Lines
http://www.clivejones.i12.com/archives.htm

Manilla Road
http://www.truemetal.org/manillaroad

Mekong Delta
http://www.nightmarepatrol.net/mekongdelta

Mercyful Fate
http://www.covenworldwide.org/

Metallica
http://www.metallica.com

Moonspell
http://www.moonspell.com

Morbid Angel
http://www.morbidangel.com

NecronomicoN
http://welcome.to/necronomicon

Nile
http://www.nile-catacombs.net/

Nox Arcana
http://www.noxarcana.com
http://www.myspace.com/noxarcana.com

The Old Ones
http://www.9productions.net/theoldones/index.html

Philosopher
http://www.philosopher-music.de

Rage
http://www.rage-on.de

Rudimentary Peni
http://www.southern.com/southern/band/RPENI/

Samael
http://www.samael.info

Septimania
http://www.myspace.com/septimania

Niko Skorpio
http://nikoskorpio.net
http://www.myspace.com/nikoskorpio

Tom Smith
http://www.tomsmithonline.com

Solitude Aeturnus
http://www.eternalsolitude.com

Stormclouds
http://www.clivejones.i12.com/menu.htm

T.O.Y
http://www.toy-music.com

Oliver Taranczewski
http://www.toy-music.com

Thergothon
http://nikoskorpio.net
http://www.myspace.com/nikoskorpio

Therion
http://www.megatherion.com

Tiamat
http://www.churchoftiamat.com

Univers Zero
http://www.univers-zero.com

The Unnameable
http://the_unnameable.tripod.com
Unquiet Void
http://www.theunquietvoid.com
http://www.myspace.com/theunquietvoid

Vader
http://www.vader.pl

White Flag
http://www.chaser.net/whiteflag
http://www.myspace.com/whiteflagofficialmyspacesite

Yavin 4
http://www.toy-music.com

Yyrkoon
http://www.yyrkoon.net

Sites Dedicated To H.P. Lovecraft:
The H.P. Lovecraft Archive
http://www.hplovecraft.com

The H.P. Lovecraft Film Festival
http://www.hplfilmfestival.com

Lovecraftian Writers and Writers on Strange Aeons
Ramsey Campbell
http://www.ramseycampbell.com

John B. Ford
http://www.terrortales.co.uk

S. T. Joshi
http://www.stjoshi.net

Brian Lumley
http://brianlumley.com

Lovecraftian Publishers
Chaosium
http://www.chaosium.com

Hippocampus Press
http://www.hippocampuspress.com

Necronomicon Press
http://www.necropress.com

Lovecraft Based Games
The Call of Cthulhu - Dark Corners of the Earth
http://www.callofcthulhu.com

Chaosium – The Call of Cthulhu Role Playing Game
http://www.chaosium.com/

Cthulhu Lives!
http://www.cthulhulives.org/toc.html

Other Sites of Interest
The Call of Cthulhu – The Film
http://www.cthulhulives.org/cocmovie/index.html

Jowita Kaminska – Artist who will be doing the Philosopher covers
http://www.jowita-kaminska.com

Monolith Graphics – The artwork of Joseph Vargo
http://www.monolithgraphics.com

Rainfall Records and Books – Steve Lines' company
http://www.rainfallsite.com

Unfilmable – A Site Devoted To Lovecraftian Film and Other News
http://www.unfilmable.com

INDEX

There are some considerations regarding the material covered in this book that necessitate using a unique set of notations. So, here is the legend for this index.

Stories, poems and song titles will be enclosed in quotation marks – e.g. "song", unless the title is used for a grouping of varied items.

A book or album (EP, etc.) title will be italicized, except in the same case as above – e.g. *album*.

Names of actual people or artists (when used as the item in question) will be bolded – e.g. **real person**.

The parenthetical after a title is the artist who created it. When that artist is the author H. P. Lovecraft (as opposed to the band by that name) it will be bolded. Any further notes necessary will also be in parenthesis in the entry.